Forensic Mental Health

Criminal Justice Series

Forensic Mental Health, by Mary McMurran, Najat Khalifa and
    Simon Gibbon
Crime Prevention, by Nick Tilley

Forensic Mental Health

Mary McMurran, Najat Khalifa
and Simon Gibbon

WILLAN
PUBLISHING

Published by

Willan Publishing
Culmcott House
Mill Street, Uffculme
Cullompton, Devon
EX15 3AT, UK
Tel: +44(0)1884 840337
Fax: +44(0)1884 840251
e-mail: info@willanpublishing.co.uk
website: www.willanpublishing.co.uk

Published simultaneously in the USA and Canada by

Willan Publishing
c/o ISBS, 920 NE 58th Ave, Suite 300
Portland, Oregon 97213-3786, USA
Tel: +001(0)503 287 3093
Fax: +001(0)503 280 8832
e-mail: info@isbs.com
website: www.isbs.com

First published 2009

ISBN   978-1-84392-389-3 paperback
       978-1-84392-390-9 hardback

British Library Cataloguing-in-Publication Data

A catalogue record for this book is available from the British Library.

FSC
Mixed Sources
Product group from well-managed
forests and other controlled sources
Cert no. SGS-COC-2482
www.fsc.org
© 1996 Forest Stewardship Council

Project managed by Deer Park Productions, Tavistock, Devon
Typeset by GCS, Leighton Buzzard, Bedfordshire
Printed and bound by T.J. International Ltd, Padstow, Cornwall

MM: For Mike Coogan, a man of wisdom, integrity and compassion.

NK: For my late mother, my wife Vian and my children Dana and Adam.

SG: For Polly, Oscar and Maisie – hope this helps to make up for the late nights and early mornings.

Contents

Foreword   *xi*
List of abbreviations   *xv*
About the authors   *xix*

**1   Introduction: the criminal justice system and mental
      health legislation**   **1**
     The aim of this book   1
     The criminal justice system   1
     The National Offender Management Service   8
     The Mental Health Acts 1983 and 2007   11
     Conclusion   26

2   Mental disorder and offending   **27**
     Introduction   27
     Mental disorders   27
     Mental illnesses   30
     Personality disorders   40
     Learning disability   48
     Substance abuse disorders   51
     Disorders of sexual preference (paraphilias)   52
     Conclusion   53

3   Entering the forensic mental health system   **54**
     Introduction   54
     Police custody   55
     The court   58

Prison transfers   69
Conclusion   69

4   Forensic mental health services   **70**
Introduction   70
Prison mental health services   70
Secure hospitals   73
Specialised forensic services   78
Community forensic mental health services   84
Forensic telepsychiatry   86
Conclusion   87

5   The multidisciplinary team   **88**
Introduction   88
Forensic psychiatrists   89
Clinical psychologists and forensic psychologists   93
Nurses   95
Healthcare assistants   96
Social workers   97
Occupational therapists   99
Art, drama and music therapists   100
Pharmacists   102
An example of multidisciplinary teamwork   103
Conclusion   104

6   Risk assessment   **105**
Introduction   105
Empirical identification of risk factors   106
Risk factors   109
Assessment instruments   113
Conclusion   120

7   Treatments in prison and probation services   **121**
Introduction   121
Risk-Needs-Responsivity   121
Programme accreditation   123
Accredited cognitive-behavioural treatment programmes   124
Accredited therapeutic communities   134
Do correctional treatments work?   135
Sentence management and throughcare   136
Conclusion   136

8   **Treatments in mental health settings**   **138**
     Introduction   138
     The Care Programme Approach   139
     Treatment of mental health problems   141
     Learning disability   157
     Substance misuse   160
     Conclusion   163

9   **Leaving the system, patients' rights and advocacy**   **165**
     Introduction   165
     Mental Health Review Tribunals   165
     The Parole Board   170
     Multi-Agency Public Protection Arrangements   175
     Legal representation   178
     The Mental Health Act Commission   181
     Mental health advocacy   183
     Voluntary groups   185
     Conclusion   186

Afterword   188

References   190

Index   211

Foreword

The field of forensic mental health is currently undergoing a major expansion. While this is to be welcomed, we also need to recognise that this is partly as a result of some unwelcome publicity from some high-profile incidents involving mentally disordered offenders that have gone spectacularly wrong, often with disastrous consequences. Cases involving Anthony Rice, Christopher Clunis, Michael Stone and John Barrett are paradigmatic of this process. All have been followed by a statutory homicide inquiry. The findings from such inquiries are drearily predictable: systemic failures within the organisation, inadequate attention to risk indicators, occasional negligence on the part of the professionals involved (usually the Responsible Medical Officer) and so on. While unfortunately many of these criticisms are warranted, what appears to underlie many of these failings is the common factor of poor communication between the differing agencies and the professionals within them.

This ought not to surprise us as forensic mental health is attempting to conjoin two very different structures (i.e. the criminal justice system (CJS) with forensic mental health (FMH)), each of which has evolved independently from the other. Consequently, each has different priorities. The priority for the CJS is to reduce offending (largely a societal rather than an individual good), while that of FMH is to maximise the mental well-being of the individual involved (largely an individual rather than a societal good). Not only are these very different objectives, the professional etiquette surrounding such matters as confidentiality and the sharing of information is also very different.

This traditional compartmentalisation of the CJS versus FMH is now being challenged. Epidemiological evidence, for instance, demonstrates very clearly that many of those within the CJS have a very high level of mental abnormality. There is also compelling evidence that the CJS already uses many psychological interventions to reduce further reoffending and does so with a rigour (particularly as regards their implementation) that would seriously embarrass many mental health practitioners. Nonetheless, many FMH practitioners criticise these programmes as being too formulaic with insufficient attention to the individual needs of those that they are deemed to treat. As a consequence, instead of a mutually supportive and rewarding relationship between these two organisations, what currently exists is hostility and separation. One has only to experience the difficulties in transferring an individual from one of these organisations to another to realise the divide between them. There is also a similar lack of recognition of the strengths (and limitations) of either organisation by the other. How is this organisational antipathy to be overcome?

Just as it is difficult for adults to learn a new language if one has not picked this up as a child, I would argue that those at either side of the CJS/FMH divide will struggle to hear what the other is saying as they fail to understand that each is using a different language. I believe that this new book *Forensic Mental Health* by Professor Mary McMurran and colleagues will be especially useful in bridging the gap in both the nomenclature and processes between these two organisations.

Here, the provenance of the authors is important as they straddle the divide between the CJS and FMH in different ways. Professor McMurran, for instance, commenced her clinical career by working as a psychologist within one of the country's largest Young Offenders Institutions – HMP YOI Glen Parva – before developing this further within the provision of high and medium NHS secure care. Hence she brings to the field a wide and wise understanding of the issues involved. Drs Gibbon and Khalifa – currently clinical lecturers in forensic psychiatry – offer a contrasting perspective as they are recent entrants to the field and so are still in a position of being able to learn languages that many of us elders are unable to understand. Moreover, they are able to bring a real-lived experience of working at the coalface between these two organisations that is very evident from their contributions to the text.

This is not a scholarly, heavily referenced textbook that is likely to gather dust in an academic library. No, it is more useful than that and comprises a *vade mecum* that practitioners from many different disciplines will find essential in carrying out their work. A point that is not sufficiently recognised is that multidisciplinary working involves members from many differing perspectives and levels of sophistication. Hence, a common level of understanding is essential if there is to be a sensible discourse between different professionals using differing languages. This text provides a basis for a common understanding between the CJS and FMH.

Here, for instance, the practitioner will find comprehensive summaries of such important topics as mental disorder and offending (Chapter 2), entering and exiting the forensic mental health systems (Chapters 3 and 9 respectively), the multidisciplinary team and its components (Chapter 5) and risk assessment (Chapter 6). There is also a very useful contrast (in Chapters 7 and 8) between therapeutic programmes in the CJS and FMH. Each of these chapters is backed up with very useful information boxes that summarise the points made in the text. In my opinion the authors have been very fair-minded in their approach to the many controversial issues that are endemic to this field.

I believe that this will be an invaluable reference guide to anyone who is entering (or thinking of entering) the field. While it may have its greatest appeal to the novice practitioner who wishes to understand the difficult terrain, it will also benefit the more established practitioner provided that he/she is prepared to listen to what it has to say.

Professor Conor Duggan
Professor of Forensic Mental Health
University of Nottingham

List of abbreviations

ACCT	Assessment, Care in Custody and Teamwork
ADHD	Attention-Deficit Hyperactivity Disorder
AMHP	Approved Mental Health Professional
APA	American Psychiatric Association
ART	Aggression Replacement Training
ASRO	Addressing Substance-Related Offending
ASW	Approved Social Worker
BMA	British Medical Association
BME	Black and minority ethnic (patients)
CALM	Controlling Anger and Learning how to Manage it
CBT	cognitive behaviour therapy
CCT	certificate of completion of training
CCTV	closed-circuit television
CJA	Criminal Justice Act
CJS	criminal justice system
CPA	Care Programme Approach
CPIA	Criminal Procedure (Insanity) Act
CPS	Crown Prosecution Service
CTO	community treatment order
DBT	dialectical behaviour therapy
DNA	deoxyribonucleic acid
DPP	Director of Public Prosecutions
DSM	Diagnostic and Statistical Manual of Mental Disorders
DSPD	Dangerous and Severe Personality Disorder
ECG	electrocardiograph
ECHR	European Court of Human Rights

ECT	electroconvulsive therapy
ETS	Enhanced Thinking Skills
FBC	full blood count
FME	forensic medical examiner
FMH	forensic mental health
GLM	Good Lives Model
GMC	General Medical Council
GP	general practitioner
HMCS	Her Majesty's Court Service
HoNOS	Health of the Nation Outcomes Scales
ICD	International Classification of Diseases
IPP	imprisonment for public protection
IQ	intelligence quotient
JETS	Juvenile Enhanced Thinking Skills
LAC	local area command (police)
LS/CMI	Level of Service/Case Management Inventory
LSI-R	Level of Service Inventory – Revised
LSU	low-secure units
MACT	manual-assisted cognitive therapy
MAOI	mono-amine oxidase inhibitor
MAPPA	Multi-Agency Public Protection Arrangements
MAPPP	Multi-Agency Public Protection Panel
MHA	Mental Health Act
MHAC	Mental Health Act Commission
MHRT	Mental Health Review Tribunal
MI	motivational interviewing
MORM	Multifactorial Offender Readiness Model
MSU	medium-secure unit
NASSA	noradrenergic and specific serotonin antidepressant
NHS	National Health Service
NHSHSW	National High Secure Healthcare Service for Women
NICE	National Institute for Health and Clinical Excellence
NOMIS	National Offender Management Information System
NOMS	National Offender Management Service
NRI	noradrenaline re-uptake inhibitor
NVQ	National Vocational Qualification
OASys	Offender Assessment System
OGRS	Offender Group Reconviction Scale
PACE	Police and Criminal Evidence Act
PCL-R	Psychopathy Checklist – Revised
PICU	psychiatric intensive care unit
PMETB	Postgraduate Medical Examinations and Training Board

POPH	psychoanalytically orientated partial hospitalisation
PRISM	Programme for Reducing Individual Substance Misuse
PSR	pre-sentence report
PTSD	Post-Traumatic Stress Disorder
R&R	Reasoning and Rehabilitation
RaPT	Rehabilitation of Prisoners Trust
RC	Responsible Clinician
RMO	Responsible Medical Officer
RNR	Risk-Needs-Responsivity
RRASOR	Rapid Risk Assessment for Sexual Offence Recidivism
RSU	regional secure unit
RSVP	Risk of Sexual Violence Protocol
SHO	Senior House Officer
SMI	severe mental illness
SNRI	serotonin-noradrenalin re-uptake inhibitor
SOAD	Second Opinion Appointed Doctor
SOGP	Sex Offender Group Programme
SOTP	Sex Offender Treatment Programme
SpR	Specialist Registrar
SSRI	selective serotonin re-uptake inhibitors
SVR-20	Sexual Violence Risk-20
TC	therapeutic community
TFT	thyroid function test
U&E	urea and electrolytes
VRAG	Violence Risk Appraisal Guide
WCU	witness care unit
WEMSS	Women Enhanced Medium Secure Services
WHO	World Health Organisation
YOI	Young Offenders Institution

About the authors

Professor Mary McMurran BSc, MSc, PhD, CPsychol, FBPsS is Professor in the Section of Forensic Mental Health, Division of Psychiatry, University of Nottingham, UK. She has worked in prisons, secure psychiatric services, and a community forensic mental health service. Her research interests are: (1) social problem-solving theories and therapies for understanding and treating people with personality disorders; (2) the assessment and treatment of alcohol-related aggression and violence; and (3) understanding and enhancing offenders' motivation to change. She has written over 100 academic articles and book chapters, and this is her tenth book as author or editor. She is a Fellow of the British Psychological Society and former Chair of the Society's Division of Forensic Psychology. She was founding co-editor of the British Psychological Society journal *Legal and Criminological Psychology* and is currently co-editor of *Criminal Behaviour and Mental Health* and the *Journal of Forensic Psychiatry and Psychology*. In 2005, she was recipient of the Division of Forensic Psychology's Award for a Significant Lifetime Contribution to Forensic Psychology.

Dr Najat Khalifa MBChB, MRCPsych is a Clinical Lecturer in Forensic Psychiatry in the Section of Forensic Mental Health, Division of Psychiatry, University of Nottingham, UK and also Specialist Registrar in Forensic Psychiatry in Nottinghamshire Healthcare NHS Trust. His research interests are: (1) personality disorder and offending; (2) the neurobiology of offending behaviour; and (3) religion and mental health. He has published a number of academic articles on telepsychiatry, the use of sniffer dogs in secure settings and the professional practice of psychiatry in Europe.

Dr Simon Gibbon MBBS, MRCPsych is a Clinical Lecturer in Forensic Psychiatry in the Section of Forensic Mental Health, Division of Psychiatry, University of Nottingham, UK. He is also an Honorary Specialist Registrar in Forensic Psychiatry, Nottinghamshire Healthcare NHS Trust and he has worked in a variety of secure settings. His research interests include: (1) the neuropsychology of violence in mentally disordered offenders; (2) the assessment and management of the co-morbidity between schizophrenia and personality disorder in this group; and (3) the family background and early experiences of mentally disordered offenders. He has a number of publications on topics that include approaches to the assessment of personality disorder, psychopharmacology, ethical issues in the treatment of those with personality disorder and the adaptation of therapeutic community principles to working with deaf mentally disordered offenders.

Chapter I

Introduction: the criminal justice system and mental health legislation

The aim of this book

This book is intended for the newcomer to the topic of forensic mental health. This person might be a student of psychology, criminology, law or mental health on a formal educational course, or someone with no exam to pass but who seeks to know more about this particular aspect of the society in which he or she lives. Our aim is to give this newcomer a clear and succinct overview of the contexts in which forensic mental health professionals work and the kinds of services and treatments that they provide. The provision of forensic mental health services is intimately bound with the legal and criminal justice systems of the country in question. The focus in this book is on practice in England and Wales. Our starting point, therefore, is to describe both the criminal justice system and mental health legislation relating to England and Wales. This will provide a foundation for understanding how offenders enter probation and prison services, and how mentally disordered offenders come to be treated as inpatients or outpatients in forensic mental health services.

The criminal justice system

In England and Wales, the criminal justice process is delivered by a number of agencies that work collaboratively under the umbrella of the criminal justice system (often referred to by its initials – CJS).

These include the police, the Crown Prosecution Service, Her Majesty's Court Service, the National Offender Management Service (which incorporates the prison and probation services), the Youth Justice Board (a body that works with young people and communities to prevent offending and reoffending) and the Serious Fraud Office. The work of these agencies is overseen by the Ministry of Justice, the Home Office and the Attorney General's Office (see Information Box 1.1). The overall aims of the criminal justice system are: (1) to detect and prevent crime; (2) to rehabilitate and punish offenders; and (3) to support victims and witnesses of crime.

The criminal justice process is depicted in Figure 1.1. Once a crime has been reported to the police, the important tasks then are to investigate, gather evidence and, crucially, find the culprit. Following arrest, the suspect is interviewed and forensic materials may be obtained from the suspect for analysis. The police may obtain further advice from the Crown Prosecution Service (another body often referred to by its initials – CPS) as to whether the suspect should be charged or not. This decision is based upon whether there is sufficient evidence to indicate that a conviction might be likely and also whether pursuing a conviction is in the public interest. Once the suspect is formally charged, the Crown Prosecution Service prepares a case and presents it at court. Most major cases of fraud are prosecuted by the Serious Fraud Office, which specialises in such crime.

Some minor offences can be dealt with by the police using the powers available to them, such as serving a reprimand or a caution;

Information Box 1.1 The government departments responsible for the criminal justice system

- *The Ministry of Justice* – responsible for criminal law and sentencing, reducing reoffending, and prisons and probation. The Ministry of Justice also oversees Magistrates' Courts, Crown Courts, the Appeals Courts and the Legal Services Commission.

- *The Home Office* – responsible for crime and crime reduction, policing, security and counter-terrorism, borders and immigration, passports and identity.

- *The Office of the Attorney General* – oversees the Crown Prosecution Service, the Serious Fraud Office and the Revenue and Customs Prosecutions Office.

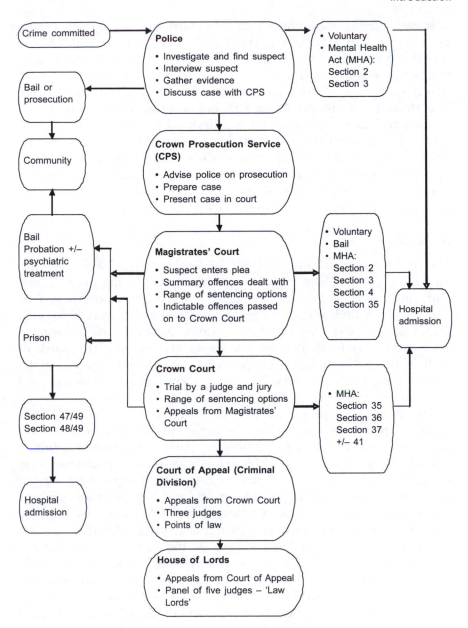

Figure 1.1 The criminal justice process and diversion mechanisms

however, more serious offences are dealt with by the courts. Virtually all criminal cases start in the Magistrates' Court or the Youth Court which is a section of the Magistrates' Court dealing with most cases involving young people under the age of 18 (from the age of 10, which is the age of criminal responsibility in England and Wales). The majority of minor (summary) offences are dealt with in the Magistrates' Court, whereas serious (indictable) offences are passed on to the Crown Court for trial by a judge and jury. The courts have a range of sentencing options (disposals) available to them to deal with convicted offenders. Of course, the criminal justice process may not end here; an appeal against a conviction may be pursued provided there are sufficient grounds for making one.

The police

The overall responsibility for policing England and Wales lies with the Home Office. There are 43 police forces employing over 228,000 personnel (Home Office 2007). Each police force is comprised of a number of divisions, each of which is divided into local area commands (LACs). Police stations within the local area commands deliver policing to local neighbourhoods and estates. The work of each of the police forces is overseen by a local police authority, an independent body comprised of local councillors, magistrates and independent members of the public.

The police represent the point of entry to the criminal justice system. Crimes are reported to the police in the first instance and the role of the police is to investigate, gather evidence and find a suspect. Police interviews involving witnesses and crime suspects remain a crucial part of the evidence gathering process. Advances in technology have made it possible to utilise other materials, such as closed-circuit television (CCTV) footage and DNA (deoxyribonucleic acid) techniques. The Police and Criminal Evidence Act (PACE) 1984 and the PACE Codes of Practice provide the framework for the use of police powers and they provide procedures for stop and search, arrest, detention, investigation, identification and interviewing detainees (Home Office Police 2008). PACE also presents a number of safeguards for individuals with mental disorders and mental handicaps. These safeguards include the presence of an appropriate adult or a solicitor or both during police interviews. In addition, PACE allows judges to exclude unreliable confessional evidence from trials. Of particular relevance is the issue of fitness for interview in police custody, which will be addressed in Chapter 3.

Crown Prosecution Service

The Crown Prosecution Service (CPS) is the body that prosecutes criminal cases on behalf of the Crown. Its principal aim is to bring offenders to justice firmly, fairly and effectively. The Service is staffed largely by barristers and lawyers, and is headed by the Director of Public Prosecutions (DPP). The work of the Crown Prosecution Service is overseen by the Attorney General, who is the government Minister answerable for the Crown Prosecution Service in Parliament. In 2005, the Crown Prosecution Service was expanded to incorporate three new divisions which deal with organised crime, counter-terrorism and specialised crime.

The Crown Prosecution Service has 42 areas across England and Wales, divided into 15 regional groups, with each area headed by a Chief Crown Prosecutor. The Crown Prosecution Service works closely with the police to decide whether or not to charge a suspect. Such a decision is based on two tests: the evidential test and the public interest test. In other words, the public prosecutor has to be satisfied that there is enough reliable evidence against the suspect for a conviction to be possible, and that prosecution is in the public's best interest. Once these tests are satisfied, the suspect is formally charged and the Crown Prosecution Service will then have to prepare a case and present it in court. The aim is to prove beyond reasonable doubt that the defendant committed the act or made the omission of which they were accused.

Justice can only be served if victims and witnesses are prepared to testify in court. Therefore, the Crown Prosecution Service has developed a role in supporting witnesses and victims of crime throughout their potentially stressful court appearances. Witness care units (WCUs) allocate an officer to attend to every victim and witness, explaining what happens in court and helping them attend sessions. The Crown Prosecution Service may apply for special measures such as allowing the victim to be shielded from the defendant's view in the courtroom or to give evidence through a live television link, clearing the public gallery, or reducing the formality of the court by asking for wigs and gowns to be removed.

The Crown Prosecution Service may also seek opinion from an 'expert witness', that is a person who, by virtue of their training or experience, has specialised knowledge that may help the court interpret facts or evidence. Mental health professionals may be called for an expert opinion in relation to mental health matters, such as the defendant's fitness to plead or psychiatric defences such as insanity, diminished responsibility, automatism and insanity (refer to Chapter 3 for more details). The Crown Prosecution Service may also instruct an expert witness to respond to the views expressed by the defence's expert witness. For further information on the Crown Prosecution Service, see their website (http://www.cps.gov.uk).

The Court Service

Her Majesty's Courts Service (HMCS) is an executive agency of the Ministry of Justice and is responsible for managing the Magistrates' Courts, the Crown Court, County Courts, the High Court and Court of Appeal in England and Wales. The Court Service in England and Wales is depicted in Figure 1.2 and the types of courts are described below.

Magistrates' Court

Virtually all criminal cases start at the Magistrates' Court. In addition, a range of civil cases and cases which involve people under the age of 18 (only if they are tried with an adult) are dealt with in the Magistrates' Court. Cases which involve people aged between 10 and 17 are dealt with in the Youth Court – a specialised form of Magistrates' Court. Almost 95 per cent of less serious (summary) offences are dealt with at the level of the Magistrates' Courts, whereas more serious (indictable) offences are passed on to the Crown Court for trial by a judge and jury. The majority of the cases in the Magistrates' Court are heard by a 'bench' consisting of three magistrates (justices of the peace), who are supported by a legally qualified court clerk. Magistrates do not hold any formal legal qualifications, although they receive a significant amount of legal training. Their work is unpaid but they are reimbursed for expenses and loss of earnings. Within some of the Magistrates' Courts, district judges (who are legally qualified and paid) sit alone and deal with more complex matters, for instance, cases related to extradition and serious fraud. A range of sentencing options are available to the magistrates; in addition to community sentences, they can order terms of imprisonment of up to 6 months (or 12 months for consecutive sentences) or fines up to £5,000.

Crown Court

More serious (indictable) offences such as murder, manslaughter, rape and robbery are dealt with in the Crown Court. Appeals from the Magistrates' Court, sentencing decisions transferred from

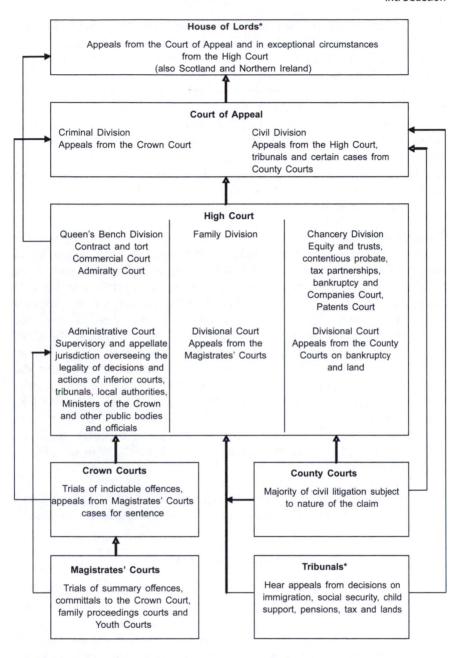

House of Lords*
Appeals from the Court of Appeal and in exceptional circumstances from the High Court
(also Scotland and Northern Ireland)

Court of Appeal

Criminal Division
Appeals from the Crown Court

Civil Division
Appeals from the High Court, tribunals and certain cases from County Courts

High Court

Queen's Bench Division
Contract and tort
Commercial Court
Admiralty Court

Family Division

Chancery Division
Equity and trusts, contentious probate, tax partnerships, bankruptcy and Companies Court, Patents Court

Administrative Court
Supervisory and appellate jurisdiction overseeing the legality of decisions and actions of inferior courts, tribunals, local authorities, Ministers of the Crown and other public bodies and officials

Divisional Court
Appeals from the Magistrates' Courts

Divisional Court
Appeals from the County Courts on bankruptcy and land

Crown Courts
Trials of indictable offences, appeals from Magistrates' Courts cases for sentence

County Courts
Majority of civil litigation subject to nature of the claim

Magistrates' Courts
Trials of summary offences, committals to the Crown Court, family proceedings courts and Youth Courts

Tribunals*
Hear appeals from decisions on immigration, social security, child support, pensions, tax and lands

*Not managed by HMCS

Figure 1.2 The structure of court service in England and Wales (reproduced with permission from HMCS)

the Magistrates' Court and 'either-way' offences (i.e. cases that are triable either by the Magistrates' Court or the Crown Court) are also dealt with in the Crown Court. Crown Court trials are heard by a judge and jury of 12 persons – members of the public whose role it is to decide, based on the facts, whether a defendant is guilty or not guilty of an offence. When the jury returns a 'not guilty' verdict, the accused will be acquitted, but a 'guilty' verdict will result in a conviction and subsequent sentencing. A range of sentencing options are available to the trial judge, including imposing fines, prison sentences, community sentences (some of which have a condition of treatment) and hospital orders under the Mental Health Act (this is explained more fully later in this chapter).

The appeal process

Appeal against a conviction may be pursued at various stages of the criminal justice process, provided there is sufficient ground for making one (see Information Box 1.2). As mentioned earlier, appeals from the Magistrates' Court are heard at the Crown Court. Appeals from upper courts (i.e. all courts above Magistrates' Courts) are heard at the Court of Appeal, which is in two divisions: the Civil Division and the Criminal Division. The former hears appeals from the High Court, County Courts and certain tribunals, whereas the latter hears appeals from the Crown Court. The House of Lords is the highest appellate authority, i.e. the final court of appeal in the UK. It deals with appeals from the Court of Appeal and, in exceptional circumstances, from the High Court. In the House of Lords there are only 12 Lords of Appeal in Ordinary ('Law Lords'), who usually sit in panels of five.

More information on the courts is available on Her Majesty's Court Service website (http://www.hmcourts-service.gov.uk).

The National Offender Management Service

The National Offender Management Service (NOMS) was established in 2004 to 'bridge the divide between custody and community' and incorporates both the prison and probation services. The National Offender Management Service is responsible for the system through which correctional services and interventions are commissioned and provided, and thus it helps to deliver punishments and also coordinates rehabilitative, health, educational and resettlement opportunities for offenders to help them reduce reoffending.

Information Box 1.2   Grounds for appeal

- Misdirection of law
- Non-direction on the law
- Failure to refer to a defence
- Misdirection on the facts
- Inappropriate comment by the judge
- Wrongful admission or exclusion of the evidence
- Defects in the indictment
- Rejection of no case to answer
- Jury irregularities
- Irregularity in relation to verdict
- Prosecution responsibilities such as non-disclosure or late change in nature of the case
- Important new evidence

The National Offender Management Service has introduced a new 'Offender Management Model', whereby an offender management team (made up of an offender manager, offender supervisor, key workers and case administrators) helps to design and support individual intervention programmes that will help the offender change his or her offending behaviour. The help of mental health professionals may also be sought, particularly in relation to the management of mental disorder and risk. Central to the work of the National Offender Management Service is 'end-to-end offender management' and the National Offender Management Information System (NOMIS) is an information technology system designed to enable prison and probation services to share information, manage risk and manage sentencing. In this section we will describe the work of the two key agencies of The National Offender Management Service, namely the Prison and Probation services.

The Prison Service

Depriving an offender of his or her liberty through imprisonment is designed to: (1) deter the offender from committing further crime; (2) punish the offender for breaking the law; (3) prevent the prisoner from committing another offence; and (4) reform and rehabilitate the offender (Morris and Rothman 1995). In February 2008, there were approximately 82,000 prisoners held in prisons across England and Wales, and this figure is predicted to rise by about 10,000 every two years over the next ten years (de Silva *et al.* 2006).

There are currently 141 prisons in England and Wales, including 11 prisons run on contract by the private sector. Of all prisons, 14 are women-only prisons and a further four have some accommodation for women. Prisons are categorised based on their function and the level of security they provide (Reed 2002). Regarding function, some prisons are 'local prisons' where people are held on remand or are housed immediately after conviction by the courts, and some are 'training prisons' where there are educational, vocational and therapeutic opportunities for prisoners who have enough time to participate in these activities. Regarding security, Category A prisons are high-security prisons that hold the most dangerous prisoners; intermediate levels of security are provided within Category B and Category C prisons; and Category D prisons are open prisons which hold those prisoners who are deemed of lesser risk and who may require contact with the community to advance their rehabilitation.

National Probation Service

A gift of five shillings from London printer Frederic Rainer to the Church of England Temperance Society in 1876 launched what was to become the National Probation Service for England and Wales. Rainer hoped that the money would be used to rescue people who fell into crime through drunkenness, regarded as the main social evil of the time and the cause of most petty crime. (National Probation Service 2007, p. 2)

The National Probation Service is responsible for supervising offenders in the community – those subject to a court order and those released on licence from prison. Today, the National Probation Service for England and Wales has 42 probation areas under its umbrella and employs around 200,000 personnel. The probation caseload on any given day is in excess of 200,000, most of whom are aged 21 and over, with approximately 90 per cent male and 10 per cent female clients (National Probation Service 2007). The National Probation Service works closely with the courts. Probation officers prepare pre-sentence reports (PSRs) on offenders appearing before courts, covering issues such as risk assessment, offence formulation and proposed sentencing options. After conviction, probation officers supervise offenders and offer community-based treatment programmes. Probation officers also work within prisons, assisting with sentence planning, treatment and liaison with the Probation Service in the area into which the prisoner will be released. The National Probation Service also runs approved probation hostels which provide controlled environments for offenders on bail, community sentences and post-custody licences. Probation staff may also work with the victims of violent or sexual crime, keeping the victim informed about the progress of the sentence, and they may also consult the victim about conditions of release (National Probation Service 2007). For high-risk sexual and violent offenders, probation, police and mental health services, and housing agencies may work together under the umbrella of MAPPA – Multi-Agency Public Protection Arrangements (see Chapter 9). More information is available on http://www.probation.homeoffice.gov.uk.

The Mental Health Acts 1983 and 2007

The main piece of specific legislation concerning the care of mentally disordered offenders is the Mental Health Act (MHA) 1983, recently amended by the Mental Health Act 2007. This section will describe the main components of the Mental Health Act 1983, and will also explain how this Act's operation has recently been changed by the 2007 Act. Scotland has different mental health legislation to that which covers England, Wales and Northern Ireland, and this chapter will describe only the mental health legislation applying to England, Wales and Northern Ireland.

A brief history of mental health legislation

The first recognisable piece of English mental health legislation was the Poor Law of 1601. This made it the responsibility of each parish to provide support for 'pauper lunatics' who were incapable of looking after themselves. While this Act was laudable in seeking to protect those who could not look after themselves, it did not provide any protection to the individual who did not want to be the responsibility of the parish. This did not come about until the 1891 Lunacy Act imposed rigid admission criteria for the newly established asylums. All patients in these asylums were detained under the Lunacy Act and there was no option for a patient to seek voluntary admission. The 1930 Mental Treatment Act allowed voluntary admission for the first time. It is interesting to note the differences in language and purpose between the Poor Law of 1601 and the Mental Treatment Act of 1930. While the 1601 Act was principally concerned with preventing vagrancy and ensuring that each area provided appropriate social care to 'lunatics', the 1930 Act was concerned with the 'treatment' of those with 'mental disorder'.

The 1959 Mental Health Act substantially changed how patients could be admitted to hospital against their will. Under previous legislation, a magistrate or justice of the peace was required to authorise admission. However, the 1959 Act took this power from the judiciary and instead gave it to the medical profession. It is noteworthy that this change was opposed by both the British Medical Association (BMA) and the Royal Medico-Psychological Association (a forerunner of the present Royal College of Psychiatrists) at the time. The Mental Health Act 1983 updated the 1959 Act by introducing additional safeguards for patients (such as the Mental Health Act Commission and Mental Health Review Tribunals – see Chapter 9), together with providing a duty upon social services and health authorities to provide appropriate aftercare for those discharged from compulsory hospital care.

In the late 1990s, a number of concerns were raised about the operation of the Mental Health Act 1983. This followed a series of high-profile cases in which it was felt that insufficient attention had been given to the right of the public to be protected from harm by psychiatric patients. Specifically, there was concern that those with severe personality disorders (classified as suffering from 'psychopathic disorder' under the Act) were being excluded from services because of the additional 'treatability test' which had to be passed for this category of patient to be compulsorily detained. It was also felt by some that the Act was remiss in not allowing the compulsory treatment of patients in the community. Changes in European Court of Human Rights legislation also necessitated some minor changes to the Mental Health Act to avoid it being ruled in breach of this legislation.

Changes to the mental health legislation were many years in formulation; there was an eight-year period of drafts, public consultations and revisions. Psychiatrists, other mental health professionals, patients and lawyers united under the auspices of the Mental Health Alliance, a coalition of mental health and other organisations, to oppose many aspects of the proposed legislation. Of particular concern was the fear that the new Act was concerned much more with public protection than the provision of appropriate care to a vulnerable group of people. Other concerns were: the wide definition of mental disorder; the proposal to allow compulsory treatment in prison; the loss of the right of the patient's doctor to discharge the patient; proposals to allow compulsory treatment in the community; and the loss of clinical discretion in deciding whether the Act should be applied if the criteria for compulsory admission were met (Mullen 2005; Zigmond 2004). After much debate it was finally agreed that, instead of an entirely new Mental Health Act, the 2007 Act should be only an amendment to the Mental Health Act 1983. The Mental Health Act 2007 received Royal Assent in July 2007, and comes into full operation in November 2008. Although most of the changes are less radical than those originally proposed (Zigmond 2007), the precise effect and meaning of some parts of the amendments are unclear and look set to be tested by case law.

The remainder of this chapter will describe the main features of the 1983 and 2007 Mental Health Acts. Readers requiring a more in-depth description of this legislation are advised to consult Jones (2008) or Bowen (2008) for further information.

Definition of mental disorder

Under the 1983 Act mental disorder was loosely defined as 'mental illness, arrested or incomplete development of mind, psychopathic disorder and any other disorder or disability of mind'. Four legal categories of mental disorder were given: Mental Illness, Psychopathic Disorder, Mental Impairment and Severe Mental Impairment. Although what constituted Mental Illness was not defined in the Act, the other three forms of mental disorder were defined. Psychopathic Disorder was defined as a 'persistent disorder or disability of mind (whether or not including significant impairment of intelligence) resulting in abnormally aggressive or seriously irresponsible conduct'. This was taken by most clinicians to equate to severe personality disorder. Mental Impairment was defined as 'a state of arrested or incomplete development of mind (not amounting to severe mental impairment) which includes significant impairment of intelligence and social functioning and is associated with abnormally aggressive or seriously irresponsible conduct on the part of the person concerned'. Severe Mental Impairment was similarly defined except that the word 'significant' was replaced with 'severe' and the part in parentheses removed. These definitions were taken by most clinicians to equate to mild to moderate learning disability and severe learning disability respectively.

In the Mental Health Act 2007, these four forms of mental disorder have been abandoned and instead a single definition of mental disorder has been introduced: 'any disorder or disability of the mind'. This is a wide definition and how it will be applied in clinical settings is not yet known. However, it is clear that this definition is sufficiently vague to mean that there will be few conditions which mental health professionals could not consider to be a mental disorder. Furthermore, under the 1983 Act, there were specific exclusion criteria stating that substance dependence and sexual deviancy should not be the sole grounds for making an application for admission to hospital. In the 2007 Act, the exclusion of sexual deviancy has been removed, although that for substance dependence remains. Again, how this change will affect clinical practice is not yet clear but it theoretically means that a person with paedophilia but no other evidence of mental disorder could now be detained in hospital if thought appropriate.

Criteria for compulsory hospital admission

In order for a person to be liable to be detained under the Mental Health Act 2007, four criteria must be met. These criteria are:

1 the individual must have, or be suspected to have, a mental disorder;
2 the mental disorder must be of a nature or degree to warrant detention in or to receive medical treatment in hospital;
3 detention must be in the interests of the patient's health and safety or for the protection of others; and
4 appropriate treatment must be available.

Medical treatment is broadly defined as being treatment 'the purpose of which is to alleviate, or to prevent a worsening of, the disorder or one or more of its symptoms or manifestations'. Under the 1983 Act this had been established as including nursing care, psychological interventions, specialist mental health habilitation, rehabilitation and care. Thus, like the definition of mental disorder, this definition is sufficiently wide as to potentially include almost any intervention provided by mental health professionals. In the 2007 Act, the criterion that 'appropriate treatment is available' is clarified as 'that medical treatment is available which is appropriate in the patient's case, taking into account the nature or degree of his mental disorder and all other circumstance of the case'.

Professional roles and the Mental Health Act 2007

In the 1983 Act, the person responsible for the detained patient was the Responsible Medical Officer (RMO). The 2007 Act replaces this with the Responsible Clinician (RC) who is the mental health professional in overall charge of a patient's care. This role is no longer exclusively the province of medical doctors (psychiatrists) and can now be undertaken by others with appropriate expertise and training, including psychologists, occupational therapists, social workers and nurses. Another new position is that of Approved Mental Health Professional (AMHP), which replaces the narrower Approved Social Worker (ASW) role. The Approved Mental Health Professional is the person responsible for making an application, after obtaining appropriate medical recommendations, for admission to hospital under civil sections of the Mental Health Act 2007. This person also has other rights and responsibilities regarding the compulsory admission of patients to hospital; in particular, he or she is required to act by taking into account the wishes of the patient and the patient's family and to pay particular attention to the patient's overall social well-being. Following appropriate expertise and training, any mental health professional, except for psychiatrists, can apply to take on this role.

Common civil sections authorising hospital detention

Admission for assessment (section 2)

Section 2 of the Mental Health Act allows compulsory admission of someone suspected as suffering from mental disorder but who is refusing to be admitted to be detained in hospital for up to 28 days to allow for assessment. To detain someone under a section 2 order requires the agreement of an Approved Mental Health Professional and two doctors, one of whom must be 'section 12 approved', that is certified as having special expertise in psychiatry and the use of the Mental Health Act. Although the primary purpose of admission under section 2 is for assessment, this may also include treatment, and patients detained under section 2 can be treated with psychiatric medication against their will if this is thought to be appropriate. A patient detained under section 2 can be discharged from the section by his Responsible Clinician before the end of the 28-day period if thought appropriate. The patient's nearest relative also has the power to order the patient's discharge. In addition, the patient can appeal against their detention to the Hospital Managers or a Mental Health Review Tribunal (see Chapter 9 for more details on Mental Health Review Tribunals). Detention under section 2 is not renewable, but the Responsible Clinician can apply for the patient's continued detention after 28 days under section 3 of the Mental Health Act.

Admission for treatment (Section 3)

Section 3 of the Mental Health Act is a six-month hospital treatment order that is renewable for a further six months and then renewable annually. To make an application for admission under section 3, an Approved Mental Health Professional and two doctors (including at least one section 12 approved doctor) must certify that the criteria for compulsory admission are met. Patients detained under section 3 have similar rights of appeal against detention as those detained under section 2. The patient's nearest relative retains the power to order the discharge of the patient but, if it is thought that the patient may be a risk to others, the Responsible Clinician can apply to the County Court for a 'barring order' to prevent discharge, although in practice this situation rarely occurs. Unlike a section 2, the nearest relative can oppose the making of an application for detention under section 3.

Common sections authorising detention in hospital of mentally disordered offenders

Hospital order (section 37)

Those who have been convicted of an imprisonable offence but are thought to be mentally disordered and in need of hospital treatment at the time of sentencing can be made the subject of a hospital order under section 37 of the Mental Health Act 1983. In many respects this is similar to a section 3 treatment order in that it lasts for six months, can then be renewed for a further six months and can then be renewed annually. The rules concerning consent to treatment and rights of appeal to the Hospital Managers and Mental Health Review Tribunals which apply to section 3 patients also apply to those detained under section 37. However, unlike section 3, the nearest relative has no right to oppose admission or seek discharge from a hospital order. Both Magistrates' Courts and Crown Courts have the power to make a hospital order, but they must have medical evidence from two doctors (one of whom must be section 12 approved) that the convicted person is mentally disordered and requires treatment in hospital. It is important to note that such an order is made or not made on the basis of how the person is *at the time of sentencing*. Thus it is perfectly possible that a person may have been extremely unwell at the time of their offence but by the time of sentencing has recovered sufficiently to make a hospital order inappropriate. Conversely, a person may have been mentally well at the time of his offence but developed a mental disorder in the intervening period which now requires the making of a hospital order. Once the court has made a hospital order an appropriate hospital bed must be found for the patient within 28 days.

Restriction order (section 41)

If a person who is eligible for a hospital order at the time of sentencing is thought to pose a risk of serious harm to others, a Crown Court may impose a restriction order, under section 41 of the Mental Health Act, which is additional to the section 37 hospital order. Only a Crown Court has the power to impose a restriction order, but if a Magistrates' Court thinks that a patient's risk is sufficiently serious, the case may be sent to the Crown Court for consideration of this. To make a restriction order, a Crown Court must hear oral evidence from a doctor (in addition to the two written medical recommendations required for a section 37 hospital order). A restriction order is made on the grounds of public protection and imposes obligations both on the patient and their Responsible Clinician. It limits the power of the Responsible Clinician to grant leave or transfer the patient to another hospital; these moves must be authorised by the Minister of Justice via the Mental Health Unit at the Ministry of Justice. The patient can only be discharged on the order of the Ministry of Justice or a Mental Health Review Tribunal. Thus a patient subject only to a section 37 hospital order may be discharged by the Responsible Clinician, but the Responsible Clinician of a patient detained under a hospital order with restrictions can only make a recommendation for discharge to either the Ministry of Justice or a Mental Health Review Tribunal. In addition, the Ministry of Justice must receive an annual report from a restricted patient's Responsible Clinician detailing the patient's progress and current presentation. A patient detained under a hospital order with restrictions (section 37/41) who is no longer thought to require hospital treatment may be the subject of either an absolute discharge or, more commonly, a conditional discharge. Patients subject to a conditional discharge are obliged to comply with certain conditions specified by the Ministry of Justice or the Mental Health Review Tribunal. Such conditions may include a condition of residence at a certain place, the requirement to take medication, to abstain from illicit drugs and alcohol, or to maintain regular contact with mental health services. If a patient does not follow these conditions or if there is evidence of deterioration in mental state, which is associated with evidence of increased risk, then the patient can be compulsorily recalled to hospital.

Transfer of sentenced prisoners to hospital (section 47)

Section 47 of the Mental Health Act allows for a sentenced prisoner to be transferred from prison to hospital if such a transfer is thought appropriate for the treatment of a suspected mental disorder. Such a transfer order is made by the Ministry of Justice, after receipt of two medical reports stating that this is necessary, although the Minister has discretion as to whether to act upon these medical recommendations. When a serving prisoner is transferred to hospital, the original prison sentence will remain but the time they spend in hospital is counted against this sentence. When the patient is sufficiently recovered such that hospital treatment is no longer appropriate, the patient is returned to prison to serve the remainder of his or her sentence. If a patient is still in hospital and thought to continue to require hospital treatment at the time that their sentence expires (i.e. if they were still in prison they would have been released), then they will become subject to continued detention under what is known as a 'notional section 37 hospital order'. In essence, this means that the patient is now treated as if he or she had been made the subject of an unrestricted hospital order.

Transfer of unsentenced prisoners to hospital (section 48)

Section 48 is similar to section 47 but, rather than applying to convicted prisoners, it allows for the transfer of remanded and civil prisoners to hospital. Prior to the Mental Health Act 2007, the provisions of section 48 applied only to patients suffering from mental illness or severe mental impairment, but these have now been extended to patients with any mental disorder. A section 48 transfer may sometimes be made to allow further assessment in hospital of a remanded prisoner to determine if the making of a hospital order under section 37 is appropriate. The requirements for making a section 47 transfer order also apply to section 48, as do the other provisions regarding the powers of the Mental Health Review Tribunal and liability to remission back to prison.

Section 49 restriction order

In all but exceptional cases, the Ministry of Justice will impose a restriction order under section 49 of the Mental Health Act when making a transfer order under sections 47 or 48. These restrictions are similar to those that apply when a patient is given a restriction order under section 41 in that the Ministry of Justice must authorise all leave, transfer and discharge and must receive a yearly progress report. Patients detained under a section 47 or 48 transfer direction with restrictions under section 49 (i.e. section 47/49 or section 48/49) can appeal against their detention to a Mental Health Review Tribunal. However, unlike patients detained under section 3 or section 37, if they are successful they are remitted back to prison rather than being discharged into the community.

Information Box 1.3 summarises the sections of the MHA allowing compulsory hospital admission.

Other provisions of the Mental Health Act

Leave (section 17)

Section 17 of the Mental Health Act allows the Responsible Clinician to grant leave to the patient (although for patients subject to restrictions under either sections 41 or 49 approval must also be granted by the Ministry of Justice). This leave may be to the community or to another hospital and may be unescorted or may require the patient to be escorted by hospital staff. The purpose of such leave is typically to allow the patient to attend for medical treatment in a general hospital, to aid rehabilitation back into the community, to allow a trial transfer of care to another hospital of lower security (while still retaining the ability to rapidly recall the patient if any problems arise), to allow for assessment of the patient's ability to cope in the community (i.e. testing out) or for compassionate reasons (e.g. to attend a family funeral).

Community treatment order (section 17A–G)

Community treatment orders (CTOs) were introduced under the Mental Health Act 2007. Under a community treatment order, a patient, who must first have been subject to either a section 3 (admission for treatment) or section 37 (hospital order), can be obliged to comply with a treatment regimen and certain other conditions (for example attending appointments with mental health professionals) when they have been discharged into the community. The Responsible Clinician can apply for the community treatment order and is able to specify what the conditions of the order should be. If a patient breaks a condition of his community treatment order, he or she can then be recalled to hospital and treated as if subject to a section 3 or section 37. While a community treatment order does not actually allow medication to be given against the patient's will in the community, if compliance with medication is a condition of the order he or she can be recalled to hospital and given this medication against his or

Information Box 1.3 Sections of the Mental Health Act authorising admission to hospital

Section	Name	Made by	Maximum length of time	Other
			Civil sections	
s. 2	Admission for assessment	Two doctors and an Approved Mental Health Professional (AMHP)	28 days, not renewable	–
s. 3	Admission for treatment	Two doctors and an Approved Mental Health Professional (AMHP)	6 months, then renewable for a further 6 months, then renewable yearly	–
s. 4	Admission for assessment in cases of emergency	One doctor and an Approved Mental Health Professional (AMHP)	72 hours, not renewable	Should only be used where it is not possible to obtain a second medical opinion within a reasonable timescale. Once in hospital patient must be assessed for a s.2 or s.3 as soon as possible.
s. 5(2)	Doctor's holding power	Doctor	72 hours, not renewable	Can only be used to detain a voluntary patient who is already in hospital to prevent them from leaving to allow assessment for possible detention under s.2 or s.3.

s. 5(4)	Nurse's holding power	Registered mental health nurse	6 hours, not renewable	Can only be used to detain a voluntary patient who is already in hospital to prevent them from leaving to allow assessment for possible detention under s.2 or s.3.
Criminal justice sections				
s. 35	Remand to hospital for a report	Court – but requires 1 medical recommendation	4 weeks, renewable up to 12 weeks maximum	Can only be discharged by the court
s. 36	Remand for treatment	Crown Court only – but requires 2 medical recommendations	4 weeks, renewable up to 12 weeks maximum	Can only be discharged by the court
s. 37	Hospital order	Court – but requires 2 medical recommendations	6 months, then renewable for a further 6 months, then renewable yearly	Patient must have been convicted of an offence potentially punishable by imprisonment
s. 38	Interim hospital order (trial of treatment)	Court	Up to 12 months	Imposed following conviction but prior to sentencing to determine if a hospital order (s. 37) is appropriate

s. 45A	Hospital and limitation direction (hybrid order)	Crown Court	As specified by court	In effect a custodial sentence with an immediate hospital transfer direction so that if patient does not comply with treatment/decided that treatment no longer appropriate, they can be returned to prison to complete their sentence; very rarely used
s. 47	Transfer of a sentenced prisoner	Two doctors with agreement of Ministry of Justice	Until end of sentence	–
s. 48	Transfer of a remanded prisoner	Two doctors with agreement of Ministry of Justice	Until convicted	–
s. 135	Power to enter premises	Magistrate upon application of an AMHP	72 hours	–
s. 136	Power to remove to a place of safety	A policeman	72 hours	–

her will in hospital. These powers are far-reaching and potentially decrease a community patient's autonomy, even when he or she is mentally well. The use of community treatment orders has been one of the most controversial aspects of the 2007 Act and has generated much debate. While those who oppose these orders argue that they decrease a patient's autonomy and rights, supporters of community treatment orders argue that it is unfair to allow chronically ill patients to deteriorate in the community to the point that they become sufficiently unwell to require hospital admission, after which they are discharged to the community only to deteriorate once again (the 'revolving door patient').

Duty to provide aftercare (section 117)
Section 117 of the Mental Health Act imposes a duty upon the patient's responsible health authority and local authority to provide appropriate aftercare. This duty only applies for patients who have been detained under sections 3, 37, 47 and 48 of the Act. Prior to any proposed discharge of a previously detained patient it is good practice to hold a section 117 pre-discharge meeting to discuss the patient's likely aftercare needs with representatives of the relevant healthcare and social services.

Removal from a public place to a place of safety (section 136)
Section 136 of the Mental Health Act allows a police officer to detain and remove a suspected mentally disordered person to a place of safety to allow further assessment. If this assessment concludes that the person may be mentally disordered and either at risk of self-neglect or at risk of harm to themselves or others, assessment for admission under sections 2 or 3 can then take place. The definition of a place of safety is a matter for local policy but is typically a designated police station, psychiatric hospital or emergency department of a general hospital. This section can last a maximum of 72 hours and is not renewable. This section automatically terminates if a person is assessed as not requiring hospital treatment.

Right to enter premises (section 135)
Section 135 allows for an Approved Mental Health Professional, acting on medical advice, to apply to a Magistrates' Court for a warrant to allow the police to enter private premises and remove to a place of safety a person who is thought to be mentally disordered. This section is typically used when someone who is thought to be mentally disordered refuses to see or allow mental health professionals to enter

his home to make an assessment for admission under sections 2 or 3 of the Mental Health Act. Once at the place of safety, the person is treated as if subject to section 136.

Consent to treatment

The rules concerning consent to treatment for patients detained under the Mental Health Act are complex, and readers are advised to consult a more detailed source such as Jones (2008). As a general rule, patients detained under sections of the Mental Health Act which only last up to 72 hours (e.g. section 136) cannot be given medication against their will except in cases of emergency where there are serious risks to the patient or others, in which case medication can be given under the Common Law doctrine of necessity. Patients detained under substantive sections of the Mental Health Act (e.g. sections 2, 3, 37, 47, 48) can be given medication against their will for three months (the 'three-month rule'), even if they have mental capacity or have a valid advance directive refusing such treatment. This period begins when the patient is first given medication, regardless of whether they are agreeing to take it. After three months' treatment, the Responsible Clinician must seek the patient's consent to continue medication. If the patient is unable to consent (i.e. lacks capacity) or refuses to consent, then the Responsible Clinician must seek a second opinion from an independent psychiatrist appointed by the Mental Health Act Commission. Medication can then only be give if the Second Opinion Appointed Doctor (SOAD) agrees with the Responsible Clinician that such treatment is appropriate.

There are particular provisions, with additional safeguards, for non-drug treatments such as electroconvulsive therapy (ECT), the use of implantable hormones and psychosurgery. It is important to note that the consent to treatment rules of the Mental Health Act apply only to patients in hospital and that prison health care centres are not regarded as hospital for the purposes of the Act. Thus those who are mentally unwell in prison cannot be compelled under the Mental Health Act to take medication. In severe cases, emergency psychotropic medication can be given when a prisoner is refusing it under Common Law.

Information Box 1.4 provides a fictitious case history showing how the Mental Health Act could be used to provide a patient with appropriate care.

Information Box 1.4 A fictional case history demonstrating appropriate use of the Mental Health Act

Background

Mr A is a 35-year-old single man who has a long history of contact with mental health services. He experienced a difficult upbringing. In early adolescence he began to use cannabis heavily and engage in petty criminality.

Section 2 admission (admission for assessment)

At the age of 20 Mr A began to believe that 'secret agents' were following him and that his family were conspiring with the agents. He also began to hear the voice of his 'commander' and this voice instructed him in how he could overcome the agents. His behaviour was increasingly disturbed and his family became concerned for their safety.

Mr A was assessed by a section 12 approved psychiatrist, his general practitioner and an Approved Mental Health Professional (AMHP). He refused voluntary admission to hospital and was showing possible signs of mental illness together with indicators of increased risk to others. As a result of this he was admitted to hospital under section 2 of the Mental Health Act (MHA) to allow further assessment to be made. While in hospital he was diagnosed with paranoid schizophrenia and started on antipsychotic medication. He rapidly responded to this medication and agreed to stay as a voluntary inpatient for several weeks to allow his mental state to fully stabilise before he was discharged back into the community.

Section 3 admission (admission for treatment)

When he returned to the community, Mr A would frequently fail to attend planned outpatient appointments. He soon also stopped taking his medication and resumed his previous pattern of heavy cannabis use. His illness relapsed and he again became paranoid and hostile towards others. Mr A continued to refuse medication or voluntary admission to hospital. He was assessed and admitted to hospital under section 3 of the MHA. After three months of hospital treatment Mr A became well enough to be discharged from this section 3 by his Responsible Clinician (RC) and was discharged back home to live with his parents.

Index offence

Mr A's mental state again deteriorated and he began to believe that his parents were poisoning him. He argued with them about this and during the course of this argument attacked his mother with a kitchen knife. The police were called and Mr A was charged with attempted murder and remanded into custody at his local prison.

Section 48/49 admission (hospital transfer of a remanded prisoner)
While in prison he complained that he was being experimented on by the prison officers and that the agents had instructed them to poison his food. Mr A refused psychiatric medication and also began to refuse food as he believed it was poisoned. He was assessed by two psychiatrists who agreed that Mr A was in need of hospital treatment for his mental disorder.

Acting on the advice of the two psychiatrists the Ministry of Justice issued a transfer warrant directing that he be transferred to his local medium secure psychiatric hospital under section 48/49 of the MHA.

Section 37/41 admission (hospital order with restrictions)
In hospital Mr A continued to display symptoms of schizophrenia but began to accept antipsychotic medication. He was found guilty of the index offence of attempted murder but, following psychiatric evidence that Mr A still required hospital treatment for his illness, the judge made a hospital order under section 37 of the MHA. After hearing oral evidence from a psychiatrist the Judge also imposed a restriction order under section 41 of the MHA in order to protect the public.

Conclusion

The purpose of this chapter has been to provide background information about the agencies, procedures and legislation which offenders are dealt with in the criminal justice system. This knowledge is an essential foundation for the work of forensic mental health practitioners, wherever they are employed. Against this background, the following chapters will describe in greater detail the major issues in forensic mental health, namely what are psychiatric disorders, how are they connected with offending and how do they affect the criminal justice process. Later in the book, service provision for mentally disordered offenders and methods of treating offenders will be described. Last, but by no means least, attention will turn to the mentally disordered offender's route out of the forensic mental health and criminal justice systems, hopefully to return to a successful life in the community.

Chapter 2

Mental disorder and offending

Introduction

In this chapter, a general description of the common types of mental disorder encountered in forensic mental health services will be given. Within a book such as this, it is possible only to give a brief overview of how these disorders may present (i.e. the main signs and symptoms of each disorder). Aetiology (causation) and prognosis (long-term outcome) will not be covered. Treatment issues will be covered in Chapter 8 on treatments in mental health settings. Readers seeking a more in-depth coverage of mental disorders should consult one of the standard psychiatry texts, such as the *Shorter Oxford Textbook of Psychiatry* (Gelder *et al.* 2006) or the *Companion to Psychiatric Studies* (Johnstone *et al.* 2004). A detailed description of the symptoms that can occur in mental disorder is given in *Sims' Symptoms in the Mind: An Introduction to Descriptive Psychopathology* (Oyebode 2008).

Mental disorders

The term 'mental disorder' is an umbrella term used to refer to any abnormality that leads to impaired mental functioning or mental distress. Thus it encompasses everything from mild anxiety to schizophrenia and dementia. In discussing the main mental disorders encountered in forensic settings, five subtypes will be described in turn: mental illness, personality disorder, learning disability, substance misuse disorder and disorders of sexual preference (paraphilias).

While each of these will be described separately, it is important to remember that among psychiatric patients in forensic settings, co-morbidity (i.e. the co-occurrence of more than one mental disorder) is common and patients will often have mental illness in combination with a substance misuse disorder and/or personality disorder.

Terminology and classification

As in any specialist area, mental health professionals have developed a particular vocabulary and terminology in order to aid clear professional communication. Unfortunately, this terminology can often be a source of confusion for those new to this field. This initial section will thus try to clarify some of these areas. Information Box 2.1 provides a glossary of some of the specialist language that may be used to describe psychiatric symptoms.

A diagnosis informs clinicians as to the likely aetiology, prognosis and appropriate treatment of a disorder. Mental health professionals commonly use standardised diagnostic criteria to increase the reliability of psychiatric diagnoses and improve professional communication. The two most commonly used diagnostic systems are the *International Classification of Diseases*, currently in its tenth edition (ICD-10: World Health Organisation 1992) and the *Diagnostic and Statistical Manual of Mental Disorders*, currently in its fourth edition (DSM-IV: American Psychiatric Association 1994).

The ICD-10, which was produced by the World Health Organisation (WHO), was designed to be used worldwide and is available in a number of different languages. Mental disorders form only a single chapter (Chapter F) of a complete diagnostic system that can be used to classify all diseases and health problems (both mental and physical). ICD-10 uses an alphanumerical system to code each disorder. All mental disorders are prefixed by the letter 'F', along with a specific code number (e.g. paranoid schizophrenia is coded as F20.0)

In contrast, the DSM-IV was produced by the American Psychiatric Association (APA) to classify mental disorders only, and was primarily designed to be used in the USA and so is only available in English. It employs a numerical system to code each mental disorder (e.g. schizophrenia, paranoid type is coded as 295.30). The DSM-IV is multi-axial, which refers to different domains of information. Mental illness is classified on axis I, personality disorders and learning disability are classified on axis II. Other axes are used to classify the patient's general medical disorders, psychosocial and environmental stressors and general level of functioning. In a comprehensive assessment, a

Information Box 2.1   Glossary of psychiatric terminology

Aetiology – The causes or origins of a disorder.

Affect – A pattern of observed behaviours that is the expression of subjectively experienced emotion or mood.

Affective disorder – A mental disorder characterised by severe and disabling mood disturbances, e.g., depression, bipolar disorder (formerly called 'manic depression'), mania.

Delusion – A fixed, false belief that is not in keeping with the person's cultural or subcultural background and is held with absolute conviction despite overwhelming evidence to the contrary, e.g. believing that they are being poisoned by enemy secret agents.

Hallucination – A false perception arising in the absence of an appropriate stimulus. This can occur in any sensory modality, e.g. hearing voices that others cannot hear (auditory hallucination); seeing visions that others cannot see (visual hallucination).

Hypomania – If mania is mild, it may be termed 'hypomania'.

Mania – An elevated mood state characterised by heightened energy levels, increased activity levels (speech and behaviour), elation, grandiose ideas, racing thoughts, poor judgment, and inappropriate social behaviour.

Neurosis – A non-psychotic mental disorder, often characterised by excessive anxiety, e.g., post-traumatic stress disorder, obsessive-compulsive disorder, or a phobia.

Prognosis – The expected course of a disorder.

Psychosis – A mental disorder where the person experiences delusions and hallucinations that lead to severely impaired functioning.

Sign – External evidence of the disorder that may be seen by another person, for example a mental health professional.

Symptom – Internal evidence of the disorder that is experienced and reported by the patient.

Thought disorder – A pattern of speech (or writing) in which the normal connection between ideas is not apparent and the content appears vague, confusing or difficult to follow. This abnormality is thought to arise from disordered thinking.

---

patient would be assessed on all axes. In the multi-axial presentation of the ICD-10, clinical diagnoses (mental illness and personality disorders) are classified on axis I, disabilities on axis II and contextual factors on axis III (World Health Organisation 1997).

Although mental health problems are common in the population at large, most tend to be mild in severity and are usually dealt with in the community by the patient's general practitioner (GP) and primary healthcare services. These disorders are often collectively referred to as 'common mental health problems'. This group of disorders (which are similar to those conditions previously referred to as 'neurotic disorders') feature low mood, excessive anxiety and worry as their core components. Examples of common mental health problems are anxiety disorders, phobias, obsessive-compulsive disorder and depression. The symptoms of these conditions can be seen as exaggerations or prolongations of normal feeling or emotions. In these conditions insight is usually present (i.e. the patient is able to recognise that he is unwell and in need of treatment).

The term severe mental illness (SMI) is used to describe a group of conditions, including schizophrenia and bipolar affective disorder, in which the illness significantly impacts upon the patient's functioning for prolonged periods. Typically, these disorders cause the sufferer to lose contact with reality in some way and experience symptoms (such as hallucinations and delusions) that are not part of most people's normal experience. Severe mental illnesses often cause the patient to lose insight (i.e. the patient may not realise that he is unwell). In the past this group of conditions was often referred to as 'psychotic disorders'.

Offenders with common mental health problems are unlikely to be treated in forensic mental health settings as they do not usually require the high level and complexity of care that is provided in these specialised units. In the community, they tend to be managed by their general practitioners. In prisons, they are treated by the prison's primary healthcare team, who may seek support from secondary psychiatric care if appropriate. Prisoners with active symptoms of severe mental illness usually require treatment within forensic mental health settings.

Mental illnesses

In specialist forensic mental health settings, schizophrenia and bipolar affective disorder are the most commonly encountered disorders.

Schizophrenia

Schizophrenia is a complex chronic mental illness that is characterised by disturbances in thinking, emotion, behaviour and perception. The prevalence of schizophrenia is approximately 1 per cent in the British general population (Perala *et al.* 2007). It usually has an onset between the ages of 15 and 45. Men and women are equally affected but women have a slightly later age of onset than that of men (Gelder *et al.* 2006). Although the causation of schizophrenia is unknown, it is thought that schizophrenia is a neuro-developmental disorder caused by a complex interaction of both genetic and environmental factors. There is also increasing evidence that many people who later go on to develop schizophrenia display subtle abnormalities of cognition, perception and social functioning for a long period before the onset of overt schizophrenic symptoms – this is known as the prodromal period (Jones 1997).

The precise symptoms of this illness will differ from patient to patient, but in general patients with schizophrenia will present with persistent delusions, hallucinations, disturbed thinking and bizarre behaviour. Schizophrenic symptoms are often classified as positive and negative. Positive symptoms of schizophrenia are those that involve phenomena which are present in the patient but not in the general population, such as hallucinations and delusions. In contrast, negative symptoms are those where the patient lacks something that is present in the general population. Examples of negative symptoms are apathy, social withdrawal, slowness and poor self-care. Positive symptoms tend to be most obvious during the acute stages of schizophrenia, while negative symptoms are a feature of chronic schizophrenia. Although positive symptoms generally respond well to antipsychotic medication, negative symptoms, which may be as disabling as positive symptoms, respond poorly to most treatments. In addition to these two main types of symptomatology, patients with schizophrenia may also often display cognitive deficits and social impairment. The main ICD-10 features of schizophrenia are shown in Information Box 2.2.

Paranoid schizophrenia is the commonest type of schizophrenia seen in the UK, and is the most prevalent type in forensic mental health services. Paranoid schizophrenia is characterised by prominent delusions and hallucinations, typically with a persecutory or grandiose theme. Examples of symptoms of paranoid schizophrenia would be where a person believes God has sent devils to take him to hell (persecutory delusion) and he hears the devils talking about him

Information Box 2.2   Main ICD-10 features of schizophrenia

Delusions

Certain types of delusion are particularly suggestive of schizophrenia:

* delusions concerning possession of thought, e.g. thought insertion, thought withdrawal and thought broadcasting;
* delusions of bodily control or influence;
* persistent delusions that are culturally inappropriate, completely impossible and often bizarre.

Hallucinations (in any modality)

Certain types of hallucination are particularly suggestive of schizophrenia:

* voices giving a running commentary on the patient's behaviour;
* voices saying the patient's thoughts aloud;
* voices discussing the patient among themselves.

Thought disturbances

Breaks in train of thought resulting in incoherent or irrelevant speech.

(auditory hallucination), or where a person believes his food is being poisoned (paranoid delusion) and experiences physical symptoms such as a constriction of the throat or a stomach upset (somatic hallucination).

ICD-10 requires that characteristic symptomatology of schizophrenia is present for most of the time for at least one month before a diagnosis of schizophrenia can correctly be made. It also specifies that this diagnosis should not be made if the symptoms have occurred only in the course of overt brain disease or during states of drug intoxication or withdrawal.

Schizophrenia is a chronic disease that tends to have a worse prognosis than most other psychiatric disorders. The illness tends to run a prolonged course with periods of acute relapse and remission. In between episodes of acute illness, the patient may also experience impaired functioning and disability due to chronic negative symptoms and residual positive symptoms. However, there is wide variation in individual outcomes. About 80 per cent of patients will experience more than one episode of acute illness (Picchioni and Murray 2007) and relapses of illness may be triggered by psychosocial stress or poor compliance with antipsychotic medication. When full recovery occurs, it usually does so within the first two years following the onset of illness. Factors which may predict a good outcome include: paranoid type of illness, sudden onset, prominent mood symptoms, good premorbid personality, good premorbid social adjustment and good compliance with treatment (Picchioni and Murray 2007). Patients with schizophrenia have a 5 per cent lifetime risk of suicide (Palmer *et al.* 2005) and a 1.6 fold increased all-cause mortality compared with the general population (Harris and Barraclough 1998). While part of this increased mortality is due to the increased rate of suicide, the majority of this increase is due to death from natural diseases. This highlights the fact that patients with schizophrenia often also have poor physical health.

Bipolar affective disorder

Bipolar affective disorder is a severe mental illness in which those affected experience prolonged periods of severe mood disturbance. It was previously referred to as 'manic depression'. The term 'bipolar' is used to highlight the fact that these patients have mood disturbance at both poles of the mood spectrum in that they have episodes of both mania (or hypomania) and depression. The ICD-10 criteria for a diagnosis of bipolar affective disorder are repeated (at least two) episodes of significant disturbance of mood or activity level, and this mood disturbance should consist of both manic (or hypomanic) episodes and depression.

The prevalence of bipolar affective disorder in the general population is approximately 1 per cent. It affects males and female equally and has a mean age of onset of 21 years old. This illness tends to run a chronic course, with frequent episodes of mood disturbance. In between episodes of mood disturbance, patients may return to their baseline level of functioning, but a significant minority of patients do not achieve a full recovery in between episodes. Over a 25-year follow-up period, patients with bipolar disorder are likely to experience a further ten episodes of significant mood disturbance. With increasing age and number of episodes, the interval between these episodes tends to become progressively shorter. Bipolar disorder has a high co-morbidity with substance misuse disorders. As described above, those affected by bipolar affective disorder will experience episodes of both depression and mania during the course of their illness. These two conditions will now be described separately.

Depression

Depression is the most common mental illness encountered in general community settings and is a major public health problem. It is important to note that only a minority of those suffering from depression have bipolar affective disorder. The prevalence of depression in the UK is between 10 and 20 per cent, and women are twice as likely to be affected as men. It is the major cause of absenteeism from work and is associated with greatly increased mortality (Scott and Dickey 2003). The characteristic feature of depression is prolonged low mood. While depression is more common after stressful events (such as bereavement or divorce), it is different from general unhappiness in that the affected person's mood is unresponsive to changes in their circumstances and the person's general level of functioning is also decreased. Other typical features of depression are given in Information Box 2.3.

In order to meet ICD-10 criteria for a diagnosis of depression, symptoms should persist for at least two weeks. In addition to prolonged low mood, those suffering from depression tend also to have negative thoughts (depressive cognitions) such as guilt, hopelessness, pessimism and feelings of worthlessness. Weight loss, decreased appetite, reduced libido (sexual desire), diurnal mood variation (improvement in mood in the afternoon compared to the morning) are collectively referred to as 'biological symptoms' of depression. While the presence of these symptoms may indicate a more severe depression, they may also predict that the patient is more likely to respond to antidepressant drug therapy. Depression may occur as a single episode or may occur as a chronic illness with recurrent episodes. As depression is closely associated with suicide, it is essential that all those suffering from depression also have an assessment of their risk of suicide.

Information Box 2.3 Main ICD-10 features of depression

- Depressed mood that varies little day to day and is often unresponsive to circumstances
- Loss of interest and enjoyment
- Reduced energy leading to fatigue and diminished activity
- Reduced concentration and attention
- Reduced self-esteem and self-confidence
- Ideas of guilt and unworthiness
- Bleak and pessimistic views of the future
- Ideas or acts of self-harm or suicide
- Disturbed sleep
- Decreased appetite

Three levels of severity of depression are recognised in ICD-10: mild, moderate and severe. In severe depression, psychotic symptoms may occur, such as hallucinations and delusions. These are usually 'mood congruent' in that their content is in keeping with the person's mood, for example believing that the world is coming to an end or that their body is rotting away. A small proportion of people suffering from depression (about 10 per cent) will go on to have manic episodes and be diagnosed with bipolar affective disorder.

Mania

Mania is much less common than depression and can be thought of as its opposite, in that instead of prolonged low (depressed) mood someone with mania has prolonged elevated (elated) mood. This elevated mood is usually accompanied by over-activity and unrealistic, over-ambitious plans (expansive ideas). The main features of mania are shown in Information Box 2.4.

In order to make a diagnosis of mania, ICD-10 requires that these symptoms have been present for one week. Some patients with mania may not see their elated mood as abnormal and may state how well they feel and how they feel that it is others who are slow and miserable. Others may present with irritability or elated mood interspersed with brief episodes of low mood. In severe mania, over-activity may be present to such an extent that the patient is at risk of physical exhaustion. Patients with severe mania often have psychotic symptoms that are mood congruent (i.e. in keeping with their elated mood), such as a belief that they have special powers or that they are a famous person. Some patients may have a milder form of mania

Information Box 2.4   Main ICD-10 features of mania

- Elated mood (euphoria)
- Increased quantity and speed of physical and mental activity
- Increased energy
- Rapid speech
- Decreased need for sleep
- Loss of normal social inhibitions
- Marked distractibility
- Inflated self-esteem
- Grandiose ideas/delusions
- Reckless spending
- Aggression/irritability
- Increased libido

in which the characteristic symptoms of mania are present but not to such an extent that there is the severe disruption to work or social activities that is seen in mania. This is called hypomania.

Patients with a single episode of mania or a mixed episode (i.e. features of mania/hypomania and depression in the same episode) and those with at least one major depressive episode and one hypomanic episode can be diagnosed as having bipolar affective disorder.

The relationship between mental illness and offending

The relationship between mental illness and offending is complex and sometimes controversial. Most research has focused on violent offending, which is considered more serious as violence directly impacts upon the health and safety of others. Depression and mania can be implicated in offending, for example the depressed suicidal person who kills family members to rescue them from a life of desperation, or the manic person who harms another person through recklessness. However, particular research attention has been paid to investigating the relationship between schizophrenia and violence.

Prior to the 1980s, most mental health professionals thought that there was no link between schizophrenia and violence, believing that those with schizophrenia were no more likely to be violent than members of the general population. Since this time, a wealth of good quality epidemiological studies have overturned this accepted professional wisdom and conclusively shown that those with schizophrenia are more likely to be violent than those without schizophrenia. Table 2.1 summarises some of these studies.

From the studies listed in Table 2.1, the following conclusions can be drawn. First, patients with schizophrenia are at increased risk of violent behaviour compared to those without schizophrenia. Second, the approximate magnitude of this increased risk is that patients with schizophrenia are between four and ten times more likely to be violent than those without schizophrenia. Third, only a small subgroup of those with schizophrenia is responsible for this increased risk of violence. Fourth, those with schizophrenia who abuse illicit drugs and alcohol or who also have a personality disorder may be a particularly high-risk group for violent behaviour. Finally, the violence committed by those with schizophrenia contributes relatively little to overall societal violence (about 10 per cent).

One crucial point to emphasise is that, while a diagnosis of schizophrenia is associated with an increased risk of violent offending, the magnitude of this increased risk is small. Serious violence and homicide are such rare events, that is there is a low 'base rate', that even a large increase in relative risk will still only produce a low overall risk. Thus even those with schizophrenia have only a 1 in 10,000 annual risk of committing homicide (Wallace *et al.* 2004) and in any given year 99.97 per cent of those with schizophrenia will not be convicted of serious violence (Walsh *et al.* 2002). It is also important to note that the UK move from institutional care of those with severe mental illness to community care has not resulted in an increase in the number of homicides by the mentally ill (Taylor and Gunn 1999).

Now that it has largely been accepted that there is a true association between schizophrenia and violence, attention has shifted to why this association exists. This is still an area of controversy but some of the main possible reasons are shown in Information Box 2.5.

A particular difficulty in examining the aetiology of violence is that schizophrenia is a heterogeneous, chronic, relapsing and remitting disease that produces numerous deficits of psychological and social functioning. The risk factors for violence in those with schizophrenia are similar to those for violence in the general population, with previous history of violence and substance misuse being the strongest predictors (Walsh *et al.* 2002). The extent to which psychotic symptoms (i.e. hallucinations and delusions) directly contribute to the risk of

Information Box 2.5 Factors that may explain the association between schizophrenia and violence

Factors pre-dating onset of active symptoms	Factors arising as a direct result of active symptoms	Factors arising as a long-term consequence of the illness
• Developmental problems • Antisocial personality traits • Increased rate of childhood conduct disorder • Early-onset substance abuse • Poor social skills	• Hallucinations • Delusions • Substance misuse • Personality deterioration • Passivity symptoms • Disinhibition and irritability • Mood abnormality	• Stigma • Social exclusion • Unemployment • Deterioration of social skills • Side-effects of medication • Victimisation • Substance misuse

Table 2.1 Summary of evidence linking major mental illness and violent offending

Study	Setting	Methodology	Main findings
Arseneault et al. (2000)	New Zealand	Birth cohort	• Individuals meeting diagnostic criteria for schizophrenia were 2.5 times more likely than control subjects to be violent. • 10% of the cohort's violence was directly attributable to schizophrenia.
Brennan et al. (2000)	Denmark	Birth cohort study	• Males hospitalised for schizophrenia were 4.6 times more likely to have been arrested for a violent crime than matched controls without schizophrenia.
Coid et al. (2006a)	United Kingdom	Cross-sectional survey	• The five-year self-reported prevalence of violence in which the victim was injured was 2% for those with no mental disorder, 12% for those with psychosis and 7% for those with neurotic disorder. • 25% of those with drug dependence and 18% of those with alcohol dependence self-reported violence in which the victim was injured during the last five years. • 26% of those with antisocial personality disorder and 7% of those with any personality disorder self-reported violence in which the victim was injured during the last five years.
Eronen et al. (1996)	Finland	Cross sectional survey of	• Males with schizophrenia were 8 times more likely and females with schizophrenia 6.5 times

Author	Country	Study type	Findings
		homicide offenders	more likely to commit homicide than those without any mental disorder. • Males with alcohol dependence were 10.7 times more likely to commit homicide than those without any mental disorder. • Males with a personality disorder were 34.4 times more likely to commit homicide than those without any mental disorder.
Lindqvist and Allebeck (1990)	Sweden	Case-control study	• Rate of violent offending was 4 times greater among patients with schizophrenia than healthy controls.
Shaw et al. (2006)	England and Wales	National clinical survey	• 34% of those convicted of homicide had a mental disorder but most had not previously received input from psychiatric services. • 5% of those convicted of homicide had schizophrenia. • 10% of those convicted of homicide had symptoms of mental illness at the time of index offence.
Steadman et al. (1998)	USA	Case-control study	• Rates of violence were similar for discharged psychiatric patients and community controls. • Substance abuse significantly raised the rate of violence in both the discharged patient group and community controls. • 17.9% of discharged patients with major mental disorder but no history of substance abuse were violent over a 12-month period compared with 43.0% of discharged patients with substance abuse but no history of other mental disorder.

violence is still a matter of debate but it appears that this is important in at least some patients (Mullen 2006). Another complicating factor is the high prevalence of co-morbid substance use in this group.

It is likely that no single aetiological pathway can explain the link between schizophrenia and violence. Instead it is thought that a number of factors interact via several different aetiological pathways, and these pathways are also likely to vary from individual to individual. For some patients with schizophrenia their violence is directly driven by psychotic symptoms (for example assaulting a family member whom they believe is plotting to murder them), whereas other patients with schizophrenia may be violent because they are frustrated that they are unable to sustain employment or because of the effects of co-morbid substance abuse. For some, violence may be unrelated to their illness.

Despite the rarity of violence, mental health services, and especially forensic mental health services, are increasingly expected to safely contain this increased risk of violence, despite the fact that it may not be always directly linked to the symptoms of the illness. Mental health professionals are still split on whether this should be part of their core role, and if so whether they are able to carry out this role sufficiently well. Maden (2007) passionately argues that the reduction of violence arising in the context of schizophrenic illness should be part of mental health services' core business. He draws a parallel with general medicine, arguing that these services do not dismiss their role in preventing and managing the consequences of an illness just because it is very rare or difficult to predict. Maden (2007) specifically cites the example of pre-eclampsia. This is a potentially fatal complication of pregnancy that kills approximately 7 of the 600,000 women who become pregnant in England each year. Despite its rarity and unpredictability, all pregnant women are screened for the risk factors for pre-eclampsia at each antenatal visit and doctors and midwives receive detailed training in its prompt recognition and management.

Personality disorders

Personality may be defined as the characteristic way in which an individual acts, thinks and feels in a variety of circumstances. It encompasses behaviour, cognition and emotion and looks at these over the lifespan. Personality disorder is a diagnostic term used to describe individuals whose difficulties seem to arise from these characteristic ways of acting, thinking and feeling. Typically, they have difficulty managing their emotions and relating to others. These individuals often seem to be stuck in repeating patterns of maladaptive behaviour that serve only to reinforce their difficulties. DSM-IV defines personality disorder as:

> An enduring pattern of inner experience and behaviour that deviates markedly from the expectations of the individual's culture, is pervasive and inflexible, has an onset in early adolescence or early adulthood, is stable over time and leads to distress or impairment.

The key features of this definition can be summarised by the three 'Ps': the disorder is pervasive, persistent and problematic. A proper assessment of those thought to have personality disorder must take these factors into account and assess not just how the patient is currently presenting, but how he or she has been for the majority of their life and how they present to others. Such an assessment may be aided by the use of a structured clinical interview instrument (Duggan and Gibbon 2008).

Personality disorders are associated with significantly increased rates of mortality, criminality, substance use, unemployment, homelessness, relationship difficulties and self-harm (Harris and Barraclough 1998; Home Office and Department of Health 1999; Paris 2003). These disorders frequently co-occur both with other personality disorders and mental illnesses (Moran 2002). When personality disorder occurs in association with a mental illness it often has a negative impact upon the outcome of the mental illness (Newton-Howes *et al*. 2006; Tyrer and Seivewright 2000).

Types of personality disorder

In ICD-10 there are eight specific types of personality disorder while in DSM-IV there are ten. There is a broad overlap between the ICD-10 and DSM-IV, although there are several key differences. The DSM-IV personality disorders include schizotypal disorder, while ICD-10 classifies this alongside schizophrenia as a mental illness, although both classifications acknowledge that the condition is closely related to schizophrenia and may be a precursor of this illness. Narcissistic personality disorder is included in DSM-IV, but in ICD-10 it is not one of the main listed disorders (in fact, it is classified under the category of 'Other Specific Personality Disorders' without reference to its specific features). There is a key difference regarding DSM-IV borderline personality disorder. ICD-10 describes a similar condition as emotionally unstable personality disorder that is then broken down into subtypes: impulsive type and borderline type. Descriptions of the specific DSM-IV and ICD-10 personality disorders and their key features are shown in Information Box 2.6.

Information Box 2.6 also demonstrates how the various personality disorders can be arranged into three clusters that group together those with similar characteristics: cluster A, the odd or eccentric; cluster B, the dramatic; and cluster C, the anxious and fearful. It has been suggested that those patients with personality disorders involving more than one cluster may be regarded as suffering from more severe personality disorder (Tyrer and Johnson 1996).

A recent UK survey of a sample of the general public, which used a structured clinical interview to assess participants for personality disorder, found a prevalence of personality disorder of 4.4 per cent (Coid *et al.* 2006a). Rates of personality disorder were greatest in men, those who were separated or divorced, the unemployed and those living in urban areas. The prevalence of each individual personality disorder ranged between 0.06 and 1.9 per cent, with obsessive-compulsive personality disorder being the most prevalent. Personality disorder was found to be highly co-morbid with other personality disorders – those meeting the criteria for at least one personality disorder met the criteria for an average of 1.9 different types of personality disorder (Coid *et al.* 2006a).

Psychopathy

Cleckley (1941) was the first to define psychopathy in terms of lack of guilt, lack of anxiety, inability to learn from punishment, impoverished emotions, inability to form lasting emotional ties, egocentricity and superficial charm. Note that criminal behaviour is not a necessary component of psychopathy. In forensic mental health services, all patients have committed criminal or antisocial acts, and some will meet the criteria for psychopathy; these people are sometimes called 'criminal psychopaths'. Research into psychopathy has most commonly used Hare's Psychopathy Checklist – Revised (PCL-R: Hare 1991, 2003), which includes traits (grandiosity, selfishness and callousness) and behaviours (antisocial, irresponsible and parasitic lifestyle). Compared with lower scorers, those who meet the criteria for psychopathy on Hare's PCL-R begin their criminal careers earlier, commit more types of offences, offend at a higher frequency and are more likely to reoffend (Hare *et al.* 2000; Harris *et*

Information Box 2.6 ICD-10 and DSM-IV subtypes and features of personality disorder

	ICD-10	DSM-IV	Main Features
Cluster A 'Odd/ Eccentric'	**Paranoid**	**Paranoid**	Excessive sensitivity to setbacks and rebuffs Tendency to interpret others' actions as threatening Preoccupation with conspiratorial explanations Tendency to bear grudges Combative and tenacious sense of personal rights Suspiciousness Excessive self-importance manifested as self-referential attitude
	Schizoid	**Schizoid**	Emotional coldness and detachment Few activities, if any, provide pleasure Limited capacity to express emotion Apparent indifference to either praise or criticism Preoccupation with fantasy and introspection Little interest in relationships with others Preference for solitary activities
	In ICD-10 'schizotypal disorder' is classified as a mental illness	**Schizotypal**	Odd beliefs Unusual perceptual experiences Eccentric behaviour Lack of close friends/confidants Odd thinking and speech Anxiety in social situations due to paranoid fears of harm
Cluster B 'Dramatic'	**Dissocial**	**Antisocial**	Pervasive pattern of disregard for and violation of the rights of others

ICD-10	DSM	Features
		Callous unconcern for feelings of others Gross and persistent irresponsibility Disregard for social norms and rules Low tolerance to frustration Irritability and aggression Incapacity to maintain enduring relationships DSM-IV also requires clear evidence that as a child the patient would have met criteria for conduct disorder
Emotionally unstable ('borderline' and 'impulsive' subtypes)	Borderline	Labile mood and emotional instability Impulsive behaviour Recurrent thoughts/acts of self-harm Outbursts of intense anger Feelings of chronic emptiness Unclear self-image Pattern of unstable relationships that often end in patient making frantic attempts to avoid abandonment
Histrionic	Histrionic	Dramatic and theatrical exaggerated emotional expression Suggestibility – easily influenced by others or environment Flirtatious and seductive Shallow and labile emotion Constantly seeking excitement and activities in which they are the centre of attention
No equivalent in ICD-10	Narcissistic	Grandiose sense of self-importance Preoccupied with fantasies of their own brilliance/fame/success Requires excessive admiration Exaggerated sense of entitlement

Cluster C 'Anxious/fearful'	Anankastic	Obsessive-compulsive	Feelings of excessive self-doubt and caution Preoccupation with order, lists, rules and organisation Perfectionism that interferes with task completion Unreasonable insistence that others submit to exactly his way of doing things Pedantry Rigidity and stubbornness May be mean with money and hoard apparently worthless possessions
	Anxious (avoidant)	Avoidant	Persistent and pervasive feelings of tension and apprehension Belief that they are inept, inferior and socially unappealing Preoccupation with being rejected in social situations Unwillingness to become involved with others unless certain of being liked Shows restraint within intimate relationships because of fear of being shamed/ridiculed Unwilling to engage in new activities because of fear they will embarrass themselves
	Dependent	Dependent	Feeling uncomfortable or helpless when alone because of fears of inability to care for oneself Difficulty making ordinary, everyday decisions without advice/reassurance from others Subordination of own needs to those of others whom they feel dependent upon Preoccupied with fear of being left alone to care for oneself Unable to initiate a project or do things on his own

al. 1991; Hart 1998). Hare's PCL-R is the most common instrument for assessing psychopathy in those presenting to forensic services (criminal justice and health services) because it is a good predictor of violence and recidivism (see Chapter 6 for more detail). Given the potential implications of an individual's PCL-R score for future risk management and treatment, it is important that this assessment is not undertaken lightly and that it is performed by someone who has received specific training in its use (Hare 2003).

The definition and assessment of psychopathy is a controversial subject (Cooke *et al.* 2007). Its proponents argue that it is a well-validated diagnostic entity that identifies a particular population who are at greatly increased risk of criminal and antisocial behaviour (Hare 1996, 2003). Its critics argue that it represents a medicalisation of criminality and that the use of psychopathy assessments may cause high-scoring individuals to remain in hospital or prison longer than necessary (Blackburn 1988). Because the PCL-R contains items relating to criminality (such as criminal versatility, juvenile delinquency and revocation of conditional release), it is unsurprising that it is closely associated with criminality. In fact, this may be an unhelpful mix of the behaviours that we are trying to explain (crime and violence) and the explanatory variables (traits). Skeem and Cooke (in press) have argued that the core features of psychopathy may be an arrogant and deceitful interpersonal style, deficient affective experience and an impulsive and irresponsible behavioural style and that these features are what explain crime and violence.

Psychopathy lacks specific status as a personality disorder in DSM-IV and ICD-10, although aspects of it are captured in DSM-IV's antisocial and narcissistic personality disorders and ICD-10's dissocial personality disorder. Psychopathy may be considered as a severe form of antisocial personality disorder in which antisocial behaviour is accompanied by emotional impairments such as callousness and lack of empathy, guilt and remorse. As the diagnosis of psychopathy is more closely based on personality traits than antisocial personality disorder (the diagnosis of which is largely based on behaviour), it is argued that psychopathy represents a more valid diagnostic category of personality disorder (Hare 1996) and it is likely that it will be included in the forthcoming DSM-V (the successor to DSM-IV).

It should be noted that clinical psychopathy, as measured by the PCL-R, is different from the legal classification of 'psychopathic disorder' which was used in the Mental Health Act 1983. Legal 'psychopathic disorder' was a much wider term and was taken to equate to any personality disorder, not just psychopathy as defined by the PCL-R. This confusion should soon be eradicated, since the new Mental Health Act 2007 no longer uses the term psychopathic disorder.

Finally, in the UK there are services for offenders with Dangerous and Severe Personality Disorder (DSPD) (see Chapter 4 for more details). While the criteria for assigning someone a label of DSPD have been defined, this is not a true psychiatric diagnosis. Instead it is an administrative label, encompassing both psychiatric and social references, that is used to help define if a person may meet admission criteria for entry into the DSPD programme. In order to receive this label a person must fulfil the following criteria (Department of Health *et al.* 2004): (1) be assessed as 'more likely than not' to commit a serious violent or sexual offence; (2) have a 'severe personality disorder', as defined by a high PCL-R score and/or number of different personality disordered diagnoses; and (3) there should be a 'functional link' between the offence and the personality disorder. The nature of this 'functional link' is not clearly specified, but has been interpreted as the personality disorder *causing* the offending (Duggan and Howard, in press).

Personality disorder and offending

Those with cluster B personality disorders (antisocial, borderline, histrionic and narcissistic) are more likely than those in the general population to be violent, and, in particular, the relationship between antisocial personality disorder and violence appears to be strong. People with cluster B personality disorders have been found to be ten times more likely to have a criminal conviction than those without, whereas people with cluster A (paranoid, schizoid, schizotypal) and cluster C (obsessive-compulsive, dependent and avoidant) personality disorders showed no increased risk of violent offending (Coid *et al.* 2006b).

While the link between cluster B personality disorders and violent offending appears impressive, the potential circularity of this association must be borne in mind. This circularity arises because many of the diagnostic criteria for these disorders (especially antisocial personality disorder) include features that are likely to be associated with criminality, for example irresponsibility, callousness, anger, impulsivity and anger. The nature of the aetiological link between violent offending and most cluster B personality disorders has not been established; however, longitudinal studies have identified the risk factors over the lifespan for antisocial personality disorder (Farrington 2005), and these include early impulsivity, low intelligence, poor parental supervision, harsh and erratic discipline, maltreatment by parents, parental conflict, lone mother, disrupted families, antisocial parents, large families, low socio-economic status, low commitment to school, poor educational attainment and delinquent peers. Additionally, people with cluster B disorders are more likely to abuse alcohol and other substances and are often socially excluded and economically deprived.

As would be expected there is a particularly high prevalence of personality disorder in criminal justice settings. A review of 28 prison surveys that assessed personality disorder identified 65 per cent of men diagnosable with any personality disorder and 47 per cent with antisocial personality disorder, with the figures for women being 42 per cent and 21 per cent respectively (Fazel and Danesh 2002). Those offenders with personality disorder are also at increased risk of reoffending post-conviction. It has been argued that criminal justice interventions need to be specifically tailored to meet the needs of the majority of personality disordered offenders (Dowsett and Craissati 2007).

Learning disability

Learning disability is a term used to describe those who have a global impairment in intelligence that has arisen during the developmental period (i.e. it emerges before the brain is fully mature), persists across the lifespan and results in impairment of the affected person's global level of functioning. While ICD-10 and DSM-IV both refer to 'mental retardation', other terms are more commonly used in clinical practice. In the UK, 'learning disability' is the most common term, as it is considered to carry less stigma and be more acceptable to those affected by this disorder. Other acceptable terms are intellectual disability and developmental disability. Although the key feature of learning disability is abnormally low intelligence, it is the degree to which this affects the person's level of social, occupational and personal functioning that is most important in determining the level of support that a person may need. Thus, although those with a measured intelligence quotient (IQ) of less than 70 may be regarded as having a learning disability, it is their degree of adaptive functioning, rather than absolute IQ level, which determines the severity of impairment. The ICD-10 features of learning disability and its four levels of severity are shown in Information Box 2.7.

Information Box 2.7 ICD-10 features of learning disability (ICD-10 uses the term 'mental retardation')

Impairment of skills (cognitive, motor, language and social abilities) manifested during developmental period that contribute to an overall decreased level of intelligence. Reduced level of intellectual functioning resulting in diminished ability to adapt to daily demands of the normal social environment.

Four severities of mental retardation are defined:

- **Mild** – Intelligence Quotient (IQ) will be in range 50–69; understanding and use of language is delayed and executive speech problems may persist into adult life; can achieve full independence in self-care, practical and domestic skills but rate of development of these skills may be considerably slower than normal; main difficulties are seen in academic school work and may have particular difficulties reading and writing; potentially capable of work demanding practical rather than academic abilities; behavioural, emotional and social difficulties and needs are more closely akin to those found in people of normal intelligence than to those with moderate/severe/profound learning disability.

- **Moderate** – IQ in range 35–49; slow in developing comprehension and use of language with limited eventual achievement in this area; achievement of self-care and motor skills is also retarded and some patients will need supervision throughout life; usually able to do simple practical work if tasks are carefully structured and supervision provided; completely independent living is rarely achieved; able to engage in simple social activities.

- **Severe** – IQ in range 20–34; similar clinical picture to those with moderate difficulties but overall lower level of achievement; likely to also suffer from marked degree of motor impairment or other associated deficits; will not be able to live independently.

- **Profound** – IQ less than 20; limited comprehension and use of language limited to, at best, understanding basic commands and making simple requests; organic causation identifiable in most cases; severe neurological or physical disabilities affecting mobility are common, as is epilepsy and sensory impairment; possess little/no ability to care for their own needs and require constant help and supervision.

The precise prevalence of learning disability in the UK is not known; however, it is estimated that there are approximately 1.2 million people in the UK who have mild or moderate learning disability, with a further 210,000 people who have severe or profound learning disability (Department of Health 2001). The aetiology of learning disability is complex due to the heterogeneity of this condition. For most people with mild learning disability, there is no obvious cause of their disability. Among those with more marked degrees of learning disability, organic causes are much more prevalent and these may be due to genetic abnormalities (e.g. Down's syndrome), birth injury, infection or metabolic disorders.

People with learning disability often have multiple difficulties. In addition to their learning disability, patients with these disorders are also at increased risk of also having mental illnesses, behavioural problems, sensory deficits, neurological disorder such as epilepsy and other physical health problems. The incidence of these associated disorders dramatically increases with increasing severity of learning disability. People with mild learning disability tend to present with similar types of psychiatric problem to the general population, while those with moderate, severe and profound disability show an increased frequency of disorders such as autism, attention-deficit hyperactivity disorder (ADHD), and self-injury.

Learning disability and offending

Low intelligence has previously been found to be a good predictor of juvenile delinquency and subsequent adult criminality (Farrington 1995). However, the association between learning disability and offending is less clear (Lindsay 2002). Aside from the usual methodological difficulties encountered when researching the link between any mental disorder and offending, learning disability poses particular difficulties. Those with learning disability comprise a heterogeneous group ranging from comparatively able individuals able to function and live independently in the community to those who are unable to care for themselves and in need of constant care. Thus most individuals with severe learning disability and many of those with moderate learning disability will be in long-term care placements in which they will have little opportunity for serious offending. Another problem is that the label of 'learning disability' may lead some individuals to be excused responsibility for their actions leading to an under-reporting of their offending. Conversely, people with learning disability who commit crime may be less able to avoid detection than those without learning disability. Those with learning disability are also at increased risk of having other mental disorders.

Having said this, it is likely that there is a true association between mild and borderline learning disability and violent offending, but, as with schizophrenia, the magnitude of this association is small. There is also some evidence that there is an increased prevalence of arson and sexual offending in those with learning disability compared to the general population (Simpson and Hogg 2001). The reasons for the increased risk of offending is likely to be multifactorial and heterogeneous, but factors such as increased impulsivity, poor social and communication skills and social exclusion may be particularly important.

Substance abuse disorders

In the ICD-10 and DSM-IV classification systems, there are three broad categories of substance abuse disorder. *Intoxication* is a transient condition following the administration of the substance and results in disturbances in consciousness, cognition, perception, affect or behaviour. *Abuse* is a pattern of use causing damage to health, risk of accident, legal or social problems. *Dependence* is a feeling of compulsion to take the substance, with impaired control over use, tolerance to the substance's effects, the experience of withdrawal when intake is reduced or stopped and an all-consuming focus on getting and using the substance, with progressive neglect of other activities and persistence in use regardless of evident harm.

A history of substance abuse is common among forensic populations. In England and Wales, 63 per cent of male sentenced prisoners reported hazardous drinking the year before coming into prison, and 30 per cent had severe alcohol problems, with the percentages for convicted women being 39 per cent and 11 per cent respectively (Singleton *et al.* 1999). Of male sentenced prisoners, 43 per cent reported moderate or severe drug dependence the year prior to imprisonment, with the percentage for sentenced women prisoners being 42 per cent (Singleton *et al.* 1999). These proportions of problematic substance users are far in excess of those observed in the general population.

Patients in forensic mental health settings are not admitted solely because of a substance misuse problem, but those with mental disorders show high rates of substance misuse. In studies of the

UK high-secure (special) hospital population, co-occurring substance misuse disorders in those diagnosed as personality disordered may be as high as 53 per cent for a lifetime alcohol misuse diagnosis and 47 per cent for a lifetime drug misuse diagnosis (Coid *et al.* 1999). Among high-secure hospital patients suffering from schizophrenia, as many as 54 per cent may have a co-occurring alcohol problem and 41 per cent may have a co-occurring drug misuse problem (Steele *et al.* 2003).

Substance abuse is a major risk factor for offending. Where illegal drugs are concerned, the crimes of principal concern are acquisitive offences driven by the economic necessity of sustaining an expensive drug habit. The main concern regarding alcohol relates to crimes of violence. The relationship between substance use and crime in mentally disordered offenders is complex (see McMurran 2008). Substance use may bring mentally disordered offenders into social contexts where crime is more likely, some substances may exacerbate underlying aggressive tendencies, and drug and alcohol use may further impair a mentally ill person's thoughts and perceptions to increase the likelihood of antisocial behaviour. Substance use can make correct diagnosis of mental disorder difficult, in addition to complicating the management and worsening the prognosis of the mental disorder.

Disorders of sexual preference (paraphilias)

Sexual deviance is a major predictor of sexual offending recidivism. In a meta-analysis of 61 recidivism studies, providing information on 28,972 sexual offenders in treatment, with an average follow-up period of four to five years, Hanson and Bussière (1998) identified that about 18 per cent of rapists and about 13 per cent of child abusers reoffend sexually, although these figures are likely to be underestimations. Although data relating to previous convictions were the best predictors of recidivism, the most powerful dynamic predictor (i.e. a factor potentially open to change) was having a deviant sexual preference. Some offenders are highly deviant in their sexual preferences, e.g. being aroused by young children or by the victim's distress. While assessment of sexual deviance need not follow a diagnostic system, both ICD-10 and DSM-IV include disorders of sexual preference, as illustrated in Information Box 2.8.

Information Box 2.8 ICD-10 subtypes and features of disorders of sexual preference.

- **Fetishism** – reliance on some non-living object as a stimulus for sexual arousal/gratification. The fetish must be the most important source of sexual stimulation or essential for satisfactory sexual response.
- **Fetishistic transvestism** – wearing of clothes of opposite sex principally to obtain sexual excitement.
- **Exhibitionism** – recurrent or persistent tendency to expose the genitialia to strangers.
- **Voyeurism** – recurrent or persistent tendency to look at people engaging in sexual or intimate behaviour such as undressing.
- **Paedophilia** – sexual preference for children.
- **Sadomasochism** – preference for sexual activity that involves bondage or the infliction of pain or humiliation.
- **Multiple disorders of sexual preference**.
- **Other disorders of sexual preference**.

Conclusion

This chapter has provided basic information regarding the diagnoses that may divert a person from the criminal justice system into forensic mental health services for treatment. Many of the patients seen in non-forensic mental health services may show challenging behaviours that could be defined as crimes, but these patients have been diverted from the criminal justice system. Forensic mental health services generally deal with those mentally disordered people who have committed the most serious kinds of offences. The next chapter will explain how these people enter forensic mental health services.

Chapter 3

Entering the forensic mental health system

Introduction

Diversion from custody refers to arrangements that allow the transfer of mentally disordered offenders from the criminal justice system to mental health facilities, whether hospital or community based. The aim of diversion is to ensure that mentally disordered offenders receive health and social care in suitable facilities (Riordan *et al.* 2000). Diversion mechanisms have existed for over two centuries (Birmingham 2000), but in 1990, the Home Office issued a directive that paved the way for establishing a large number of police and court diversion schemes across England and Wales. This document – Home Office Circular 66/90 – encouraged cooperation between criminal justice, health and social services to ensure that those suffering from mental disorder received appropriate care and treatment, whether or not proceedings were brought.

There is some debate about whether or not mentally disordered individuals should enter the criminal justice process at all. Clearly, such people require treatment, but at what stage should diversion to mental health services occur? Mentally disordered offenders can now be diverted at any stage of the criminal justice process (see Figure 1.1), regardless of whether or not criminal proceedings would have been pursued. It is important to note that diversion does not necessarily result in discontinuation of prosecution, although it is not uncommon for the Crown Prosecution Service to discontinue proceedings during the early stages of prosecution and in cases involving less serious offences (Birmingham 2000).

Prins (1995) lists five main stages at which diversion may occur: (1) informal diversion by the police; (2) formal diversion by the police; (3) psychiatric referral before the court hearing and discontinuation of prosecution; (4) diversion to mental health services at court; and (5) diversion to mental health services after sentence. In this chapter, we will focus principally on diversion at the police and court stages, with a brief reminder that prisoners who develop mental health problems can be diverted to forensic mental health services.

Police custody

Mentally disordered offenders may be diverted away from the criminal justice system by the police who, after dealing with an incident, may take no further action or may issue an informal caution. Alternatively, under mental health legislation, a police officer may 'remove to a place of safety' a person who appears to be mentally disordered and is in need of immediate care and control. Such persons who pose a risk to themselves or others may be detained in a police station for up to 72 hours to allow for examination by mental health professionals (under section 136 of the Mental Health Act – see Chapter 1).

A mentally disordered person who is suspected of committing a crime may be detained in police custody. If an arrested person is mentally vulnerable, the custody sergeant must arrange for attention by an appropriate healthcare professional, that is a mental health professional who is trained in mental health legislation and whose duty it is to ensure that the mentally disordered person is provided with assessment and treatment in a psychiatric hospital. The forensic physician (formerly called a forensic medical examiner (FME) or police surgeon) or appropriate healthcare professional will be required to assess whether the arrested person is 'fit to be detained' and 'fit to be interviewed' (see below). If they assess the person to be mentally vulnerable they should advise the custody sergeant that an appropriate adult will be necessary for any subsequent interview. An appropriate adult supports the person being interviewed, and is normally a relative, guardian or a mental health professional. Also involved at this point are the person's solicitor, who represents the detained person. Criminal justice liaison workers and arrest-referral scheme workers, who are typically community psychiatric nurses and probation officers, are often present to assist the police in identifying people with mental health problems and advise the police on the treatments available.

Mental health problems are common among individuals held in police custody. Robertson et al. (1995) observed all detainees in seven police stations for three weeks and found 1.4 per cent to be actively mentally ill and a further 1.3 per cent were possibly ill or were known to have had hospital admissions for psychotic illnesses. Riordan et al. (2000) reported on 420 individuals referred to a 'diversion at point of arrest' scheme in Birmingham over a four-year period and found that schizophrenia was the most frequent diagnosis, followed by drug or alcohol dependence and neuroses.

Diversion from police custody can be achieved through a number of mechanisms. Police diversion schemes are usually based on collaboration between police and local health and social care agencies (Birmingham 2000). James (1999) reported that by 1999 there were 50 police diversion schemes in England and Wales. Although deficiencies in these arrangements have been noted, including lack of coordination between the agencies involved, lack of awareness among police officers about mental health problems and lack of psychiatric training among forensic physicians (James 2000; Laing 1995), diversion schemes are effective. For example, in the study by Riordan et al. (2000), of the 420 detainees assessed, almost 60 per cent received psychiatric help – 154 were admitted to hospital and 94 had outpatient treatment arranged for them.

Fitness for interview in police custody

Fitness for interview is mainly related to the effects of mental factors on the suspect's functioning while in police custody (Gudjonsson et al. 1993). Although in the majority of cases fitness for interview is determined by forensic physicians, the expertise of psychiatrists and clinical psychologists is increasingly called upon, particularly if the suspect is deemed to have mental disorder or learning disability (Gudjonsson et al. 2000). A major concern is that such individuals are 'vulnerable' or 'at risk' as they may not fully understand the implications of the interview and, in certain circumstances, they may unintentionally provide unreliable or self-incriminating information during the police interviews. Improperly obtained confessional evidence can result in the dismissal of evidence in court and convictions being quashed in the appeal process (Gall and Freckelton 1999).

Fitness for interview may be influenced by a number of conditions. These include: (1) temporary conditions, such as drug or alcohol intoxication; (2) treatable severe mental illness (particularly psychosis and mood disorders); and (3) permanent conditions including dementia, learning disability and acquired brain injury (Norfolk 1997). Currently there are no universally agreed criteria for determining fitness for interview. Gudjonsson (1995) suggested three broad criteria including: (1) inability to comprehend the police caution; (2) disorientation in time, place and person; and (3) the likelihood that the detainee will give answers which could be misconstrued. Rix (1997) suggested a format for assessing fitness for interview which is presented in Information Box 3.1.

Rix (1997) argues that fitness for interview must be distinguished from the notion of *reliability* of interview material. Gudjonsson *et al.* (2000) argue that certain personality traits, such as suggestibility and compliance (eagerness to please), may affect the suspect's ability to give reliable answers to questions put to them during police interviews. That is not to say that such individuals, by the virtue of their personality characteristics, are not fit to be interviewed but that special precautions should be taken during police interviews involving suggestible or eager to please suspects. These may, for example, involve the use of protection under the safeguards of the Police and Criminal Evidence (PACE) Act, part of which addresses fair methods of interviewing suspects.

If the police decide to charge the mentally disordered person, they will first discuss the case with Crown Prosecutors, then remand the person in custody to appear before the courts the next day or remand the person on bail for a subsequent appearance at court.

Information Box 3.1 Rix's (1997) suggestions for assessing fitness for interview

---

- Use the sources of information available to you including:
  - the suspect's existing medical and psychiatric records;
  - custody record;
  - speaking to forensic physician and police officers.
- Obtain the suspect's consent and explain the nature of the assessment.
- Conduct the assessment in a suitable room.
- The assessment should include:
  - psychiatric and medical history;
  - substance misuse history;
  - mental state examination paying particular attention to assessing mood, abnormal beliefs and perceptions, and cognitive function;
  - physical examination.
- Document the outcome of your assessment.

The court

Pre-trial diversion from custody

Mentally disordered persons who are charged with offences may also be diverted from custody at the pre-trial phase. Court diversion schemes were set up to avoid the situation where a mentally disordered offender could spend weeks or months on remand awaiting psychiatric reports (Maden 2008). Court diversion schemes are run by community psychiatric nurses, psychiatrists and social workers (Birmingham 2000). An initial psychiatric assessment upon first appearance at the Magistrates' Court can lead to referral to mental health services, referral to other specific treatments (e.g. drug and alcohol) or admission to hospital on a voluntary basis. The offender may also be compulsorily admitted under non-criminal sections of the Mental Health Act. In many cases the criminal prosecution will be dropped, but in some cases the person may have to return to court for trial and sentencing.

Mental health professionals' reports to the court

Mental health professionals, most commonly psychiatrists and psychologists, may be asked to provide reports to the court. These reports advise on fitness to plead and psychiatric or psychological factors that may provide a defence or mitigation, and provide advice on disposal (Maden 2008). These reports can be requested by the prosecution, defence or judge if it is felt that a mental health issue may be pertinent to the case. Such cases usually occur in the criminal courts but may also occur in the civil court (for instance where the complainant is seeking damages based on having sustained a psychiatric injury as a result of another party's negligence) or the family courts (for example where a mental illness may impact upon an individual's parenting capacity). With the advent of new sentencing powers (e.g. Indeterminate Public Protection Orders) the expertise of psychiatrists and psychologists is increasingly called upon in relation to the assessment of 'dangerousness' as defined in the Criminal Justice Act 2003. Typical issues are presented in Information Box 3.2.

In writing such reports, the mental health professional takes on the role of an 'expert witness', in that their involvement is to give a specialist opinion which the court may use to inform its decisions rather than attesting to the facts of the case. It is also important to remember that, regardless of who commissioned the report, its contents must not be partisan and should present the author's

Information Box 3.2 Issues upon which mental health professionals may be asked to give an opinion for the criminal courts

- Fitness to plead
- Reliability of witnesses
- Intent (*mens rea*)
- Contribution of mental disorder to the offence
- Not guilty by reason of insanity (special verdict)
- Automatism
- Whether defendant has an abnormality of mind which may diminish his/her responsibility (homicide cases only)
- Appropriateness of a psychiatric hospital disorder
- Need for future psychiatric supervision
- Risk assessment or 'dangerousness' assessment

unbiased and considered expert opinion. If there is any dispute as to the opinion given by the expert, then the other parties involved may commission their own reports by mental health professionals. While reports are given in written form, the expert witness may also be called to the court to give verbal evidence. A typical outline format for a report to the criminal courts is given in Information Box 3.3.

When assessing an individual for a report to court, it is important to make the purpose of the report clear at the outset. Following this, it should be emphasised that the normal rules of clinical confidentiality do not apply; any relevant information disclosed during the interview may be used in the report which will be disclosed to all parties involved in the case. In addition to interviewing the individual, relevant collateral information should be actively sought and included as part of the overall assessment. Such information may include: witness statements, transcripts of police interviews, records of previous convictions, probation service reports, general practitioner records and previous psychiatric records.

The involvement of mental health professionals so directly in the legal process can pose ethical dilemmas. A particular example of this relates to risk assessment. In performing a mental health risk assessment, a clinician may report to the court that the defendant is at high risk of reoffending but that a mental health disposal is not indicated. A possible outcome of such a scenario is that, if convicted, the offender may receive a longer (or even an indeterminate) custodial sentence than if a mental health professional had not been involved in the assessment. While this outcome may be desirable in terms of public protection, it is usually less desirable for the person concerned.

59

Information Box 3.3 Structure for an expert report to the criminal courts

Introduction – brief demographic outline of the subject, the offence(s) with which he/she is charged and who requested the report and why.

Sources of information – list the available information which was taken into account when preparing the report.

Qualifications and experience – brief summary of the report author's professional background, qualifications and expertise.

Background history – include family history, early development, educational and occupational history, psychosexual history, relevant personal history and past medical history.

Previous psychiatric history – include contact with any mental health professional or history of symptoms of mental disorder; also include any previous history of self-harm and current treatment.

Substance misuse history – establish which substances the subject has used (including alcohol) and to what extent this use has been problematic both to the subject and others.

Previous forensic history – in addition to previous convictions, also mention previous risk behaviours which may not have resulted in conviction (for example weapon use/carrying, fire setting, interpersonal violence).

Index offence – subject's description of the offence and events leading up to it including mental health and psychiatric symptoms occurring at this time, recent drug use, motivation and appropriate collateral information.

Current mental state and interview with subject – description of current mental state to include attitude to the offence and insight.

Summary – list the main points from the report.

Risk assessment

Conclusions:
(i)   **Diagnostic issues**
(ii)   **Relationship between mental state and current offence**
(iii) **Recommendations**

Some would argue that in this example the involvement of a mental health professional has done the offender harm by increasing his or her length of confinement and that this directly conflicts with the beneficence principle of medical ethics (i.e. that clinicians should seek to do good for their patients). Others may argue against this view by saying that mental health professionals also have a duty of beneficence to the general public, and that their intervention is justified by preventing others from being harmed by the offender. Another view of this ethical dilemma is that it is not in the offender's own best interests for him to reoffend, given that this is likely to result in a further substantial period in custody. By ensuring that the offender is dealt with appropriately, the mental health professional is ultimately acting in the person's best interests, thus preserving the principle of beneficence. While the debate on this issue continues, the General Medical Council made it clear in its latest guidance on good medical practice that doctors have a duty to protect and promote the health of patients and the public (General Medical Council 2006).

Fitness to plead

Fitness to plead is a legal term used to describe the defendant's mental state at the time of the trial. In contrast to this, psychiatric defences (including insanity, diminished responsibility, infanticide and automatism) concern the defendant's state of mind at the time of the offence (see below). In essence, a finding of unfitness to plead (also known as 'disability in bar of trial') means that it is thought that the defendant's current mental state would not allow him to conduct a proper defence.

The origins of this term lie in the medieval courts in which a defendant first had to enter a plea, and if he or she did not, then the court had to decide if he or she was 'mute by malice or by visitation of God'. In 1836, the judge in the case of Pritchard, a deaf mute charged with bestiality, established the criteria for fitness to plead that pertain to this day. In order to be fit to plead a defendant must be able to:

1 enter a plea with understanding of the charges;
2 comprehend the evidence against him/her;
3 follow the court proceedings;
4 instruct legal advisers; and
5 know that a juror can be challenged.

It can be seen from these criteria that fitness to plead is a specialised capacity test in which intellectual performance is assessed. Psychiatric diagnosis is irrelevant as the Court is only concerned with how the mental disorder may affect intellectual capacity to conduct a defence.

The original statute law regarding unfitness to plead was the Criminal Procedure (Insanity) Act (CPIA) 1964. This was subsequently modified by the Criminal Procedure (Insanity and Unfitness to Plead) Act 1991 which itself was recently modified by the Domestic Violence, Crime and Victims Act 2004. Under the 1964 Act, all those found to be unfit to plead were admitted to hospital as if they were detained under a notional hospital order with restrictions (sections 37 and 41 of the Mental Health Act 1983). This had two unfortunate effects. First, those found unfit to plead could potentially be detained indefinitely in hospital and subjected to restrictions, regardless of the severity of the original offence with which they were charged or whether the person actually needed inpatient hospital treatment. Second, an unfit to plead defendant was automatically detained without the court ever having heard any evidence to prove that he or she had done the act or the omission (i.e. neglected to perform what the law requires) of which he was accused.

This unsatisfactory situation was modified by the Criminal Procedure (Insanity and Unfitness to Plead) Act 1991 which gave the judge the power to make a range of disposals rather than a mandatory hospital order. This Act also allowed for a 'trial of the facts' to take place after a finding of unfitness to plead, in which it could be determined if the defendant actually did the act or omission of which he was accused (although this finding was not the same as one of guilty or not guilty).

In 2004, the Domestic Violence, Crime and Victims Act 2004 made further substantial changes to this area. Fitness to plead is now decided by the judge rather than a jury. If the judge finds that a defendant is unfit to plead, then a trial of the facts will proceed in which the jury decides whether the defendant did the act or omission with which he is charged. If he is not found to have done the act or omission, then he will be acquitted of the charges in the usual way. If he is found to have done the act or omission (again, this is not the same as a guilty verdict because the defendant has not been able to give his version of events or advance his defence), then the judge now has three disposal options: a hospital order, a supervision order or an absolute discharge. These are elaborated upon in Information Box 3.4. These same disposal options apply to insanity cases (see below).

Information Box 3.4 Disposal options following a finding of unfitness to plead or not guilty by reason of insanity

---

Hospital order:
- under section 37 of the Mental Health Act 1983, with a restriction order under section 41 if thought appropriate;
- court must hear medical evidence is supportive of such an order being made.

Supervision order:
- enables treatment to be given under supervision for both physical and mental disorders;
- cannot include requirement for person to receive inpatient treatment;
- this is a framework for treatment – there is no sanction for breach of the order.

Absolute discharge.

If a person who is found unfit to plead and is sent to hospital for treatment subsequently recovers and becomes fit to plead, the Ministry of Justice can remit him back for trial and he or she is then dealt with in the usual manner. In deciding whether to remit back for trial, the Ministry of Justice must judge if it is in the public interest for a trial to take place, particularly given that the outcome could be that the person is sent back to hospital under a hospital order, and whether a proper trial could take place given the length of time that may have now passed between the offence and the trial, for example key witnesses or evidence may now be unavailable.

Grubin (1991) reviewed the case files of all 295 defendants who had been found unfit to plead between 1976 and 1988 (i.e. under the old CPIA 1964). On average, there were 24 findings of unfitness to plead each year. The majority of those found unfit were male and had either schizophrenia or learning disability. Most had previous criminal convictions and prior contact with either social or psychiatric services. In terms of the offences with which they were charged, a third were judged to be of mild severity, a third of moderate severity and a third severe. Reassuringly, there appeared to be good evidence linking the defendant with the crime in 80 per cent of cases. A third of the sample were admitted to a high-secure hospital. Just under half subsequently became fit to plead and 80 per cent of those who became fit did so within a year.

Recent changes to fitness to plead judgments and procedures have given defendants a fairer deal; however, there is concern that the fitness to plead capacity test does not appear to be in keeping with recent developments in civil law concerning capacity and in particular the newly introduced Mental Capacity Act 2005 (Scott-Moncrieff and Vassal-Adams 2006). The latter relates to circumstances where decisions need to be made on behalf of others who may have lost mental capacity, for example as a result of dementia or brain injury, or where an incapacitating condition has been present since birth. The Mental Capacity Act 2005 states very precisely how capacity should be assessed and the help people should receive in understanding information required for decision-making and communicating their wishes. Perhaps because of its complexity, unclear relationship with mental disorder, the previous mandatory imposition of a hospital order with restrictions and the poorly specified assessment of capacity, fitness to plead is still only rarely raised at trial.

Psychiatric defences

There are four specific legal issues that psychiatrists and psychologists are often asked to address, which are sometimes referred to as psychiatric defences. These are insanity, diminished responsibility, infanticide and automatism. Addressing these issues requires a good understanding of a number of legal terms. These will be explained first, before moving on to describe the psychiatric defences.

In Anglo-Saxon jurisdictions, crime requires the conjunction of two elements: (1) *actus reus*, a Latin term for the guilty act; and (2) *mens rea*, a guilty mind. Crimes of 'basic intent' are those where proof is required only that the defendant committed the act, with no need to prove that harm was intended (e.g. criminal damage, theft), hence only *actus reus* needs to be established. Crimes of 'specific intent' are those where there is an intention to cause harm, and both *actus reus* and *mens rea* need to be established. *Mens rea* concerns the state of mind at the time of committing an act, including:

1 'intent', which is when the accused foresees and desires that his act will lead to unlawful consequences (think of throwing a stone deliberately to hit someone on the head as opposed to throwing a stone and accidentally hitting someone on the head);

2 'recklessness', which is when the accused foresees that his act will lead to unlawful consequences, but he is not concerned whether

these consequences occur or not, that is the deliberate taking of an unjustifiable risk;

3 'negligence', which is when the accused has neither foreseen nor desired unlawful consequences, but a reasonable person with the same abilities as the accused would have foreseen and taken the necessary steps to prevent undesirable consequences; and

4 'accident', which is when it would not have been possible, either for the accused or another person in similar circumstances, to predict the outcome.

The following example, taken from *Smith and Hogan Criminal Law – Cases and Materials* (Ormerod 2006), succinctly summarises the different states of mind with which an act may be committed: 'If D, driving his car, runs V down and kills him this will be murder if D did so intending to kill V; manslaughter if, though he wished no harm to anyone, he was driving with such gross negligence as a jury thinks to deserve condemnation as to that offence; and accidental death if the collision occurred in spite of the fact that he was concentrating on what he was doing and exercising the care that a prudent and reasonably skilful driver should' (p. 14).

Insanity

In the English jurisdiction, the defence of insanity is based on the M'Naughten (pronounced McNaughten and spelled in various ways, including McNaughton) test. They derive from the trial of Daniel M'Naughten in 1843. M'Naughten, who was probably suffering from paranoid schizophrenia, had delusions about the Tory party, believing them to be conspiring against him. He decided to kill their leader, the Prime Minister Sir Robert Peel, but he mistakenly killed Peel's private secretary, Edward Drummond. M'Naughten was subsequently charged with murder and faced capital punishment if found guilty (the defence of diminished responsibility was not introduced until the twentieth century). At the beginning of his trial at the Old Bailey he said, 'I was driven to desperation by persecution ... I'm guilty of firing.' A not guilty plea was recorded. The court found M'Naughten not guilty by reason of insanity and he was admitted to Bethlem hospital (West and Walk 1977). After the case, the House of Lords asked how the judges handled this case, and their reply forms the M'Naughten test, still used today. The test is presented in Information Box 3.5.

Information Box 3.5 M'Naughten test of insanity (1843)

'The jury ought to be told in all cases that every man is to be presumed to be sane, and to possess a sufficient degree of reason to be responsible for his crimes, until the contrary be proved to their satisfaction; and to establish a defence on the grounds of insanity, it must be clearly proved, that at the time of committing the act, the party accused was labouring under such a defect of reason, from disease of the mind, as to not know the nature and quality of the act he was doing, or if he did know it, that he did not know what he was doing was wrong.'

Notes:

- 'Defect of reason' has to be a consequence of disease of mind **not** brutish stupidity without rational power, absent mindedness or uncontrollable urges.

- 'Disease of mind' includes psychotic disorder, depression, arteriosclerosis resulting in melancholia and sleep walking **not** if the disease is caused by external factors such as alcohol, drugs, anaesthetics or hypnotic influences.

- 'Nature and quality' refers to the physical **not** moral aspect.

- 'Not knowing' refers to the legal **not** moral aspect.

The defence of insanity can be raised to any charge. However, since its criteria are so difficult to fulfil, it tends to be raised only to serious charges. Although a successful defence on the grounds of insanity (also called the 'special verdict') leads to an acquittal, the defendant remains subject to sentencing. The Domestic Violence, Crime and Victims Act 2004 sets out three disposals for insanity cases, including a hospital order under the Mental Health Act, a supervision order or an absolute discharge (see Information Box 3.4).

Diminished responsibility

A defence of diminished responsibility can only be raised to the charge of murder and is defined in the Homicide Act 1957 as:

Where a person kills or is a party to the killing of another, he shall not be convicted of murder if he was suffering from such abnormality of mind as substantially impaired his mental responsibility for his acts and omissions in doing or being a party to the killing.

The 'abnormality of mind' could arise from a condition of arrested or retarded development of mind, or any inherent causes, or could be induced by disease or injury. If the defence of diminished responsibility is successful (i.e. accepted by the court), the charge will be reduced from murder to manslaughter. This in turn will affect the sentencing decision. A murder conviction attracts a mandatory life sentence, whereas a manslaughter conviction may be dealt with by a broader range of sentencing options, including a hospital order (with or without a restriction order) under the Mental Health Act. (See Information Box 3.6 for an example.)

Infanticide

A defence of infanticide may be raised when a woman has killed her child of under the age of 12 months. The Infanticide Act 1938 provides the following definition:

> Where a woman by any wilful act or omission causes the death of her child, being a child under the age of 12 months, but at the time of the act or omission the balance of her mind was disturbed by reason of her not having fully recovered from the effect of giving birth to the child or by reason of the effect of lactation consequent upon the birth of the child, then, notwithstanding that the circumstances were such that but for this Act the offence would have amounted to murder, she shall be guilty of felony, to wit of infanticide, and may for such offence be dealt with and punished as if she had been guilty of the offence of manslaughter of the child.

A successful defence of infanticide will result in a charge of murder being reduced to manslaughter, giving the sentencing judge some discretion over sentencing. A wide range of disposals are available to the trial judge including the use of hospital order with or without restriction. (See Information Box 3.6 for an example.)

Automatism

Automatism is a defence raised when it is alleged that the accused lacked *mens rea* for his or her offence because the act was involuntary and beyond the control of the individual's mind (Haque and Cumming 2003). In the English jurisdiction, two types of automatism are recognised – insane and sane. Insane automatism is due to 'defect of reason' and is subject to M'Naughten Rules. Insane automatism

Information Box 3.6   Case examples of psychiatric defences

Diminished responsibility
Y is known to psychiatric services with a diagnosis of paranoid schizophrenia. He stops taking his antipsychotic medication and starts smoking cannabis. He develops a complex delusional system that he has invented new computer software which will bring him fame. He believes that Microsoft Corporation has been spying on him through his partner's computer. He starts hearing voices telling him to kill his partner. He stabs his partner to death. He pleads guilty to manslaughter on grounds of diminished responsibility. Psychiatric evidence indicates that Y was suffering from acute schizophrenia at the time of his offence. The court accepts the defence of diminished responsibility and deals with the case by the way of hospital order under section 37/41.

Infanticide
X gives birth to her first child after an uneventful delivery. A few weeks later she develops delusions that her child is possessed by the devil. She believes that the child will bring harm into the world. She smothers her child to death. The court, based on evidence from two psychiatrists, accepts that X suffered from post-partum psychosis. X is convicted of infanticide and receives a hospital order.

Automatism
Z is a 50-year-old man of blameless character. He suffers from epilepsy, but has been free from fits for a number of years. Z drives his car erratically, then onto the opposite lane of the road, and collides with an oncoming vehicle. R, the driver of the other car, dies at the spot. Z is accused of causing the death of R by dangerous driving. Z denies any memory of the actual offence. Witness statements indicate that Z appeared dazed at the time of his alleged offence and was driving his car erratically. His legal team raise the defence of automatism. Medical evidence indicates that Z was experiencing a generalised epileptic seizure at the time of his offence. The court accepts the defence of automatism and the accused is acquitted.

may occur in a variety of contexts including epilepsy, narcolepsy and dissociative states. Sane automatism may be related to reflex, sleepwalking, insulin induced hypoglycaemia or head injury. The defence of automatism may also be raised in cases of illicit drugs or alcohol intoxication. (See Information Box 3.6 for an example.)

Prison transfers

Mental health services in prisons are provided by the National Health Service. Most prisoners with mental health problems can be treated by prison-based primary healthcare teams and mental health in-reach teams, who provide treatment similar to that offered to the wider community (Senior and Shaw 2008). However, where a remand or sentenced prisoner has severe mental health problems, he or she may be transferred to hospital for assessment and treatment under the terms of the Mental Health Act, as described in Chapter 1. The treatment transferred prisoners receive is the same as that for mentally disordered offenders with hospital orders.

Conclusion

In this chapter, we have seen that people with mental health problems can be diverted to general mental health services as an alternative to being prosecuted and tried by the criminal justice system. These people are generally not attended to in forensic mental health services. Forensic mental health professionals can contribute to the legal process by giving expert advice on a defendant's fitness to plead, psychiatric defences and psychological factors that may mitigate culpability. In some of these cases, the prosecution may not be pursued and the defendant again may end up in general mental health services. In other cases, the defendant may be found guilty of an offence and receive a mental health disposal. This person will usually be treated in forensic mental health services, as will a prisoner who becomes seriously ill in prison and requires transfer to hospital. The following chapters describe forensic mental health services and the professionals who work in them.

Chapter 4

Forensic mental health services

Introduction

The purpose of this chapter is to describe the mental health services that are available to mentally disordered offenders. These services are of varying levels of security and the underlying principle is that no person should be detained in a greater level of security than is necessary. This principle may not always be applied in practice. One reason is the differential rate of progress through levels of security. Patients in high-secure services may be stabilised relatively quickly to the point of being fit to move on to services offering lower security. However, rehabilitation often takes a long time, and low-secure places do not become available at the rate required. This problem is often compounded by a lack of connection between services, so that there is no clearly planned route for a patient's movement from high-secure through to low-secure services. However, over the past decades, there have been many improvements in the provision of mental health services for offenders in prisons, in secure hospitals and in the community and these are reflected in the descriptions below.

Prison mental health services

Epidemiological surveys have shown a high prevalence of mental disorder among prisoners (Gunn *et al.* 1991; Maden *et al.* 1995; Singleton *et al.* 1998). Singleton *et al.*'s (1998) study for the Office for National Statistics showed that 90 per cent of prisoners suffered from one or more mental disorder (psychosis, neurosis, personality disorder, or drug- and alcohol-related disorders) (see Table 4.1.). Psychiatric-comorbidity was common, with almost 70 per cent of prisoners having two or more of these disorders. A more recent study by Harris *et al.* (2007) suggests that those in the prison population (as compared with the general population) are more likely to have suffered some form of social exclusion, have significantly greater degrees of mental health problems and substance abuse and worse physical health. It also shows that women, young offenders, older prisoners and those from minority ethnic groups have distinct, and often unmet, health needs. Suicide and deliberate self-harm is a serious problem in prison. In 2006, the prison suicide rate was 90 per 100,000. Although this figure represents a reduction in prison suicides from 2004 (127 per 100,000), suicide continues to be a major concern in prisons (Shaw and Humber 2007).

Historically, the provision of prison healthcare was the responsibility of the Home Office. The provision of mental healthcare within the prison system was repeatedly criticised, particularly in relation to

Table 4.1 Psychiatric morbidity among prisoners[1] and the general population[2] in England and Wales (after Birmingham 2003)

ICD-10 diagnosis	Male (%)			Female (%)		
	General	Remand	Sentenced	General	Remand	Sentenced
Psychotic disorder	0.5	10.0	7.0	0.6	–	–
Neurotic disorder	12.0	59.0	40.0	18.0	76.0	63.0
Personality disorder	5.4	78.0	64.0	3.4	–	–
Hazardous drinking[3]	38.0	58.0	63.0	15.0	36.0	39.0
Drug dependence[4]	13.0	51.0	43.0	8.0	54.0	41.0

1 Singleton *et al.* (1998).
2 Meltzer *et al.* (1995).
3 In the year prior to imprisonment.
4 Current.

the quality of care provided, isolation from the National Health Service (Her Majesty's Inspectorate of Prisons 1996), inadequacies in reception screening and failure to meet the treatment needs of mentally disordered prisoners (Birmingham 2003). In April 2003, the responsibility of providing healthcare to the prison population was devolved to the National Health Service. There followed major reforms in prison mental health services with the aim of achieving equivalence of healthcare – that is to 'give prisoners access to the same quality and range of health care services as the general public receives from the NHS' (Health Advisory Committee for the Prison Service 1997).

Two levels of healthcare services are provided within prisons – primary healthcare and secondary healthcare. Primary healthcare services are led by nurses and general practitioners and act as the first point of contact in most prisons. Primary healthcare services in some prisons offer specialist drug and alcohol services, such as education, detoxification and methadone maintenance programmes. Secondary mental healthcare services are mainly represented by mental health in-reach teams, which have been established in most prisons (Shaw and Humber 2007). These should be equivalent to community mental health teams, but most are represented only by community psychiatric nurses and only a few offer proper multidisciplinary mental healthcare. Psychiatric input to prisons is usually provided by visiting psychiatrists, most of whom are forensic psychiatrists. Although in some prisons general adult psychiatrists also provide input, there is a perception among general psychiatrists that the provision of prison mental healthcare lies in the domain of forensic psychiatry. A small number of psychiatrists work in prisons full time. Some predict that prison psychiatry may become a distinct speciality in the future, although this seems unlikely to become a reality soon.

Suicide prevention has become a major target in prisons. The risk of suicide is increased during the transitional stages of imprisonment such as pre-custody, reception and post-custody (Pratt et al. 2006; Shaw et al. 2004). There are now calls for mental health service improvements to occur at all stages of imprisonment, particularly during these transitional stages (Shaw and Humber 2007). There currently exist no formal arrangements to support prisoners pre-custody, although some work has been undertaken to improve health screening upon reception into prison (Grubin et al. 2002). Health screening at reception may help to identify those with mental health problems and those at risk of suicide. Moreover, there are now initiatives to train prisoners (also known as 'wing listeners') to provide emotional support to fellow prisoners, particularly those at risk of self-harm or suicide. The Assessment, Care in Custody and Teamwork (ACCT) approach has been introduced to manage prisoners at high risk of self-harm and suicide. ACCT promotes a multidisciplinary approach and good quality engagement with the at-risk prisoner.

Intensive care beds, staffed round the clock, are now available in some prisons (mostly Category A and B prisons). A large proportion of these beds are occupied by prisoners with mental health problems, particularly those awaiting transfer to secure hospital facilities (Birmingham 2003). A few prisons offer specialised interventions for people with personality disorder. The therapeutic community at HMP Grendon Underwood has been in operation for over 40 years. More recently, therapeutic communities have been established in Gartree and Dovegate prisons. Recent years have seen the development of two prison-based units in Frankland and Whitemoor high-security (Category A) prisons for the treatment of prisoners with 'dangerous and severe personality disorder' (DSPD). In the future, step-down DSPD units may also be developed in category B and C prisons.

Secure hospitals

Forensic mental health services are provided both within the National Health Service and the independent (private) sector. Inpatient services are usually delivered at secure hospitals which are stratified, based on the level of security measures they provide, into three levels of security – high (only available within the NHS), medium and low. Within secure hospitals, three types of security measures are provided – physical, relational and procedural (Exworthy and Gunn 2003; Kennedy 2002). Physical security refers to the use of physical measures to prevent escape from hospital, such as a perimeter fence, locked doors, airlocks and escape-proof windows. Relational security is concerned with a detailed knowledge of the patient, a high staff-to-patient ratio and the therapeutic rapport established between staff and patients. Procedural security is concerned with policies and procedures used to control risk within the unit, including room searches, escorting patients as they move within the unit and rules regarding visits.

Secure hospitals consider referrals from a range of agencies including prison, probation, other forensic mental health services, general psychiatric services and sometimes the Ministry of Justice. The level of risk posed by the patient determines the level of security that will be required. A decision to admit a patient or not is usually informed by a gatekeeping assessment conducted beforehand. Such an assessment is usually carried out by professionals working in the receiving hospital. The manner in which forensic services currently operate means that patient movement or transfer between one level of security and another and between hospitals and community settings is integral to the practice of forensic mental health. The emphasis on a multidisciplinary and inter-agency approach to the management of mentally disordered offenders means that professionals have to liaise, co-work and share care for these patients.

High-security 'special' hospitals

Historically, high-security (also known as special) hospitals were the main providers of secure hospital care until the 1970s. High-secure care is currently provided at three English hospitals – Broadmoor in Berkshire, Ashworth in Merseyside and Rampton in Nottinghamshire – and also at the Scottish State Hospital in Carstairs. These hospitals provide multidisciplinary mental health services to mentally disordered individuals with 'dangerous, violent or criminal propensities' (National Health Service Act 1977). Due to concerns over the safety of the public, the UK government has shown long-standing involvement in the operation of special hospitals. Their work has come under considerable scrutiny through a number of public inquiries, for example the 'Fallon Inquiry' (Fallon et al. 1999), which investigated allegations that staff at Ashworth Hospital were not in control of the personality disorder treatment unit. The effects of such inquiries are usually to increase security. Increases in physical security and some procedural security measures are often seen as intrusive and anti-therapeutic; however, increases in relational security through improving the staff–patient ratio may lead to a better treatment environment.

All of the patients in special hospitals are formally detained under mental health legislation. The main criterion for detention at high security is that the patient should present a 'grave and immediate danger to the public if at large' (National Health Service Act 1977). A study by Taylor et al. (1998) showed that the population of high-security hospitals is mainly male, white and aged between 20 and 50. Of the 1,740 patients included in this study, 58 per cent had psychosis (mainly schizophrenia), a quarter of whom also had a co-morbid personality disorder, 26 per cent had personality disorders and 16 per cent had learning disability. Substance misuse prior to admission was common among patients with psychosis and those with personality disorder. Serious violence against another person (including homicide) was the most common precipitant of admission to high-secure hospitals. Other serious precipitants included sexual offending and arson. In a systematic review of 38 reports relating to the British special hospitals, Badger *et al.* (1999) identified the average length of stay as eight years, although there is a wide range of lengths of stay with some high-profile patients being hospitalised for a very long time. Many patients in high-secure hospitals actually required long-term treatment and care in lower levels of security, but were unable to progress because of a shortage of medium- and low-secure provision. The review also found that minority ethnic groups were over-represented in the special hospitals, making up almost 20 per cent of the population.

A follow-up study of patients discharged from high security over a ten-year period showed that 34 per cent of patients had been reconvicted of any offence, 15 per cent of a violent offence, 7.5 per cent of a sex offence and 15 per cent of any serious offence (Buchanan 1998). Factors associated with reconviction after discharge included a legal category of psychopathic disorder and prior criminal record.

Medium-secure units

In the 1960s, an emphasis on reducing the number of beds in psychiatric hospitals and increasing community provision highlighted the need for an additional level of security between general psychiatric hospitals and high-security hospitals (Coid *et al.* 2001). Two influential reports commissioned by the government of the time – the Glancy Report (Department of Health and Social Security 1974) and the Butler Report (Home Office 1975) – paved the way for the development of regional (medium) secure units (RSU or MSU) in most regional health authorities in England and Wales. The first interim medium-secure unit was opened in 1980 and by 1998 there were 29 health service and eight independent sector units providing 1,663 medium-secure beds for adults with mental disorders in England and Wales (Grounds *et al.* 2004). In 2005, there were 2,800 medium-secure beds. The development of secure units led to the emergence of forensic psychiatry as a new specialty within psychiatry with its own academic infrastructure (Coid *et al.* 2001).

Today, the care delivered in secure units is multidisciplinary and underpinned by the principles of the Care Programme Approach (see Chapter 8). There is, however, considerable variation in the operation of services delivered by secure units across England and Wales (Coid *et al*. 2001). The majority provide services for individuals with mental illness, and only a few provide services for women and people with personality disorder or learning disability. The Department of Health (2007) has recently published a document outlining quality principles, specifications and high-level indicators for all medium-secure services in England and Wales (see Information Box 4.1).

Information Box 4.1 Quality principles for adult medium-secure services (Department of Health 2007)

A – Safety

Patients are detained in safe and secure environments with the aim of preventing or reducing the risk of harm to themselves and others.

B – Clinical and cost effectiveness

The healthcare provided should be evidence-based and tailored to meet the individual needs of patients.

C – Governance

Probity, quality assurance, quality improvement and patient safety are central to all the activities of the healthcare organisation.

D – Patient focus

Healthcare is provided in partnership with patients, their carers and relatives, respecting their diverse needs, preferences and choices, and in partnership with other relevant organisations.

E – Accessible and responsive care

Patients have choice in access to services and treatments without unnecessary delay at any stage of service delivery or of the care pathway.

F – Care environment and amenities

Care is provided in environments that are designed for the effective and safe delivery of healthcare (both for staff and patients), providing as much privacy as possible and are well maintained to optimise health outcomes for patients.

G – Public health

Programmes and services are designed and delivered in collaboration with all relevant organisations and communities to improve the quality of healthcare provided and reduce health inequalities between different population groups and areas.

Lelliott *et al.* (2001) described patients in medium-secure care in inner London and reported that the majority were male, single and had been unemployed prior to admission. The mean age was 36 and more than half were black. Most of the cohort had been diagnosed with a psychotic illness, and 10 per cent had a primary or secondary diagnosis of personality disorder. The majority were detained under the criminal part of the Mental Health Act 1983. Over one-third were admitted from courts and prisons, 8 per cent from high security, 15 per cent from other medium-secure units and the remainder from community and general psychiatric services. For over a quarter, the specific offence which may have led to admission was not recorded. The remainder committed a range of offences including murder, manslaughter, sexual offences, arson, assault and criminal damage.

A number of studies report on the long-term follow-up of patients discharged from secure units, with reconviction rates of 10–50 per cent over a twenty-year period (Davies *et al.* 2007; Edwards *et al.* 2002; Falla *et al.* 2000; Maden *et al.* 1999; Maden *et al.* 2004). Factors such as past offending history, diagnosis of personality disorder, shorter duration of admission, younger age on admission and a history of substance misuse were positively associated with reconviction. The study by Davies *et al.* (2007) reported on the long-term follow up of 550 patients discharged from a medium-secure unit over a twenty-year period. The results showed that 10 per cent of the patients had died, of whom one-third died by suicide, and the risk of death was six times greater than in the general population. Half were reconvicted and almost two-fifths were readmitted to secure care. The authors concluded that patients discharged from secure units are a highly vulnerable group requiring careful follow-up.

Low-secure mental health services

Low-secure mental health services are provided within two types of units – psychiatric intensive care units (PICU) and low-secure units (LSU). In 2006, there were 170 PICUs treating 1,242 patients and 137 LSUs treating 1,583 patients in the UK (Pereira *et al.* 2006). Generally speaking, PICUs are managed by general adult mental health services and are concerned with the management of acutely disturbed patients who are difficult to manage on ordinary wards. LSUs, in contrast, are managed by community forensic mental health services which also manage patients discharged into the community. Moreover, LSUs accept referrals from a wide range of agencies including prisons, other secure services, probation and general psychiatric services.

PICUs offer a more time-limited, medically-oriented treatment than LSUs. In contrast, the treatment in LSUs tends to be long-term with a rehabilitation focus (Pereira *et al.* 2006).

Specialised forensic services

Within secure hospitals, there are services that are highly specialised, providing treatment for groups with particular needs.

Dangerous and severe personality disorder services

The criteria for entry to the DSPD programme are that: (1) offenders are more likely than not to commit an offence within five years that might be expected to lead to serious physical or psychological harm from which the victim would find it difficult or impossible to recover; (2) offenders have a significant disorder of personality; and (3) the risk presented appears to be functionally linked to the significant personality disorder (Home Office and Department of Health 2001). The DSPD concept is based on the belief that there is a functional link between personality disorder and dangerous criminal behaviour, a notion that has been a subject of debate, both by the general public and within the mental health profession (Duggan and Howard, in press; Mullen 2007).

The UK government first coined the term DSPD in a consultation paper in 1999 (Department of Health and Home Office 1999). In this document, proposals were made for the detention and treatment of a small proportion of people with severe personality disorder who pose significant risks of harm to others and themselves. The consultation paper was largely driven by long-term frustration within government with mental health services which actively excluded personality disordered individuals from their provisions on the grounds of treatability (Maden 2007). Following a period of consultation, the Home Office and the Department of Health jointly initiated a DSPD assessment and treatment programme in prisons and high-security hospitals, with plans to develop more than 300 high-security placements over a three-year period. Money was also set aside for developing medium-security and community DSPD services. Initially, the DSPD concept and services attracted much criticism (see Information Box 4.2); nevertheless, the DSPD programme has been described by Mullen (2007) as 'a genuine attempt to address the psychological and interpersonal difficulties of recidivist violent offenders in a manner which it is hoped will decrease the damage these people do to others and to themselves' (p. 6).

The current DSPD programme provides services within two Category A prisons (HMP Whitemoor and HMP Frankland) and two high-security hospitals (Rampton and Broadmoor). A case illustration of a DSPD patient is presented in Information Box 4.3. Treatment programmes vary across sites, but their common and original feature is that programmes are designed for highly psychopathic individuals. This includes attention to methods of motivating and managing these individuals in therapy, as well as working with and around their cognitive and emotional strengths and deficits. Work is underway to develop DSPD services for women (the Primrose Project) and services at lower levels of security and in the community.

Women's services

The quality of care provided to women, particularly those detained in special hospitals and medium-secure units, has been repeatedly criticised for being insensitive to their specific needs (Bartlett and Hassell 2001; Fallon *et al.* 1999; Lart *et al.* 1999). In 2000, women constituted less than one-fifth of the patients detained in secure settings in the UK and as a group they differed from men on diagnosis, psychiatric history and criminal records (Coid *et al.* 2000). According to Coid *et al.* (2000), women admitted to high-security and medium-security hospitals are more likely (as compared with men) to have been transferred from other psychiatric hospitals following challenging behaviour; have been admitted under the category of psychopathic disorder; have been convicted of arson and have histories of fire-setting behaviour; have fewer criminal convictions and more previous psychiatric admissions; and be diagnosed with personality

Information Box 4.2 Criticisms of the DSPD concept (after Feeney 2003)

- The term DSPD is a political term with no legal or medical basis.
- Lack of conclusive evidence to support the functional link between severe personality disorder and dangerousness.
- The assumption that dangerousness is a trait and that treatment of a personality disorder would reduce the level of dangerousness.
- Problems of predicting future violence.
- Ethical problems in relation to stigmatisation and detention solely for public protection.

Information Box 4.3   Illustrative case of a DSPD patient

X is a 30 year old man admitted to the DSPD unit from a high-security prison where he was serving a life sentence for murder. X grew up in a disturbed family environment where he experienced domestic violence. He was also a victim of sexual abuse. His father was a heavy drinker who had an extensive criminal history. His mother had a dysfuctional upbringing and a history of violent offending. There has been extensive social services involvement with X and his family and X was on the child protection register for three periods. X was bullied at school and displayed some childhood behavioural problems including truancy and fighting throughout his education. He has never sustained any periods of employment. He has a history of serious sexual and violent offending. X has a long history of contact with mental health services. As a child he was diagnosed with attention deficit disorder and conduct disorder. He was later diagnosed with personality disorder, alcohol dependence and poly-drug dependence. Assessment prior to his admission to the DSPD unit revealed high psychopathy scores and diagnoses of antisocial, paranoid, borderline and narcissistic personality disorders. He also met the diagnosis of recurrent depression, alcohol dependence and poly-drug dependence. There was a high risk of future sexual and violent offending.

disorder, particularly borderline type. It is also documented that a high proportion of women in secure care have histories of substance misuse/dependence, sexual abuse, physical abuse and self-harm (Lart *et al.* 1999). Moreover, women patients are often detained at greater levels of physical security than required (Bartlett and Hassell 2001).

Historically, women were either managed in segregated wards, an approach often described as 'women as afterthought', or mixed wards tailored to the needs of men (Lart *et al.* 1999). The past few years have seen major reforms in women's secure services. In 2002, the Department of Health (2002a) published a consultation paper, *Women's Mental Health: Into the Mainstream,* which highlighted the need for gender-sensitive and gender-specific services, and outlined broad areas for the development of women's mental healthcare. In 2003, a guidance document was issued recommending a way for establishing a network of secure services for women (Department of Health 2003a; see Information Box 4.4). A national group was established to oversee the 'reprovision' of women's secure services, which included an accelerated discharge programme for women patients from high-secure care; establishment of a national high-secure women's service

Information Box 4.4   The national policy for women's secure services
(Department of Health 2003a)

The aim is to provide:

- gender-sensitive and specific women services;
- the least restrictive environments necessary to promote safety and shortest length of stay required;
- a high level of relational security that will enable women to address their mental distress, risk behaviours, trauma issues and offending behaviours;
- evidence-based therapeutic interventions;
- a holistic approach to care, meeting the women's cultural, ethnic, religious and spiritual needs;
- individualised care plans;
- multidisciplinary care and inter-agency liaison.

---

at Rampton hospital; closure of the women's service at Ashworth and Broadmoor hospitals and transfer of all women patients to Rampton Hospital; and establishment of therapeutically enhanced services for women with very challenging behaviours.

Currently, specialised women's services are available across all levels of security. The care provided is multidisciplinary and delivered under the Care Programme Approach. The National High Secure Healthcare Service for Women (NHSHSW) based at Rampton Hospital is currently the sole provider of high-secure services for women in England and Wales. The NHSHSW has a total of 50 beds within four wards, covering three functional clinical streams including learning disability and complex needs, mental illness and personality disorder. There are also three pilot Women Enhanced Medium Secure Services (WEMSS). Standard women's services are also available in medium-secure and low-secure units both in the NHS and the independent sector.

Learning disability services

In England and Wales, services for offenders with learning disabilities are provided across all levels of security. Rampton high-security hospital is the national provider of learning disability services for men. Medium- and low-security learning disability services are provided both within the NHS and the private sector. Looking at the national picture, the results of the 'Count Me In' census showed that in 2006 there were 4,609 inpatients with learning disabilities distributed among 124 organisations (75 in the NHS and 49 in the private sector) in England and Wales (Commission for Healthcare Audit and Inspection 2006). The majority were men (65.8 per cent), under 50 years of age (71.4 per cent) and from the white British ethnic group (89 per cent). The median length of stay in hospital was higher for women than men (36 and 32 months respectively). Ninety per cent had either a learning disability or autistic spectrum disorder or both. Of these, 38 per cent were detained under the Mental Health Act 1983, with more detained patients in independent organisations (76 per cent of patients) than in NHS organisations (24 per cent of patients). Eighteen per cent of all inpatients were on a medium- or high-secure ward. Only 6 per cent were referred from high- and medium-secure forensic units.

There are concerns that offenders with learning disabilities are often placed in 'remote and costly' independent sector units because of the lack of suitable local NHS facilities (Yacoub et al. 2008). In 2006, around 20 per cent of inpatients with learning disabilities were placed in independent sector units. There are now calls to reduce reliance on independent sector providers through the development of local NHS facilities (Yacoub et al. 2008).

Services for Deaf mentally disordered offenders

Before describing services for Deaf patients, the key term will be clarified: the word 'deaf', using the lower case, is the term used to describe those with hearing impairment, while the capitalised 'Deaf' is used to refer to those with hearing impairment who consider themselves part of Deaf culture and use sign language as their main method of communication. While the overall number of Deaf mentally disordered offenders is small, Deaf people are over-represented in forensic settings and have higher rates of violent and sexual offending (Young et al. 2000). Possible explanations for this are factors such as: social exclusion, communication difficulties, organic brain damage and poor educational and occupational opportunities (Miller and Vernon 2003). Another important factor is that many Deaf people receive inappropriate interventions from the criminal justice system, often being excused responsibility for minor offences, and may not come into formal contact with forensic services until they have committed a more serious offence (Miller and Vernon 2003; O'Rourke and Reed 2007).

The needs of Deaf mentally disordered offenders may be very different from hearing mentally disordered offenders. This was reflected in the publication *A Sign of the Times* (Department of Health 2002b) that suggested the need for the development of specific centres and care pathways to meet the needs of Deaf people with psychiatric problems who present a risk to others. There are now several independent sector medium-secure units which provide such a service and a National High-secure Deaf Service has been established at Rampton Hospital (Izycky *et al.* 2007).

Black and minority ethnic (BME) groups

Existing literature indicates that African-Caribbean patients differ from their white counterparts on measures of psychiatric diagnosis (Coid *et al.* 2000), pathways to care (Bhui *et al.* 2003) and the treatment they receive from mental health services (Lyall 2005). Coid *et al.* (2000), in their study of admissions to forensic psychiatry services over a seven-year period, found that African-Caribbean patients were more likely than their white counterparts to be diagnosed with psychosis; have co-morbid substance misuse problems; be admitted following minor violent offences, serious sexual offences and robbery; have more previous convictions; and have been compulsorily admitted following criminal behaviour. Asian patients, by contrast, were less likely than white patients to have had previous criminal convictions, to have previously spent time in secure institutions and to have previous history of drug misuse. Moreover, white patients were more likely than patients from Black and minority ethnic groups to be referred from other psychiatric services and receive a diagnosis of personality disorder. There is also evidence that African-Caribbean patients show greater dissatisfaction with mental health services (Bhui and Sashidharan 2003). They are also more likely to present to services late, be detained under civil sections of the Mental Health Act 1983, be secluded and be given multiple psychotropic medications (Lyall 2005). While these differences may reflect true differences between the groups, it may also indicate the failure of psychiatric services to detect illness and intervene early. Moreover, it may also indicate that the behaviour of black patients is more likely to be criminalised and dealt with through the criminal justice route (Coid *et al.* 2000).

There currently exist no separate forensic services for Black and minority ethnic groups. Some commentators, however, argue in favour of establishing specialist services for this group. Bhui and Sashidharan (2003) argue that:

Culturally informed staff develop innovative ways of engaging and working with distressed people from Black and ethnic minority groups. They develop new methods of ensuring engagement and functional improvement beyond symptom alleviation. They focus on personal contact and relationship-building in the context of culturally congruent thinking. (p. 11)

The counter-argument is that there is no evidence that different ethnic groups have different mental health needs. Furthermore, establishing separate services may imply that cultural issues in healthcare are only applicable to the minority groups, thus 'bleaching' culture out of mainstream services (Bhui and Sashidharan 2003). While the arguments for and against specialist services continue, a 'third approach' to meeting the needs of minority groups has also been suggested (Waheed *et al.* 2003). This has been based on a 'cultural consultation model' (Kirmayer *et al.* 2003). This model proposes that specialist multidisciplinary teams assess patients from minority backgrounds and provide a clear cultural formulation, diagnosis and treatment plan. A team built on this model comes mainly in an advisory role. Professionals working in such teams will provide advice and training to other professionals in primary care, social services, mental health and other related disciplines (Waheed *et al.* 2003).

The inquiry into the death of David Bennett rekindled the debate on the care and treatment of ethnic minority patients detained in secure hospitals. David Bennett was a 38-year-old African-Caribbean patient who died in 1998 at a medium-secure psychiatric unit while being restrained by staff. The independent inquiry into his death made a number of recommendations, most of which were incorporated into the five year action plan outlined in the document *Delivering Race Equality in Mental Health Care* (Department of Health 2005). This action plan (see Information Box 4.5) is aimed at implementing a 10-point race equality action plan in the NHS, and helping NHS Trusts to fulfil their obligations under the Race Relations (Amendment) Act 2000.

Community forensic mental health services

Community mental health services in England and Wales have a recent history. Their development was largely driven by the Reed Report (Department of Health and Home Office 1992), following which

Information Box 4.5 Delivering race equality (Department of Health 2005)

It is envisaged that by 2010 there will be a service characterised by:

- less fear of mental health services among Black and minority ethnic (BME) communities and service users (including those of Irish or Mediterranean origin and east European migrants);
- improved satisfaction with mental health services;
- a reduction in the rate of admission of BME patients to psychiatric hospitals;
- a reduction in the disproportionate rates of compulsory detention of BME patients;
- fewer violent incidents that are secondary to inadequate treatment of mental illness;
- a reduction in the use of seclusion in BME patients;
- the prevention of deaths in mental health services following physical intervention;
- more BME service users achieving self-reported states of recovery;
- a reduction in the ethnic disparities found in prison populations;
- a more balanced range of effective therapies, such as peer support services and psychotherapeutic and counselling treatments, as well as pharmacological interventions that are culturally appropriate and effective;
- a more active role for BME groups in the training of professionals, in the development of mental health policy and in the planning and provision of services, and a workforce and organisation capable of delivering appropriate and responsive mental health services to BME communities.

---

community forensic mental health teams began to evolve. By 2006, there were 37 such services with over 80 per cent operating separately from (parallel to) generic mental health services (Judge *et al.* 2004). A study by Judge *et al.* (2004) showed that these services varied in composition, caseload (which varied from 50 to 150 per service) and services offered. Although all services offered risk assessment and case management, only half offered specific therapeutic interventions such as anger management and cognitive behavioural therapy and some offered treatments for personality disorder (40 per cent), sex offenders (36 per cent) or substance misuse (16 per cent). Only 20 per cent provided psychodynamic therapy and family therapy. The most common source of referral to these services included regional secure units, followed by generic mental health services, probation, courts and prisons.

The effectiveness of community forensic services has been researched. Sahota *et al.* (2008) compared the reconviction rates for patients discharged from a medium-secure unit to community forensic services and generic services over a twenty-year period. The median time to reconviction was significantly lower for the community forensic services than generic services (5 and 14 years respectively). Although their clinical characteristics were broadly similar at discharge, patients discharged to the community forensic services had a number of factors that have been associated with reconviction in previous studies including a longer inpatient stay, more pre-index offence convictions and being younger on admission. A more recent study compared patients discharged from medium-secure units to forensic and generic services on measures of criminal convictions, hospital readmissions and deaths over a mean follow-up period of 6.2 years (Coid *et al.* 2007). The study showed that neither service was superior in relation to subsequent offending or hospitalisation. More research is required before making definite conclusions about the efficacy of community forensic services.

Forensic telepsychiatry

Telepsychiatry is defined as the use of telecommunication technologies, particularly video conferencing, to deliver mental health services from a distance. Video conferencing involves the use of special equipment that allows live visual-audio data to be exchanged between two or more sites connected through a telephone line or a secure network. The use of telepsychiatry may save time and money and reduce the need for travel. Although telepsychiatry is not new, its use in forensic settings in the UK has a recent history. By comparison, however, the criminal justice system had allowed the use of a video link at remand hearings and for child testimony since the Crime and Disorder Act of 1998. Video link facilities are now widely available in most courts, prisons and some secure units in the UK (Saleem and Stankard 2006). Within the criminal justice system, these facilities are connected through a secure network and are readily accessible to various professionals such as lawyers, probation officers and mental healthcare professionals.

There currently exists very limited literature on the use of telepsychiatry within forensic settings in the UK (Khalifa *et al.* 2008). Leonard (2004) described the development and evaluation of a prison telepsychiatry service which linked a medium-secure hospital to a prison off the south coast of England. Saleem and Stankard (2006) used telepsychiatry to conduct psychiatric assessments both for gatekeeping and psychiatric court reports. Telepsychiatry has also been used to improve the quality of care provided to mentally disordered offenders in London's South London and Maudsley Foundation NHS Trust (see http://www.telepsychiatry.slam.nhs.uk). It is worth noting that there is a wider international literature on forensic telepsychiatry. Khalifa *et al.* (2008) reviewed the literature on the use of the video link in forensic settings and concluded that although the use of forensic telepsychiatry is promising, the evidence for its effectiveness could only be regarded as preliminary. There remain also a number of other unresolved issues in relation to the practice of telepsychiatry including lack of guidelines regulating the practice of telepsychiatry and some practical considerations in relation to privacy, confidentiality and uncertainty about how the use of a video link may affect the therapeutic relationship (Leonard 2004).

Conclusion

In this chapter, the context in which mentally disordered offenders are assessed and treated by forensic mental health professionals has been described. The next chapter describes the forensic mental health professionals – the range of specialists that make up the multidisciplinary teams that collaborate in assessing and treating mentally disordered offenders.

Chapter 5

The multidisciplinary team

Introduction

Mental health services, forensic as well as other specialities, are provided by professionals from a range of disciplines. Among these are psychiatry, nursing, clinical psychology, social work, occupational therapy, arts therapy (art, music and drama) and pharmacy. All of these professionals work for the benefit of the patient, each contributing differently to the patient's care. The work of the team is coordinated through the Care Programme Approach (see Chapter 8) and multidisciplinary team meetings. The purpose of this chapter is to describe the training required by each profession and to describe the typical input each professional makes to the patient's care and treatment.

In recent years, the Department of Health has described the tasks of health service workers in general in terms of the knowledge and skills required at various levels. Core and specialist competencies are listed in the Knowledge and Skills Framework (Department of Health 2003b), which applies to all health service staff, not just mental health service workers. These are presented in Table 5.1. A health professional will be expected to have all core competencies plus around three to six of the specialist competencies, with different specialist competencies relevant to different professional disciplines. Note that these competencies are also relevant to managers, technical and scientific staff, service staff and researchers.

The Department of Health has also recently described the capabilities that all mental health professionals are expected to have,

Table 5.1 The core and specific dimensions in the Knowledge and Skills Framework

---

Core dimensions
  1 Communication
  2 Personal and people development
  3 Health, safety and security
  4 Service development
  5 Quality
  6 Equality, diversity and rights

Specific dimensions
  7 Assessment of health and well-being needs
  8 Addressing individuals' health and well-being needs
  9 Improvement of health and well-being
 10 Protection of health and well-being
 11 Logistics (i.e. movement of people and goods)
 12 Data processing and management
 13 Production and communication of information and knowledge
 14 Facilities maintenance and management
 15 Design and production of equipment, devices and visual records
 16 Biomedical investigation and reporting
 17 Measuring, monitoring and treating physiological conditions through the application of specific technologies
 18 Partnership
 19 Leadership
 20 Management of people
 21 Management of physical and/or financial resources
 22 Research and development

---

regardless of their discipline. The ten essential shared capabilities (Department of Health 2004a) are listed in Table 5.2, and provide an ethos of working that is respectful, ethical and evidence-based. These qualities are fundamental to good practice for all mental health professionals. From this basis we can move on to look at the generic and specialist forensic mental health training that members of each profession undergo.

Forensic psychiatrists

Forensic psychiatrists are medical doctors who have chosen to specialise in psychiatry and then to sub-specialise in forensic psychiatry. Would-be forensic psychiatrists must first qualify as

Table 5.2   The ten essential shared capabilities for mental health practice

1 **Working in Partnership.** Developing and maintaining constructive working relationships with service users, carers, families, colleagues, laypeople and wider community networks. Working positively with any tensions created by conflicts of interest or aspiration that may arise between the partners in care.

2 **Respecting Diversity.** Working in partnership with service users, carers, families and colleagues to provide care and interventions that not only make a positive difference but also do so in ways that respect and value diversity including age, race, culture, disability, gender, spirituality and sexuality.

3 **Practising Ethically.** Recognising the rights and aspirations of service users and their families, acknowledging power differentials and minimising them whenever possible. Providing treatment and care that is accountable to service users and carers within the boundaries prescribed by national (professional), legal and local codes of ethical practice.

4 **Challenging Inequality.** Addressing the causes and consequences of stigma, discrimination, social inequality and exclusion on service users, carers and mental health services. Creating, developing or maintaining valued social roles for people in the communities they come from.

5 **Promoting Recovery.** Working in partnership to provide care and treatment that enables service users and carers to tackle mental health problems with hope and optimism and to work towards a valued lifestyle within and beyond the limits of any mental health problem.

6 **Identifying People's Needs and Strengths.** Working in partnership to gather information to agree health and social care needs in the context of the preferred lifestyle and aspirations of service users, their families, carers and friends.

7 **Providing Service User-centred Care.** Negotiating achievable and meaningful goals, primarily from the perspective of service users and their families. Influencing and seeking the means to achieve these goals and clarifying the responsibilities of the people who will provide any help that is needed, including systematically evaluating outcomes and achievements.

8 **Making a Difference.** Facilitating access to and delivering the best quality, evidence-based, values-based health and social care interventions to meet the needs and aspirations of service users and their families and carers.

Table 5.2 continued

9 **Promoting Safety and Positive Risk Taking.** Empowering the person to decide the level of risk they are prepared to take with their health and safety. This includes working with the tension between promoting safety and positive risk taking, including assessing and dealing with possible risks for service users, carers, family members and the wider public.

10 **Personal Development and Learning.** Keeping up-to-date with changes in practice and participating in lifelong learning, personal and professional development for one's self and colleagues through supervision, appraisal and reflective practice.

Source: Department of Health (2004a). Reproduced with permission.

medical doctors by completing a five- or six-year undergraduate course at a medical school attached to a university. Most medical school entrants come straight after having done A levels, but there are increasing numbers of medical students who are already graduates in related subjects (such as biochemistry or physiology) who may be able to complete a shortened medical course. While at medical school, the student learns both the basic and clinical sciences relevant to the practice of medicine. As well as academic teaching, there is also a large amount of vocational training to ensure that the medical student has both the clinical knowledge and the skills to perform effectively as a doctor. During their medical school training, medical students will rotate through a number of training placements in all the major medical specialties such as surgery, general medicine, obstetrics and gynaecology, general practice, paediatrics, neurology, cardiology and psychiatry.

After passing their final exams in medicine, newly qualified doctors must register with the General Medical Council (GMC). This is a professional body which acts to safeguard patients by maintaining a register of those who are suitably qualified to practise medicine and investigates allegations of malpractice made against doctors. Having provisionally registered, the newly qualified doctor must successfully complete two years working as a Foundation Year trainee (these are referred to as FY1 and FY2). The foundation years consist of six four-month periods of full-time clinical work, under the supervision of an experienced doctor, in a variety of medical and surgical specialties. After completing this stage the doctor can then apply to specialise in psychiatry.

Specialist training in psychiatry is six years which comprises three years of core training (ST1–3) followed by three years of more specialised training (ST4–6). This specialty training programme was recently introduced as part of Modernising Medical Careers (Department of Health 2004b) to replace the previous grades of Senior House Officer (SHO) and Specialist Registrar (SpR) respectively. Trainees at the level of ST1–3 will rotate through six-month training posts to give them a broad experience of the practice of psychiatry. These posts will include general adult psychiatry and old age psychiatry, as well as specialties such as child psychiatry, the psychiatry of learning disability, liaison psychiatry (i.e. the overlap of treatment for mental health and physical conditions), forensic psychiatry and substance misuse. Progression through the specialist training years is subject to satisfactory performance and the passing of postgraduate examinations in psychiatry, the completion of which allows the doctor to apply for membership of the Royal College of Psychiatrists (MRCPsych). After having gained the MRCPsych, junior doctors in psychiatry can apply to specialise in forensic psychiatry for the remaining ST4–6 years.

During training in forensic psychiatry, the specialist trainee will rotate thorough a number of different placements, at all levels of security, and begin to take on some of the responsibilities of a consultant forensic psychiatrist appropriate to their level of experience. During this period, the ST doctor will also take part in research, audit, teaching and professional development activities. At the end of successfully completing the ST6 year, the ST can apply for a certificate of completion of training (CCT) from the Postgraduate Medical Examinations and Training Board (PMETB), which ensures that trainees have the competencies required to work as a consultant. Following the award of a CCT in Forensic Psychiatry, the doctor can apply to work as a consultant forensic psychiatrist (Royal College of Psychiatrists 2008). There are separate training pathways for those who wish to specialise in academic forensic psychiatry, during which the trainee gains research experience and works toward the award of an MD or PhD in addition to their training in forensic psychiatry (Gibbon *et al.* 2008).

In addition to the generic skills of a psychiatrist, forensic psychiatrists have particular expertise in the management of challenging behaviour, risk assessment, the therapeutic use of security, and the provision of expert evidence to the courts. Traditionally, multidisciplinary teams have been led by a consultant forensic psychiatrist who also fulfilled the role of the Responsible Medical Officer (RMO) under the Mental Health Act 1983 (see Chapter 1). However, with the advent of the new Responsible Clinician (RC) role in the Mental Health Act 2007 and the introduction of changes to the professional roles of all the multidisciplinary team, in line with the principles of New Ways of Working (Care Services Improvement Partnership and the National Institute for Mental Health in England 2007), other disciplines may now take on this coordinating role.

Forensic psychiatrists work in a variety of settings including low-secure hospitals, medium-secure hospitals, high-secure hospitals, prisons, courts and the community. Most forensic psychiatrists work in the NHS but increasing numbers are now employed in private-sector hospitals or in the production of medico-legal reports. Within forensic psychiatry there are also areas of further specialisation such as forensic child and adolescent psychiatry, learning disability forensic psychiatry, forensic psychotherapy (Jethwa 2006) and academic forensic psychiatry (Gibbon *et al.* 2008).

Clinical psychologists and forensic psychologists

Clinical psychologists

Becoming a clinical psychologist requires completion of a three-year, full-time professional doctorate course at a university. A good degree in psychology is a prerequisite for acceptance into training, and some relevant postgraduate work experience is also advantageous. This includes experience as an assistant psychologist, which is a graduate worker who assists qualified clinical psychologists, a research assistant, a healthcare assistant (see below) or a social care assistant. Applicants who are successful in gaining a clinical psychology training place are employed by the NHS as trainee clinical psychologists, although this does not guarantee employment post-qualification. Clinical psychology doctoral courses consist of academic work, supervised clinical practice and research experience.

The British Psychological Society's (2006a) core competencies for clinical psychology document states that qualified clinical psychologists 'should be committed to reducing psychological distress and enhancing and promoting psychological well-being through the systematic application of knowledge derived from psychological theory and evidence' (p. 2). Clinical psychology training teaches the skills required for the practice of clinical psychology, which are:

- conducting psychological assessments;
- developing problem formulations based on psychological theories and knowledge;

93

- conducting psychological interventions;
- evaluating the effectiveness of interventions;
- using and conducting research;
- maintaining and developing personal and professional skills;
- communicating psychological information and knowledge effectively;
- working with others to deliver services effectively.

These skills are applicable in a range of settings, including forensic mental health settings. In clinical psychology training, the trainee will learn to work with clients of all ages (e.g. children, adults, older adults), with a range of problems (e.g. developmental disorders, mental illness, mood disorders, neuropsychological problems) and in a variety of settings (primary healthcare, inpatient, outpatient). Trainee clinical psychologists are likely to have some forensic clinical psychology training in their courses, but most of the specialisation comes after qualification. Qualified clinical psychologists (chartered clinical psychologists) who take posts in forensic mental health specialist teams then develop their skills further through continuing professional development activities. They may also work to become chartered forensic psychologists.

Forensic psychologists

Forensic psychology covers both legal and criminological psychology. The legal aspect includes crime investigation and legal decision-making. Criminological psychology is concerned with the understanding, assessment and treatment of criminal behaviour. In the UK, most forensic psychologists are employed by the prison and probation services, although many work in forensic mental health settings. There are two postgraduate routes to qualifying as a forensic psychologist. After obtaining a good psychology degree, there is an option to take a one-year full-time (or part-time equivalent) master's degree in forensic psychology followed by two years' supervised practice, or to undertake the British Psychological Society's Diploma in Forensic Psychology which combines academic and practical work over a period of three to six years.

The academic work covers the civil and criminal justice systems, investigative psychology, the psychology of criminal behaviour, assessment of and intervention with victims, assessment of and intervention with offenders, giving expert testimony and research, consultancy and organisational interventions. The British Psychological

Society (2006b) requires that, through supervised practice, the trainee forensic psychologist will become competent in four key roles:

1 Conducting psychological applications and interventions, which involves an iterative process of problem identification, assessment, formulation, intervention and evaluation. This may be aimed at producing changes in offenders, staff, investigations or organisations.

2 Research, which is concerned with the design, conduct, analysis and interpretation of research and the implementation of relevant findings.

3 Communicating psychological knowledge, which includes giving professional information and advice, for example regarding offender risk or treatability, policy development or regime development.

4 Training other professionals in psychological skills and knowledge, including training non-psychology staff in suicide prevention, hostage awareness and psychological interventions.

After completing the academic and supervised practice requirements, the psychologist may use the title Chartered Forensic Psychologist.

Nurses

Nursing training is a three-year university degree or diploma course, and mental health nursing is one branch of training. As well as academic work, nurses-in-training undertake supervised placements in hospitals and community mental health settings. All nursing training has a common foundation, including: learning observational, communication and caring skills; studying anatomy, physiology, psychology, sociology, social policy; and learning core practical skills. In the second two years, training focuses on the specialist area. The Department of Health (2006) identified the core competencies for the practice of mental health nursing as follows:

• *Putting values into practice* – promote a culture that values and respects the diversity of individuals and enables their recovery.
• *Communication* – use a range of communication skills to establish, maintain and manage relationships with individuals who have mental health problems, their carers and key people involved in their care.

- *Physical care* – promote physical health and well-being for people with mental health problems.

- *Psychosocial care* – promote mental health and well-being, enabling people to recover from debilitating mental health experiences and/ or achieve their full potential, supporting them to develop and maintain social networks and relationships.

- *Risk and risk management* – work with individuals with mental health needs in order to maintain health, safety and well-being.

- *Multidisciplinary and multi-agency working* – work collaboratively with other disciplines and agencies to support individuals to develop and maintain social networks and relationships.

- *Personal and professional development* – demonstrate a commitment to the need for continuing professional development and personal supervision activities, in order to enhance knowledge, skills, values and attitudes needed for safe and effective nursing practice.

Bowring-Lossock (2006) described forensic mental health nurses as requiring a range of specific skills over and above the skills required for non-forensic mental health nursing. These skills relate to: safety and security (e.g. escorting patients, visitor control, searching patients and their property); assessment and management of risk (e.g. risk of violence, escape, abscond or hostage-taking); knowledge of offending behaviour and its treatment; knowledge of legal and ethical matters; knowledge and understanding of public attitudes towards mentally disordered offenders; and understanding what it means to the patients to be locked up or under supervision. Because of the mixed control and therapeutic role, forensic mental health nurses require excellent interpersonal skills, a calm approach to decision-making and a respectful attitude to the patients in their care to enable them to facilitate therapeutic gain.

Healthcare assistants

Healthcare assistants work within hospital or community settings under the guidance of qualified healthcare professionals, usually nurses. No specific qualifications are required to become a healthcare assistant, although evidence of suitability for a caring role will be required. Once in post, healthcare assistants are given training in areas such as the principles of care, understanding the role of a care worker, health and safety, and developing as a care worker. There are usually opportunities to work towards a National Vocational Qualification (NVQ) in Health and Social Care, which may provide the basis for entry to nurse training. Healthcare assistants help with the smooth running of a service by attending to the practicalities of patient care. More experienced healthcare assistants will assist nurses and other professionals with actual treatments.

Social workers

Social work training is a three-year degree course covering human development, mental health and disability, assessment and interventions, law, communication skills, and partnership and inter-agency working. Practical experience is an integral component of the social work degree. Course entry requirements vary between universities, and each may specify particular subjects, grades, qualifications and experience. Experience may be voluntary or paid work, but it needs to be sufficient to demonstrate an interest in and a commitment to a career in social work. There are also opportunities for graduates in social sciences subjects (plus practical experience) to undertake social work training for a Masters degree.

The Department of Health (2002c) has identified national occupational standards of practice which should be reached by a newly qualified social worker. There are six key roles as follows:

- *Key Role 1: Prepare for and work with individuals, families, carers, groups and communities to assess their needs and circumstances*
  - Prepare for social work contact and involvement.
  - Work with individuals, families, carers, groups and communities to help them make informed decisions.
  - Assess needs and options to recommend a course of action.

- *Key Role 2: Plan, carry out, review and evaluate social work practice with individuals, families, carers, groups and communities and other professionals*
  - Respond to crisis situations.
  - Interact with individuals, families, carers, groups and communities to achieve change and development and to improve life opportunities.

- Prepare, produce, implement and evaluate plans with individuals, families, carers, groups, communities and professional colleagues.
- Support the development of networks to meet assessed needs and planned outcomes.
- Work with groups to promote individual growth, development and independence.
- Address behaviour which presents a risk to individuals, families, carers, groups, communities.

• *Key Role 3: Support individuals to represent their needs, views and circumstances*
  - Advocate with and on behalf of individuals, families, carers, groups and communities.
  - Prepare for and participate in decision-making forums.

• *Key Role 4: Manage risk to individuals, families, carers, groups, communities, self and colleagues*
  - Assess and manage risks to individuals, families, carers, groups and communities.
  - Assess, minimise and manage risk to self and colleagues.

• *Key Role 5: Manage and be accountable, with supervision and support, for your own social work practice within your organisation*
  - Manage and be accountable for your own work.
  - Contribute to the management of resources and services.
  - Manage, present and share records and reports.
  - Work within multidisciplinary and multi-organisational teams, networks and systems.

• *Key Role 6: Demonstrate professional competence in social work practice*
  - Research, analyse, evaluate and use current knowledge of best social work practice.
  - Work within agreed standards of social work practice and ensure own professional development.
  - Manage complex ethical issues, dilemmas and conflicts.
  - Contribute to the promotion of best social work practice.

Social workers in forensic mental health services apply all these skills with offender-clients and their families and carers. Additionally, they are often also 'Approved Social Workers' (ASWs), this being the term for those specially trained to be eligible to contribute to decisions about detaining a person under mental health legislation. The updated mental health legislation has made other appropriately qualified and trained mental health professionals eligible for this role, which is now called 'Approved Mental Health Professional' (AMHP – see Chapter 1). Along with the psychiatrist, an ASW/AMHP may help decide if a person is suffering from a legally defined mental disorder of a nature or degree that warrants compulsory admission to hospital for assessment or treatment in the interests of the person's health or safety or for the protection of other people.

Occupational therapists

In forensic mental health services, the role of the occupational therapist is to help people overcome difficulties that result from their mental disorder. Using specific, purposeful activity, the aim is to promote independent functioning and prevent disability where possible. Occupational therapy training is usually a three-year degree course of study and clinical placement experience. Trainees learn biological and behavioural sciences, creative programme development, care management, therapeutic interventions and practical and environmental adaptations.

The Health Professions Council (2007a) lists standards of proficiency for occupational therapists. Of these standards, those that reveal the key roles of occupational therapists refer to specific areas of knowledge, understanding and skills. A proficient occupational therapist will:

- be able to understand and analyse activity and occupation and their relation to health and well-being;

- understand and be able to apply the theoretical concepts underpinning occupational therapy, specifically the occupational nature of human beings and how they function in everyday activities;

- be aware of the origins and development of occupational therapy, including the evolution of the profession towards the current emphasis on autonomy and empowerment of individuals, groups and communities;

- understand the use of the current philosophical framework for occupational therapy that focuses on service users and the social model of disability;

- understand the impact of occupational dysfunction and deprivation on individuals, families, groups and communities and recognise the importance of restoring opportunities;

- recognise the socio-cultural environmental issues that influence the context within which people live and work;

- recognise the impact of inequality, poverty, exclusion, identity, social difference and diversity on occupational performance;

- recognise the value of the diversity and complexity of human behaviour through the exploration of different physical, psychological, environmental, social, emotional and spiritual perspectives;

- be aware of social, environmental and work-related policies and services and their impact on human needs within a diverse society;

- understand the impact of legislation on the delivery of care;

- know how to meet the social, psychological and physical health-based occupational needs of service users across a range of practice areas.

Clearly, an occupational therapist working in a forensic mental health service has to balance the development of an individual's skills with attention to risk factors and to restrictions that may be placed upon the individual (e.g. access to sharp tools must be controlled and individually risk assessed). Nevertheless, engagement in activities and occupations that are aimed at longer-term well-being and life satisfaction is as important to forensic mental health patients as to anyone else.

Art, drama and music therapists

Art, music and drama therapies are forms of psychotherapy that use the arts as their primary mode of communication. The main aim of these therapies is to enable expression and communication and so to promote personal understanding and growth. The arts-based therapies can be particularly helpful for those who find it difficult to express their thoughts and feelings verbally. Arts therapy training is a postgraduate Masters degree or diploma, which combines theoretical and experiential work and is completed over two years full-time or three years part-time. Applicants must have a first degree in the relevant arts subject (or sometimes a psychology-related subject) and usually some experience of working in an area of health, education or social care.

The Health Professions Council (2007b) lists standards of proficiency for arts therapists. Of these standards, those that reveal the expertise of each type of art therapist are as follows:

Art therapists:

- use a range of art and art-making materials and techniques competently and help a client to work with these;

- understand that while art therapy has a number of frames of reference, they must adopt a coherent approach to their therapy, including the relationship between theory and practice and the relevant aspects of connected disciplines including visual arts, aesthetics, anthropology, psychology, psychiatry, sociology, psychotherapy and medicine;

- know the practice and process of visual art-making;

- understand the role of the physical setting and the art-making process in the physical and psychological containment of emotions;

- understand the role and function of the art object as an intermediary frame and within the relationship between client and art therapist;

- understand the role and use of visual symbols in art that communicate conscious and unconscious processes;

- understand the influence of socio-cultural context on the making and viewing of art in art therapy;

- recognise that different approaches to the use of visual arts practice in therapeutic work have developed in different socio-cultural and political contexts around the world.

Drama therapists:

- use a range of dramatic concepts, techniques and procedures (including games, activities, styles and structures);

- understand core processes and forms of creativity, movement, play and dramatic representation pertinent to practice with a range of client groups;

- understand both the symbolic value and intent inherent in drama as an art form, and with more explicit forms of enactment and re-enactment of imagined or lived experience;

- know a range of theatrical representation techniques and be able to engage clients in a variety of performance-derived roles;

- recognise that drama therapy is a unique form of psychotherapy in which creativity, play, movement, voice, storytelling, dramatisation and the performance arts have a central position within the therapeutic relationship;

- recognise that different approaches to the discipline have developed from different histories in Eastern and Western Europe and the Americas;

- recognise that the discipline has deep foundations within the many cultural traditions that use ritual, play, drama and performance for the enhancement of health;

- know the key principles of influential theatre practitioners and their relevance to the therapeutic setting.

Music therapists:

- use a range of music and music-making techniques competently and help a client to work with these;

- are able to improvise music in a variety of styles and idioms;

- are able to use musical improvisation to interact and communicate with the client;

- know a broad range of musical styles and are aware of their cultural contexts;

- can play at least one musical instrument to a high level.

Pharmacists

Pharmacists are experts in medicines and they can advise the clinical team on the best medication for the patient. Pharmacists also monitor the effects of medicines on the patient. In addition to this, pharmacists play a vital role in monitoring, prescribing and ensuring that medication is appropriately dispensed. To do this competently, the pharmacist must have knowledge of the patient's problems and history. Pharmacists have a degree in pharmacy followed by a year of employment as a pharmacist before they are eligible for registration with the Royal Pharmaceutical Society of Great Britain. A registration examination must be passed before the pharmacist can become a member of the Society and begin to practise independently.

An example of multidisciplinary teamwork

To illustrate the working of a multidisciplinary team, we will describe a patient and her problems and describe how each member of the team might contribute to that patient's care and treatment.

The patient

Donna is 35 years old and has been diagnosed with borderline personality disorder (see Chapter 2). Donna has a history of challenging behaviour in childhood and adolescence which led to relationships with her parents breaking down. She was sent to live with an aunt and when she was 15 years old she set up home independently with a boyfriend. Donna's schooling was incomplete and she has no qualifications. She had a few casual jobs in the catering trade, but has had no consistent work experience. After she left home, Donna began drinking heavily and using illicit drugs. She found herself less able to control her emotions and she had dramatic arguments with friends and boyfriends. Because of this, her relationships were turbulent and unstable. This made her emotions even more difficult to control and she began to demonstrate her feelings by cutting herself, trashing her belongings and threatening suicide. Donna's drinking and drug use also increased, which made her emotions still more uncontrollable. One night, while drunk and in despair, Donna set fire to her flat. She was charged with arson and received a prison sentence but was soon transferred to hospital for treatment.

The multidisciplinary team

The psychiatrist diagnoses Donna's mental disorder, prescribes any necessary medications (often in consultation with a pharmacist) and coordinates and evaluates the effective delivery of care. The nursing team will identify Donna's needs for safety and well-being and will devise care plans to address relevant issues. For example, nurses will assess Donna's general health, they will be vigilant for self-harming behaviour and they will begin to observe and understand Donna's moods. Once Donna has settled on the ward, more intensive therapies will begin. The clinical psychologist will assess the origins of Donna's difficulties and what maintains her problems into adulthood, and will then assist her to develop emotion control and develop a more positive self-image, and control her self-destructive behaviours (drinking, drug-use, self-harm, fire-setting). An arts therapist may also work with Donna to help her express her feelings and gain a better understanding of the confusion she experiences. The occupational therapist will assist Donna to learn life skills, such as interpersonal communication, job-seeking, budgeting, cooking and leisure activities. The social worker will assess family relationships, future accommodation and sources of financial, practical and emotional support, with the eventual aim of the effective resettling of Donna in the community.

The multidisciplinary team will meet regularly to share information, set goals for Donna's care and treatment, and examine progress. Importantly, Donna will meet with the team on these occasions to discuss her treatment goals and wishes for the future with the professionals. Through these meetings, there develops a collaborative approach among professionals and with the patient.

Conclusion

Treating patients in forensic mental health services, as in other services, is a team effort with various professionals contributing in different ways according to their areas of expertise. All are working to the same end, namely the successful treatment and rehabilitation of the patient. It is essential, therefore, that everyone working with a patient communicates with other members of the team to ensure a consistency of approach with any one individual. Working as a member of an effective and collaborative multidisciplinary clinical team can be very satisfying.

Chapter 6

Risk assessment

Introduction

Many people are familiar with the concepts of risk assessment and risk management in relation to matters of health and safety in the workplace. Hazards are identified, the potential damage they may cause is assessed and the likelihood of exposure to these hazards is quantified. Hazards may be obvious, for instance trailing electricity cables that are likely to trip people up, or they may be apparent only to those with specialist knowledge, for example the toxicity of certain substances that are used in the workplace. Knowledge of what actually is hazardous and the likelihood of exposure to that hazard is *risk assessment*. Having identified the risk, reasonable steps need to be taken to minimise risk. Total elimination of risk may not be possible and may not even be desirable. Take, for example, the use of hazardous chemicals in a research laboratory. Elimination of risk could be achieved by completely banning the use of these substances, but total safety would be gained at the expense of advancing scientific knowledge. Instead, it is usually considered appropriate to manage risk to reach an acceptable level of safety. For example, research chemists are taught safe procedures for working with hazardous substances and they are provided with protective clothing and safety equipment so that they work under conditions of as low a level of risk as possible. This is *risk management*. Risk assessment and risk management are procedures that need to be repeated regularly to identify changes to risk factors and monitor compliance with risk management strategies.

The same principles of risk assessment and risk management apply when working with offenders. There are now empirically based methods of identifying the factors that predict reoffending and assessing the likelihood of reoffending. In forensic mental health, offender treatments aim to reduce the risk posed by the offender and risk management is done by means of supervision and monitoring the offender in the community. If the effectiveness of treatment in reducing the likelihood of reoffending is to be tested, then some risk needs to be taken by allowing the offender closely supervised freedom to demonstrate that she or he can manage to live safely in the community. In such cases, risk is not totally eliminated but it is monitored and managed. Of course, the least risky route would be to keep the most serious offenders locked away for their whole lives. While society's appointed decision-makers in the form of the Home Secretary, a Mental Health Review Tribunal or the Parole Board may be cautious about allowing some very serious offenders to return to life in the community, most offenders are discharged or released. In this chapter, the focus is on the science behind the identification of risk factors and the methods used by clinicians to assess risk in individuals. Risk reduction and risk management are covered elsewhere in chapters that deal with treatment and supervision.

Empirical identification of risk factors

Empirically based risk assessment is a relatively recent appearance in forensic mental health. As Webster and Bailes (2004) said, until the 1960s it was assumed that the mental health professionals knew which of their clients were 'dangerous' and which were not. (It is worth noting that the old-style terminology was the assessment of dangerousness, but this has now been replaced by the term risk assessment.) A natural experiment made it very plain that professionals were nowhere near as good at identifying dangerous people as was thought. A man named Johnny Baxtrom contested the legality of his detention in a New York psychiatric hospital for the criminally insane on the grounds of his dangerousness. He won his case and was released, but so too were almost 1,000 other patients to whom the new ruling applied. These patients were released from secure psychiatric hospitals to regular psychiatric hospitals. All of them had been considered 'dangerous' by clinicians (although not the US Supreme Court), hence it would have been expected that they would be responsible for a large amount of serious crime in the period following release from secure hospitals. Not so! Follow-up research over the next four years showed that only about 20 per cent had ever been arrested and only 2 per cent had been arrested for violence. This meant that the false positive rate was as high as 80 per cent.

The issue of accuracy is important, hence it is worth taking a moment to explain the meaning of a false positive. Table 6.1 illustrates the relationship between a professional's prediction and what is actually likely to happen. With regard to serious offenders, the accuracy of this risk prediction is not scientifically testable since, if the professional predicts reoffending, then the offender is likely to be in a hospital or prison where the opportunity to offend is strictly limited. Imagine, however, that the professional's assessment could be scientifically tested for accuracy by allowing offenders free opportunity to reoffend. There are two accurate scenarios. The first is the *true positive*, where the professional predicted reoffending and reoffending actually did occur. If in this case the offender had been detained, this would have been justified. The second is the *true negative*, where the professional predicted no reoffending and none occurred. If this offender had been released and lived a free and non-offending life, then again the decision would have been justified.

However, if the professional predicted no reoffending and re-offending actually did happen, this would be a *false negative*. This means that someone had been seriously hurt, and also the professional's reputation and perhaps even his or her job would be on the line. Because of these possible adverse consequences, the professional is likely to err on the side of caution by using a prediction of no reoffending only in the most certain of cases, and is likely drawn into the excessive use of making a prediction of reoffending where no reoffending is actually likely to occur, which is a *false positive*. This would mean that many offenders are wrongly classified as high risk and detained even though their actual risk of reoffending is low. The detention of false positives gives rise to concerns about human rights and the unnecessary waste of scarce resources. The release of false negatives gives rise to concerns for public safety. How, then, do we ensure that risk assessments have both good sensitivity (i.e. they detect risk in really risky people) and specificity (i.e. they do not detect risk in people who do not pose a risk). The first step is to identify the actual factors that should guide a professional in making a risk classification.

Table 6.1 Accuracy of risk prediction

	Professional predicts reoffending	Professional predicts no reoffending
Person actually does reoffend	True positive	False negative
Person actually does not reoffend	False positive	True negative

Longitudinal studies

Probably the best research method for identifying risk factors is a longitudinal design. In this, the researcher measures a number of relevant variables in a group of people at a certain point in time and then takes a break. The subject group is followed up at a later point in time and data are collected on who has been convicted of what type of offence. Statistical procedures can illuminate which of the variables measured at the start of the project actually predict reconviction at the end of the follow-up period. For the purposes of offender risk classification, longitudinal studies are conducted on known offenders and they may focus on general offending, violent offending or sexual offending.

In the early days, the identification of risk factors was atheoretical. This led to the identification of a range of factors that correlated with reconviction, producing simple actuarial lists that consisted mainly of *static risk factors*. Static risk factors are those that are historical and cannot be changed. For example, risk factors for later offending include being born male, being young when first convicted of an offence, having many convictions and having served many custodial sentences. These are static factors that cannot be changed; either they never were changeable (e.g. a person's sex) or they are past the point of change (e.g. early delinquency). One important point that becomes evident in mentioning early predictors is that risk factors are variables that indicate *increased risk*; they are not 'marks of Cain' that show definitely who is going to become a criminal.

As Andrews and Bonta (2003) pointed out, there was very little attention in the early days to whether risk factors made any sense in relation to reoffending. While useful actuarially for calculating an individual's level of risk and providing the basis for legal decision-making and resource allocation, these actuarial risk factors are of limited value. The next development was to focus upon variables that were underpinned by theories of what might be relevant predictors of offending rather than just taking a stab in the dark. In this way, *dynamic risk factors* were identified. These are aspects of a person's current status and functioning that relate to risk and which are, in principle, amenable to change. Examples of dynamic risk factors are drinking and drug use, emotion control problems and holding antisocial attitudes and values. In a further development, risk assessments are now being augmented through connection with case management and treatment, which guides appropriate service delivery (Andrews *et al.* 2006). Hence, it is more common these days to refer to risk-needs assessments.

Risk factors

Research into the identification of recidivism risk factors may be split into two broad domains: (1) risk of general and violent offending; and (2) risk of sexual offending. Risk factors for general and violent recidivism, that is committing further offences after being convicted, are presented in Table 6.2 (Andrews and Bonta 2003). Risk factors for sexual recidivism are similar in respect of individual and general criminal history factors, but in addition a number of sexual offending-specific factors need to be taken into account (Hanson and Bussière, 1998). These additional specific sexual offending risk factors are presented in Table 6.3.

In relation to forensic mental health, while antisocial personality disorder appears as a risk factor for both violent and sexual offending, one obvious omission from the lists of identified recidivism risk factors is mental illness.

Does mental illness make people violent?

Bonta *et al.* (1998) conducted a meta-analysis of 58 prospective, longitudinal studies investigating recidivism of mentally disordered offenders. They found that the risk factors for general and violent offending were similar, and the strongest positive predictors were

Table 6.2   Risk factors for general and violent recidivism

Individual factors	Criminal history
Male sex	Previous general offending
Youth	Previous violent offending
Single	Previous arrests
Unemployed	Juvenile arrests
Drug and alcohol abuse	Previous imprisonment
Antisocial attitudes	
Antisocial peers	
Antisocial personality	

Source: Andrews and Bonta (2003).

Table 6.3   Specific risk factors for sexual recidivism

Sexual deviance	Sexual criminal history
Deviant sexual preference	Previous sexual offences
Deviant sexual attitudes	Early onset of sexual offending
	Stranger victim
	Male victim

Source: Hanson and Bussière (1998).

length and amount of criminal history, an antisocial personality disorder, poor institutional adjustment, many hospital admissions, poor living arrangements, abuse of substances, family problems, an escape history, a history of violence, being single and having used a weapon. One striking feature of this list is the total absence of any factors relating to mental illness. In fact, factors that were *negative* predictors of risk were the presence of a mental disorder, the use of an insanity defence, a diagnosis of psychosis or mood disorder and having a history of psychiatric treatment. That is, the evidence was that offenders with a mental illness were *less likely* to recidivate than were non-mentally ill offenders. One conclusion from this research is that most mentally ill offenders are likely to need the same types of intervention to reduce offending as are non-mentally ill offenders. If the risk factors for recidivism are the same for mentally ill and non-mentally ill offenders alike, then treating an offender's mental illness may not be sufficient to reduce the likelihood of recidivism. Indeed, the fact that antisocial personality disorder and substance abuse are major risk factors for recidivism among people with a mental illness suggests that these are two principal areas that warrant attention.

There is, however, evidence to the contrary. In the 1980s, a longitudinal study of about 20,000 of the general population in the US was set up. Swanson (1994) reported on a sub-group of 7,000 who were given a psychiatric examination and whose violent behaviour was recorded. Of the entire group, 9 per cent had been seriously violent at some time in their lives, rising to 18 per cent when less serious violence was included. Looking only at recent violence, i.e. in the previous year, 1.2 per cent of the population with no mental disorder had been seriously violent compared with 3.8 per cent of those with a mental illness (schizophrenia or affective disorder). Obviously, the overall likelihood of violence was low. The odds of having been seriously violent in the past year were three times higher for those with schizophrenia or a major affective disorder compared with those without a mental illness. Thus mental illness does increase the likelihood of violence, but the overall likelihood of violence was low and three times a little is still only a little. By contrast, people who abused alcohol and drugs were nine times more likely to have been seriously violent in the past year, and those with both mental illness and substance use problems were 13 times more likely to have been seriously violent in the previous year. The conclusions that may be made from Swanson's (1994) research are as follows:

- Most people are not violent (but some are).
- Most mentally ill people are not violent (but some are).
- The overall incidence of violence is low, but nevertheless serious mental illness increases the risk of violence threefold.
- People with substance abuse disorders are much more likely to be violent than are people with a mental illness.
- Having a major mental illness plus a substance abuse disorder is the highest risk for violence.

There is a clear contradiction between the findings of Bonta *et al.* (1998), who showed that mental illness was negatively related to recidivism, and Swanson's (1994) research in which mental illness was a positive predictor of risk. How may this contradiction be explained? As an ordinary member of the community, having a mental illness, perhaps untreated, places the person at risk of offending. This may be due to the mentally ill person's social circumstances, for instance being out of work, impoverished and living in socially disadvantaged circumstances which are risk factors for crime. Also, a person with a mental illness may behave oddly, which may make other people fearful and consequently react in such a way as to inflame a situation to violence. In some cases, the symptoms of mental illness may increase the likelihood of crime, for example people with persecutory delusions may resort to violence to protect themselves if they think someone is trying to harm them, or people experiencing command hallucinations may act upon them if they believe that a higher power is telling them to harm someone (see Chapter 2). This risk is actually diminished for known mentally ill offenders because the mental illness is treated, the mentally ill offender is closely monitored in the community and, if there are signs of risk, there is a strong chance of the offender being recalled to hospital for treatment rather than be charged with a crime. These controls give the illusion of mental illness reducing the likelihood of crime, but this is only true for people who are in contact with treatment agencies. For those mentally ill people who are not in contact with services, the risk of violence is slightly elevated. Furthermore, as Jamieson and Taylor (2004) pointed out, reconviction rates among discharged mentally disordered offenders are likely to be an underestimate since they are conducted on patients who are not necessarily in the community but may be in general psychiatric hospitals or other residential units.

Personality disorder and risk of recidivism

Compared with mentally ill offenders, those with personality disorders are more likely to reoffend after discharge from hospital (Bailey and MacCulloch 1992; Steels et al. 1998). In their 12-year follow-up of a cohort of 204 patients discharged from UK high-security hospitals in 1984, Jamieson and Taylor (2004) found that 38 per cent were reconvicted, 26 per cent for a serious offence. The odds of committing a serious offence were seven times higher for those classified as psychopathically disordered compared with those classified as mentally ill. Among all the DSM personality disorders, Hiscoke et al. (2003) identified offenders with antisocial, borderline and schizoid personality disorders as most likely to be reconvicted for a violent crime.

Concerning clinical psychopathy, a meta-analysis of studies using Hare's Psychopathy Checklist–Revised (PCL–R; Hare 1991, 2003) showed that offenders defined as psychopaths were three times more likely than non-psychopaths to commit further offences and about four times more likely to commit further violent offences (Hemphill et al. 1998). Correlations between antisocial lifestyle (Factor

2) and general recidivism were stronger than those for callous and unemotional traits (Factor 1), and both factors correlated equally with violent recidivism. Personality disorder diagnoses were not as accurate as PCL-R scores at predicting recidivism. Hare *et al.* (2000) followed up 278 offenders for two years after release from prisons in England and Wales, and compared high and low PCL-R scorers, using a cut-off of 25. Of the high scorers, the reconviction rate was 82 per cent for general offences and 38 per cent for violent offences, with the rates for low PCL-R scorers being 40 per cent and 3 per cent respectively, these differences being highly significant. Antisocial personality traits are important predictors of recidivism for mentally ill and non-mentally ill offenders alike. Therefore, as we shall see, this aspect figures large in risk assessments.

Base rates

The different rates of reoffending for mentally disordered offenders and personality disordered offenders as described above are different 'base rates'. In conducting risk assessments, it is important to know the rate of occurrence of the behaviour under scrutiny in a population to which the individual under assessment might belong. This provides information about risk in general, to which information about the individual may be added to estimate that person's level of risk.

Assessment instruments

Actuarial measures that focus upon static risk factors can be highly reliable in predicting risk. The Violence Risk Appraisal Guide (VRAG – Quinsey *et al.* 2006), a 12-item checklist, is recognised as the best predictor of non-sexual violence (Andrews *et al.* 2006). There are several actuarial risk assessments for sexual offending, including the ten-item STATIC-99 (Hanson and Thornton 1999), the four-item Rapid Risk Assessment for Sexual Offence Recidivism (RRASOR – Hanson 1997) and the seven-item (plus three additional non-sexual violence items) Risk Matrix 2000 (Thornton 2007). All of these are competent risk assessment instruments. However, the actuarial approach has limited practical utility compared with those assessment instruments that both predict risk *and* identify targets for managing risk by incorporating both static and dynamic risk factors. In these, the actuarial aspect of risk assessment that focuses on static variables (e.g. criminal history) is augmented by the inclusion of clinically relevant dynamic variables that address individual differences and identify potential for change. These structured clinical risk assessments are guided by research into what is relevant in risk prediction, use explicitly identified criteria for assessing the presence of risk factors and require hard evidence for ratings of risk. Furthermore, these risk assessments are time-limited, which is an acknowledgement of the potential for change, for better or for worse.

There are several structured risk assessment instruments in existence (see Conroy and Murrie 2007, for further information). Because antisocial personality traits are important risk predictors and because psychopathy is subsumed within some risk assessment instruments, it is useful to describe the Psychopathy Checklist – Revised (PCL-R). We have selected the HCR-20 violence risk assessment (Webster *et al.* 1997) and the Sexual Violence Risk-20 (SVR-20 – Boer *et al.* 1998) to illustrate structured clinical risk assessment procedures.

Psychopathy Checklist – Revised (PCL-R)

There is no personality disorder called 'psychopathy' in the major diagnostic systems. The World Health Organisation's (1992) International Classification of Diseases-10 (ICD-10) lists dissocial personality disorder, with criteria that are largely psychopathic personality traits, namely lack of guilt, lack of anxiety, inability to learn from punishment, impoverished emotions, inability to form lasting emotional ties, egocentricity and superficial charm. By contrast, the American Psychiatric Association's (1994) Diagnostic and Statistical Manual of Mental Disorders-IV (DSM-IV) lists antisocial personality disorder, which is based more upon behavioural criteria, namely law-breaking, recklessness and irresponsibility.

Hare (1991, 2003) incorporated both personality traits and behavioural criteria in his definition of psychopathy, and these form the basis of the Psychopathy Checklist – Revised (PCL-R). The PCL-R consists of 20 items (see Table 6.4) which are scored from interview, official records and corroborative checks with significant others. Each item is scored absent (0), somewhat applicable (1) or definitely applicable (2), with the resultant total score ranging from 0 to 40, where a higher score indicates a greater degree of psychopathy. Hare (1991, 2003) recommended a score of 30 or more for determining psychopathy, although a cut-off score of 25 is more commonly used in the UK (Cooke 1995). The use of a cut-off score to diagnose psychopathy implies that the condition is a taxon, that is a distinct class whose members differ in some discrete way from non-members. This approach leads to the identification of 'the psychopath', a label with pejorative connotations. Others prefer to use the PCL-R as a continuous measure, identifying the individual's degree of psychopathic traits. Within the PCL-R, two factors have been identified: Factor 1 – affective and interpersonal characteristics such as grandiosity, selfishness and callousness, and Factor 2 – an antisocial, irresponsible and parasitic lifestyle (Hare *et al.* 1990). As noted earlier, these have different predictive powers in relation to different types of reconviction.

HCR-20: assessing risk for violence

The HCR-20 identifies risk of violence generally, including sexual and intimate partner violence, although items do not focus specifically upon these areas. The HCR-20 is so called because it examines historical (past), clinical (present) and risk management (future) issues in 20 items. These items are listed in Table 6.5. The historical items are risk markers, whereas the clinical and risk management items are targets for change. All items are empirically identified as related to risk and so following the HCR-20 assists the clinician in conducting

Table 6.4 Items of Hare's (1991) Psychopathy Checklist – Revised

1	Glibness/superficial charm
2	Grandiose sense of self-worth
3	Need for stimulation/proneness to boredom
4	Pathological lying
5	Conning/manipulative
6	Lack of remorse or guilt
7	Shallow affect
8	Callous/lack of empathy
9	Parasitic lifestyle
10	Poor behavioural controls
11	Promiscuous sexual behaviour
12	Early behaviour problems
13	Lack of realistic long-term goals
14	Impulsivity
15	Irresponsibility
16	Failure to accept responsibility for actions
17	Many short-term marital relationships
18	Juvenile delinquency
19	Revocation of conditional release
20	Criminal versatility

a comprehensive assessment of the major risk factors. To reduce bias, no single source of information should be relied upon too heavily. The HCR-20 is completed by gathering information from multiple sources, including reviewing official records, interviewing the patient and consulting with professionals working with the patient.

Criteria are set for each item to allow transparent and reliable scoring. The items of the HCR-20 are coded definitely absent (0), possibly present (1) or definitely present (2). The numerical score can be used as an actuarial scale with the H items in the range 0 to 20, the C and R scales in the range 0 to 10, and the total score in the range 0 to 40. Research has shown that scores on the HCR-20 scales are good predictors of violence in correctional, general psychiatric and forensic mental health samples (see review by Douglas *et al.* 2006). But what, if anything, do these scores mean for the individual being assessed?

Table 6.5 Items of the HCR-20

Historical scale
H1   Previous violence
H2   Young age at first violent incident
H3   Relationship instability
H4   Employment problems
H5   Substance use problems
H6   Major mental illness
H7   Psychopathy
H8   Early maladjustment
H9   Personality disorder
H10 Prior supervision failure

Clinical scale
C1   Lack of insight
C2   Negative attitudes
C3   Active symptoms of major mental illness
C4   Impulsivity
C5   Unresponsive to treatment

Risk management
R1   Plans lack feasibility
R2   Exposure to destabilisers
R3   Lack of personal support
R4   Non-compliance with remediation attempts
R5   Stress

The procedural manual for the HCR-20 explains that allocating a risk number makes little sense for the individual, but instead a clinical judgement of high, medium or low risk should be made. This permits the clinical team to use a sensible approach to decision-making, interpreting the meaning of the number or combination of risk factors displayed by a patient or giving extra weight to an obvious risk factor, for instance a stated intention to kill someone. Importantly, the HCR-20 assessment is time-limited and should be repeated every 6– 12 months or sooner if there are substantial changes to the patient's case. Meanwhile, treatment efforts should focus on any risks identified in the clinical and risk management domains.

Sexual Violence Risk-20

The Sexual Violence Risk-20 (SVR-20 – Boer *et al.* 1998) assesses the risk of actual, attempted or threatened sexual contact with a person who is non-consenting or unable to give consent. The assessment schedule has 20 items known to be risk factors for sexual offending and these are split into three domains – psychosocial adjustment, sexual offences and future plans – as listed in Table 6.6. As with the HCR-20, the SVR-20 is completed using information from multiple sources, including records, witness statements, patient interviews and consultation with professionals working with the patient. Items are rated as absent (0), somewhat or maybe present (1) or present (2). If present, a record is made of whether there has been a recent change in status regarding that factor (exacerbation, no change, amelioration).

From the information collected on these items, clinicians rate the level of risk as low, moderate or high. The authors suggest that the SVR-20 should enable reportage on the likelihood that the individual will engage in future sexual violence; the possible nature, frequency and severity of sexual violence; the likely victims; and circumstances that might exacerbate the individual's risk. Importantly, this should lead to the identification of steps that could be taken to manage the individual's risk for sexual violence.

The SVR-20 has been shown to predict sexual reoffending with a moderate degree of accuracy (de Vogel *et al.* 2004), but not in all studies (Sjöstedt and Långström 2002). It may be that specification of different subgroups of offenders, such as contact and non-contact offenders and those with child or adult victims may improve accuracy (Macpherson 2003). A new measure, building on the strengths of the SVR-20 but adding new features to it, is the Risk of Sexual

Table 6.6   Items of the Sexual Violence Risk-20 (SVR-20)

Psychosocial adjustment
1   Sexual deviation
2   Victim of child abuse
3   Psychopathy
4   Major mental illness
5   Substance use problems
6   Suicidal/homicidal ideation
7   Relationship problems
8   Employment problems
9   Past non-sexual violent offences
10   Past non-violent offences
11   Past supervision failure

Sexual offences
12   High density sex offences
13   Multiple sex offence types
14   Physical harm to victims in sex offences
15   Uses weapons or threats of death in sex offences
16   Escalation in frequency or severity of sex offences
17   Extreme minimisation or denial of sex offences
18   Attitudes that support or condone sex offences

Future plans
19   Lacks realistic plans
20   Negative attitudes towards intervention

Violence Protocol (RSVP – Hart *et al.* 2003). This is currently being researched.

Prison and probation services' risk assessment procedures

Prison and probation services in England and Wales use an actuarial risk scale developed originally for the probation service. The Offender Group Reconviction Scale (OGRS – Copas and Marshall 1998) and the revised version, the OGRS2 (Taylor 1999), are empirically derived estimates of the probability that offenders will be reconvicted within two years of release. The OGRS2 variables are presented in Table 6.7. From these variables, a percentage probability of reconviction can be calculated, representing the average reconviction rate from a group of offenders who match the individual offender on the OGRS2 factors.

Table 6.7 Items of the OGRS2

---

1   Age at time of sentence
2   Gender
3   Number of youth custodial sentences
4   Current offence
5   Age at current conviction
6   Age at first conviction
7   Rate of offending
8   History of burglary
9   History of breach of probation

OGRS2 items are embedded within the broader Offender Assessment System (OASys) developed first for the probation service and later also for the prison service (Howard *et al.* 1999). In a lengthy interview using OASys, corrections personnel assess offending history, current offence, accommodation, education and training, financial management and income, relationships, lifestyle and associates, drug and alcohol misuse, emotional well-being, attitudes, thinking and behaviour, risk of harm to self and health considerations. This information is used to assess risk and guide supervision or sentence planning. If an offender's assessment identifies any specific risk areas, further specialist assessments may be triggered.

In England and Wales, OASys predominates, having taken over from another popular risk-needs assessment measure, the Level of Service Inventory – Revised (LSI-R – Andrews and Bonta 1995). Some favour this as the better evidenced (Hollin 2002) and more practical (Raynor 2007). The LSI-R consists of 54 items over 10 domains: criminal history, education/employment, financial, family/marital, accommodation, leisure/recreation, companions, alcohol/drugs, emotional/personal and attitudes/orientation. The information permits the assessment of risk, placement decision-making, the identification of treatment targets and monitoring risk. More recently, the authors have developed the Level of Service/Case Management Inventory (LS/CMI – Andrews *et al.* 2004). In this, the original LSI items are augmented by scales intended to strengthen case management or treatment, for instance by identifying factors that are protective against offending and should be capitalised upon; social integration, health and mental health status; and issues that influence responsivity to change, such as denial of the offence, motivation to change and communication barriers.

Conclusion

Harris and Lurigio (2007) have commented on the history of risk assessment. There has been a move away from the assessment of monolithic concepts of 'dangerousness' to identifying specific risk factors that will identify the probability of a particular harmful behaviour occurring. The focus has shifted from one-off risk prediction to ongoing risk management, through addressing dynamic risk factors. Consequently, there has emerged a practice of empirically grounded professional judgement. There are further developments in risk assessment that may change clinical practice in the future, for instance the use of classification tree methods, where the choice of question asked depends upon the answer to the previous question (Monahan *et al.* 2000). Research to improve the accuracy of risk assessment and the utility of assessment instruments in guiding management and treatment is of great value. One important way of reducing risk is through treatment, and it is to this issue that we turn in the following chapters.

Chapter 7

Treatments in prison and probation services

Introduction

Treatments in prison and probation services have, in recent years, been guided by the 'What Works?' body of research. In the 1970s, there was a view that 'nothing works' in offender treatment (Martinson 1974), leading to a shift away from offender treatment. However, in the 1980s, researchers began to identify what did work in offender treatment. They were aided by the newly emerging statistical technique of meta-analysis, which permits the aggregation of data from individual studies, thus giving a more accurate representation of treatment outcomes. Over the past two decades, many meta-analyses of offender treatment outcome studies have been conducted. Along with information on factors that are predictive of recidivism (see Chapter 6), the accumulated information has led to the empirically based formulation of the Risk-Needs-Responsivity (RNR) model of offender rehabilitation (Andrews and Bonta 2003; Andrews *et al.* 2006).

Risk-Needs-Responsivity

The main tenets of the Risk-Needs-Responsivity (RNR) model of offender rehabilitation are that treatment ought to be offered to offenders who are high risk for reoffending, should focus upon criminogenic needs and should be delivered using methods and styles to which offenders will respond. Treatments that adhere to the principles of the RNR model, which is underpinned by psychological theories of criminal conduct, are effective in reducing recidivism (Andrews *et al.* 2006).

The *risk principle* is that 'service delivery to the offenders who are higher risk produces larger decreases in recidivism than it does for offenders who are lower risk' (Andrews *et al.* 2006: 18). Offenders who are higher risk benefit from intensive treatment, as long as the treatment adheres to the principles of need and responsivity (Lowenkamp *et al.* 2006). One word of warning is that low risk offenders who receive treatment may actually do worse in terms of recidivism by being included in intensive treatment programmes. This may be because they learn antisocial behaviours from higher-risk offenders or develop antisocial networks, or because protective factors such as work, accommodation and relationships are disrupted.

The *needs principle* is that treatment targets focus upon a range of issues that, when changed, reduce the likelihood of recidivism. These are 'criminogenic needs', which are a subset of offenders' overall needs. Criminogenic needs are empirically identified dynamic risk factors. Andrews *et al.* (2006) identified eight central risk-need factors which are summarised in Table 7.1. Of these, antisocial behaviour, antisocial personality, antisocial cognitions and antisocial associates are the 'Big Four', that is they are the most important risk-need factors.

The *responsivity principle* consists of two parts. The first is general responsivity, which is that effective treatments should be used. The most effective are structured cognitive-behavioural interventions, these being more effective than deterrence, punitive approaches (e.g. boot camps) and non-directive counselling (see review by McGuire 2002). Additionally, meta-analyses have shown that therapeutic communities work, at least for substance abusing offenders (Lipton *et al.* 2002). The second aspect is specific responsivity, which means that treatment programmes should be delivered to suit specific characteristics of recipients, for example their age, gender, ethnicity, motivation, ability and personality. Issues of specific responsivity are the least well researched, but it is generally accepted that programmes that use active and participatory methods to teach people new skills and encourage them to practise those skills are most effective with offenders.

Table 7.1 Major risk-needs factors

Factor	Risk	Dynamic need
History of antisocial behaviour	Learned antisocial responses	Build non-criminal alternative behaviours for use in risky situations
Antisocial personality features	Sensation-seeking, aggressiveness, impulsivity	Build problem-solving, coping and self-management skills
Antisocial cognition	Antisocial attitudes, values and beliefs, hostility, criminal identity	Reduce antisocial cognitions; build a prosocial identity
Antisocial associates	Criminal peer networks	Build prosocial peer networks
Family or relationship problems	Low bonding, low supervision	Reduce conflict; build positive relationships
School or work	Low satisfaction and performance	Enhance performance, rewards and satisfaction
Leisure	Unstructured, antisocial	Enhance performance, rewards and satisfaction in prosocial activities
Substance abuse	Use of drugs and alcohol	Reduce substance use

After Andrews *et al.* (2006).

Programme accreditation

In order to promote good practice in prison and probation services, a number of jurisdictions have set up accreditation systems. In these, the principles of RNR are set forth as criteria by which offender treatment programmes may be judged as suitable for accreditation by a panel of experts. As an example, the accreditation criteria of the Correctional Services Accreditation Panel (2003) for England and Wales are presented in Table 7.2. To judge whether a programme meets the set criteria, Accreditation Panels scrutinise a range of programme manuals which should contain all necessary information about the theory behind the programme, evidence for its effectiveness and how it is implemented, managed and evaluated. The manuals typically provided are: (1) a theory manual, (2) a treatment manual, (3) a management manual, (4) a staff training manual, and (5) an assessment and evaluation manual. Accredited programmes may then be used in prison and probation services, tied in to the organisation's performance indicators. That is, budgets are dependent upon the achievement of previously agreed numbers of offenders completing programmes, with a quality quotient factored into this budget calculation. Quality is externally assessed by auditing a range of factors that impact upon programmes, namely organisational support, the physical environment and staff training, as well as adherence to the set protocols and practices for programme implementation.

Of course, not all interventions in prisons are accredited. Accreditation is reserved for intensive programmes, hence shorter treatment programmes are not eligible for accreditation. External agencies (e.g. counsellors) and self-help groups (e.g. Alcoholics Anonymous) may work with offenders without their work being accredited. Education and vocational training have other regulatory procedures. The focus here, however, will be on accredited programmes. These will be covered in two sections: cognitive-behavioural programmes and therapeutic communities.

Accredited cognitive-behavioural treatment programmes

There are currently a large number of accredited treatment programmes in correctional services in England and Wales. These are listed in Table 7.3. Clearly, these cannot all be described in detail here. Instead, an idea of what a cognitive-behavioural treatment programme might entail can be conveyed by describing some common treatment components.

Motivating offenders to change

First, the offender's motivation to change needs to be addressed (see McMurran 2002, for more detailed information). The importance of engaging offenders in treatment is illustrated by a study of treatment non-completers. McMurran and Theodosi (2007) systematically reviewed offender cognitive-behavioural treatment outcome studies that compared treatment completers, non-completers and those not offered treatment, with all three groups being equivalent in risk for reoffending. They found that treatment completers were least

Table 7.2 Correctional Services (England & Wales) offender treatment programme accreditation criteria

1	**A clear model of change**	A clearly specified, empirically supported model of change articulated in a theory manual. This should explain for whom the programme is designed, what changes it aims to bring about in participants and how it will achieve these changes.
2	**Selection of offenders**	A statement of inclusion and exclusion criteria and how potential participants are assessed.
3	**Targeting a range of dynamic risk factors**	A list of the dynamic risk factors addressed by the programme, with evidence of how these relate to offending.
4	**Effective methods**	A description of the intervention methods used and empirical support for their effectiveness.
5	**Skills orientated**	A demonstration that skills will be taught and practised during the programme.
6	**Sequencing, intensity and duration**	A statement of the duration of the programme, the frequency of sessions and the amount of homework assignments.
7	**Engagement and motivation**	A description of how the offender is to be motivated for and engaged in treatment.
8	**Continuity of programmes and services**	A statement of how the programme fits with the offender's overall sentence plan and how progress is communicated to other staff and agencies.
9	**Maintaining integrity**	A description of the how the organisation and non-treatment staff will be encouraged to support the programme and how treatment staff will be monitored to check adherence to the treatment manual.
10	**Ongoing evaluation**	A statement of how data on throughput, changes in dynamic risk factors and recidivism outcomes will be collected.

Table 7.3 Accredited cognitive-behavioural offender treatment programmes, England & Wales

Type of programme	Title	Description
General offending programmes	Enhanced Thinking Skills (ETS)	Address antisocial thinking and behaviour (20 sessions)
	Juvenile Enhanced Thinking Skills (JETS)	Address antisocial thinking and behaviour for 15 to 18 year olds (25 group and 7 individual sessions)
	Reasoning and Rehabilitation (R&R)	Address antisocial thinking and behaviour (38 sessions)
	Think First	Social problem-solving skills training (22–30 sessions)
	Priestley One-To-One	Individual programme to reduce antisocial thinking and offending (20 sessions)
	Cognitive Skills Booster	Reinforces learning from other general offending programmes (10–12 sessions)
Violence programmes	Aggression Replacement Training (ART)	Social skills, anger management and moral reasoning (18 sessions)
	Controlling Anger and Learning how to Manage it (CALM)	Anger and emotion management (24 sessions)
	Cognitive Self-Change Programme	Reduce violence by addressing antisocial attitudes, anger management and thinking skills (136–257 sessions)
	Healthy Relationships Programme	Aims to reduce intimate partner violence by developing responsibility and control skills training (high intensity version – 68–70 sessions; low intensity version – 24–26 sessions)
	Integrated Domestic Abuse Programme (institutional and community versions)	Aims to reduce intimate partner violence by group and individual sessions, interagency risk management and work with victims (35 sessions)

	Chromis	Designed for dangerous and severe personality disorder (DSPD) clients; identification, reduction and management of risk factors (2 years duration)
Acquisitive crime	Women's Acquisitive Crime Programme	Motivation to change (31 sessions)
Substance Misuse	Addressing Substance-Related Offending (ASRO); Prison-ASRO (P-ASRO); P-ASRO for women	Skills training for reducing substance misuse (20–24 sessions)
	Programme for Reducing Individual Substance Misuse (PRISM)	Individual skills training for reducing substance misuse (20 sessions)
	Drink Impaired Drivers	Education and skills training for reducing drink-driving (14 sessions)
	FOCUS	Aims to reduce substance use for medium- to high-risk offenders with severe substance use problems and who are in high-security prisons (62 sessions)
	Action for Drugs	Teaches prosocial skills for becoming and remaining drug-free and reduce risk of reoffending (48 sessions)
	STOP	Teaches prosocial skills for becoming and remaining drug-free and reduce risk of reoffending (90 × 1-hour or 45 × 2-hour sessions)
	Short Duration Programme	Harm minimisation for short-term prisoners (20 sessions)
	Offender Substance Abuse Programme	Motivation to change, goal-setting and risk management (26 sessions)
	Control of Violence for Angry Impulsive Drinkers (COVAID)	Targeting alcohol-related violence in low to medium risk offenders (10 sessions)

Table 7.3 continues overleaf

Table 7.3 continued

Type of programme	Title	Description
Sex offender treatment	HM Prison Service Sex Offender Treatment Programme (SOTP)	Five separate programmes addressing risk factors, deviant desires, fantasies, cognitive distortions, intimate relationship skills (Core – 86 sessions; Adapted (for lower functioning offenders) – 85 sessions; Extended (for high-risk Core graduates) – 70 sessions; Rolling (for low-risk offenders) – 45–60 sessions; Booster – (a pre-release booster for Core and Extended graduates) – 32–38 sessions)
	Internet-SOTP (I-SOTP)	Individual or group treatment addressing victim awareness, cognitive distortions, intimate relationship skills, risk identification and management, compulsive collecting (35 sessions)
	Healthy Sexual Functioning	Individual programme addressing intimate relationship skills, risk identification and management and deviant fantasies (12–20 sessions)
	Community Sex Offender Group Programme (C-SOGP)	Relapse prevention (total 260 hours)
	Thames Valley Sex Offender Groupwork Programme (TV-SOGP)	Victim empathy, life skills, relapse prevention (total 196 hours)
	Northumbria Sex Offender Group Programme (N-SOGP)	Core programme addressing risk factors, deviant desires, fantasies, cognitive distortions, intimate relationship skills and relapse prevention (total 180 hours)

likely to reoffend, consistent with the evidence that treatment works. However, treatment non-completers reoffended at a *higher* rate than did those not recruited to treatment, suggesting that non-completion of treatment may exacerbate risk. Their speculations regarding how risk might be increased in treatment non-completers were that this group may have raised problems without learning solutions, failure to complete may have given rise to feelings of inadequacy, or, for those who were removed from treatment, antisocial feelings toward treatment and change may have been inflamed. It is important, therefore, to consider how to promote motivation to engage in treatment and change behaviour.

Ward *et al.* (2004) described a Multifactorial Offender Readiness Model (MORM), which identifies internal and external factors that may affect an individual's readiness to engage in treatment and change behaviour. Internal conditions relate to *cognitions* (e.g. thoughts about oneself, the treatment on offer, the people delivering treatment and one's ability to change), *affect* (e.g. feelings of guilt or shame about the offence), *volition* (i.e. choosing to pursue the goal of not offending), *behaviour* (i.e. recognising a problem, seeking help, and having the skills to enable change) and *identity* (e.g. one's overall sense of self as a non-offender and a valued contributor to society). External readiness conditions relate to what treatment programme is offered, when, where, how and by whom. Some people may be reluctant to receive treatment in prison or in probation from correctional personnel because they see them as being agents of justice and control rather than helping professionals.

Readiness to change is most commonly enhanced using the principles of motivational interviewing (MI). This approach was developed by Miller and Rollnick (2002), originally as a technique for motivating substance abusers to change. The essence of MI is to acknowledge the client's ambivalence about change. Change may be recognised as a good idea, but there is also recognition of giving up some of the pleasures of the behaviour (e.g. the material gains of stealing or the emotional release of aggression), putting in the effort required for change, and possibly having to cut off from old social networks. The strategy is to work on this ambivalence using techniques such as expressing empathy, avoiding arguing for change and giving objective advice. The aim is to elicit 'change statements' from the client, and so strengthen commitment to change. Change statements (e.g. 'I've got a problem here' or 'I've got to stop doing this') that come from the client him- or herself are much more powerful than exhortations to change that come from a therapist.

One way of assessing change in motivation is to track the individual's progress through the putative stages of change. This derives from the transtheoretical stages of change model described by Prochaska and DiClemente (1983), in which behaviour change was said to unfold though a series of stages: *precontemplation*, where a person is unaware of a problem or unconcerned by his or her behaviour; *contemplation*, where there is acknowledgement of a problem but ambivalence about change; *action*, where change attempts are in progress; and *maintenance*, where change is consolidated and temptations to relapse become less salient. Different interventions have been suggested as applicable at different stages of change, with education and awareness-raising for precontemplators, motivational interventions for contemplators, skills training for those in the action stage and relapse prevention to promote maintenance.

The stage model of change was developed originally in relation to smoking cessation and was subsequently widely applied in addiction treatment. It has been criticised as flawed in that change does not occur in genuine stages, it focuses too much on decision-making and not enough on implicit processes (e.g. when stimuli trigger responses outside conscious awareness), and it may misdirect interventions (West 2005). In relation to changing offending, the model quite simply has not been empirically validated. Despite this, it is widely used in offender treatments, if only to convey to offenders that change is a process rather than a single event, and that slippages back to earlier stages are not unusual and so setbacks should not cause people to give up trying.

Enhancing self-control

The offender then needs to learn the skills of self-control. This is relevant for a range of offending and offence-related behaviours and requires that a wide range of factors should be changed (Baumeister *et al.* 1994). The behaviour in question needs to be studied and understood in terms of what triggers it and what increases its likelihood. Once risk factors are identified, these need to be controlled or changed.

Issues relating to self-control in the treatment of sexual offending can be illustrated using offending against a child as an example (see Marshall *et al.* 2006, and Ward *et al.* 2006, for more detailed information). Sexual offending against a child is based on a sexual desire for children under the age of consent. Why there should be this desire in the first place will differ between offenders. For some, it may be because they have been witness to or victims of sexual abuse in childhood and their desires have become distorted. For others, it may be that they do not have the skills to forge satisfying relationships with an adult and they find children less threatening. The potency of the desire may be exacerbated in a number of ways, for example if the person receives a blow to his self-esteem that makes him want to do something that will make him feel better, or if the person increases his sexual arousal by the use of pornography or masturbation to deviant fantasies, or if the person drinks and his self-control is diminished. These triggers can initiate a cycle of behaviour. This may include planning an offence, identifying a child victim and accessing that child through force or 'grooming' that child into a position where a sexual offence can take place. This is followed by the commission of the offence, with the immediate experience of satisfaction, which may possibly be followed by guilt or fear. In order to commit a sexual offence against a child, the offender has to suspend any empathy for the victim and develop thoughts (cognitions) that are supportive of offending. The latter are called 'cognitive distortions' and include views that children enjoy sex with adults and that sexual contact between a child and an adult does no harm to the child.

In enhancing self-control, the offender must learn to identify the risk factors at an early stage and become enabled to interrupt the offending process. In the above example, this would mean recognising adverse emotional states, the increase of deviant fantasies, and the onset of alcohol use as circumstances of increased risk. The individual would then operate escape strategies such as seeking support or diverting his attention to another engaging activity. To build self-control strength, treatment would include work to build victim empathy and change the individual's cognitive distortions. Where there is a problem with developing intimate relationships with adults, an aim in treatment would be to improve the necessary skills. In some cases, the underpinning deviant sexual desire would be tackled through methods of behaviour modification, such as aversive conditioning (i.e. where sexual images of children are paired with unpleasant experiences, such as imagined exposure and shame, or a sniff of a noxious gas).

Encouraging self-control for violent offenders follows the same principles as outlined above (see Goldstein *et al.* 2004, for more detailed information). Aggression and violence develop over the lifespan. A difficult temperament evident in early childhood presents a risk that may flourish if the child is not disciplined appropriately and if there are models of aggression and violence within the family. As time goes on, the aggressive child may be frequently punished, which leads to the view that the world is a hostile place. The child's aggressive behaviour may get in the way of him or her benefiting from school and so there begins truancy, association with delinquent peers and involvement in antisocial behaviours. Fighting as a means of conflict resolution is commonplace and opportunities to learn negotiation skills are missed. In adulthood, a poor educational history along with a criminal record may militate against the person finding regular work, and financial constraints may force people to live in less desirable neighbourhoods where trouble is never far away. Drinking or taking drugs may be endemic, and substance use may further exacerbate the risk of violence. The person develops attitudes and values that excuse or justify violence, for example that his anger is uncontrollable, that violence is the language people understand, and that if violence is not used then he will be seen as weak and will be tormented or exploited.

Enhancing self-control in the violent offender will include identification of risk factors, for example being with specific people, being in particular places and being in negative emotional states that often precede violent incidents. Once the risks are recognised, the individual needs to learn coping skills. These might be simply to escape a situation when anger arousal is noticed so as to avoid trouble. More complex skills of conflict resolution, problem-solving, anger management and stress management will also be introduced. Exacerbating factors will be addressed in treatment, including reducing drinking and drug use, changing antisocial networks and challenging antisocial attitudes and values.

Enhancing thinking skills

The origins of cognitive-behavioural treatments for offenders actually lie in research that indicated deficits in offenders' cognitive skills (Ross and Fabiano 1985). From this, programmes aimed at developing offenders' thinking skills developed, first Reasoning and Rehabilitation (Ross et al. 1988), then Enhanced Thinking Skills (Clark 2000) and Think First (McGuire 2000) (see McMurran and McGuire 2005 for more detailed information.)

In these thinking skills programmes, offenders are taught a range of cognitive skills. Antonowicz (2005) lists these as follows:

- *Self-control*, where offenders are taught to stop, think and consider the consequences of their actions before making decisions.
- *Meta-cognition (thinking about thinking)*, where offenders learn that how they think influences what they think, which in turn influences behaviour.
- *Social skills*, in which appropriate interpersonal communications skills are taught to help the offender experience more rewarding interactions with others.
- *Interpersonal cognitive problem-solving skills*, where offenders are taught to analyse interpersonal problems, consider other people's points of view and choose appropriate solutions.
- *Creative thinking*, in which conceptual rigidity is corrected by getting people to think of alternative solutions to problems.
- *Critical reasoning*, in which the skills of logical, rational and objective analyses of problems is encouraged.
- *Social perspective-taking*, where offenders learn to imagine how other people think and feel.
- *Values enhancement*, where egocentricity is challenged through debates and discussion.

These thinking skills are taught in an engaging and lively manner. A flavour of the Reasoning and Rehabilitation approach can be conveyed by offering some examples. Creative thinking may be enhanced by asking offenders to think of as many uses as possible for a brick, or to list experiences they might have if they were coloured green. Values enhancement might be to debate who among a number of candidates might be the most worthy recipient of a donor kidney to save his or her life, for instance a mother of young children, a surgeon who saves many lives or a war veteran who was decorated for bravery. Reasoning and Rehabilitation has recently been revised and updated to incorporate recent research, particularly in the field of cognitive neuroscience (Ross and Hilborn 2008).

Relapse prevention

Working towards behaviour change can actually be very engaging and rewarding for the client. There is a job to do, progress is evident and there is support and attention from treatment personnel and others participating in programmes. The real challenge is in maintaining change over time after treatment ends. Of course, continued supervision is mandatory for many offenders on community orders, parole or licence, and this is important in supporting the maintenance of treatment gains. However, broader changes may be needed to develop a non-criminal lifestyle and identity.

Recently, the RNR model's focus on risk and criminogenic needs (i.e. those related to offending) has attracted criticism because of the emphasis on the offender's deficits. In tune with the Zeitgeist of 'positive psychology', which focuses on the study of people's strengths rather than their deficits (Seligman and Csikszentmihalyi 2000), positive approaches to rehabilitation and resettlement are emerging. Drawing upon principles of restorative justice, Maruna and LeBel (2003) have focused upon how an offender can make a positive contribution to and be accepted by society. In a similar positive vein, Ward and colleagues have developed the Good Lives Model (GLM) of offender rehabilitation (Ward 2002; Ward and Brown 2004; Ward and Stewart 2003). The underlying principle is that offenders, as all human beings, seek satisfaction in certain life areas that are the essential ingredients of human well-being, but that the offender seeks satisfaction in problematic or distorted ways. Building on the offender's existing preferences, strengths and opportunities, the GLM focuses on helping offenders attain satisfaction in appropriate ways in a range of life areas, rather than focusing purely on reducing risk. In interventions, the offender should be assisted to develop the skills and resources to equip him or her to live a more fulfilling and offence-free life.

Although the GLM has been criticised as lacking in empirical support (Bonta and Andrews 2003), the notion of working positively and holistically with offenders has currency, particularly with regard to motivation to engage in treatments and change behaviour. Recent research into what offenders themselves identify as their goals in life has shown that they want both to reduce risk and to attain satisfaction in life (McMurran *et al.* 2008). This suggests that both the risk reduction approach of RNR and the positive approach of GLM have a role to play in offender rehabilitation (Ward *et al.* 2007).

Accredited therapeutic communities

A therapeutic community (TC) is essentially a group of people who live together temporarily with the aim of helping each other to learn about themselves by openly making observations about their impact upon each other, airing conflicts and attempting to solve problems.

In this way, maladaptive interpersonal styles are open to correction. Experiences are shared and conflicts resolved in group meetings, which are facilitated by staff. Additionally, TC residents participate in education, work and psychoeducational programmes.

The TC approach to offender treatment has a long history in the UK, with HM Prison Grendon having operated on therapeutic community principles since 1962 (see Cullen *et al.* 1997, for more detailed information). HMP Grendon's therapeutic community, which is an accredited programme, takes some of the most serious violent offenders, who remain there for up to three years. Other accredited TCs are 'concept TCs', which is the name given to TCs which focus specifically on substance misuse. Of these, two use the Minnesota Model, which is a 12-step abstinence-oriented approach. These 12 steps include admitting to being powerless over one's addiction, making a commitment to self-examination, and appealing to a higher power for help in changing. The substance abuse treatment programme offered by the Rehabilitation of Addicted Prisoners Trust (RaPT – Martin and Player 2000) and the Prisons Partnership 12-Step Programme are two such abstinence-oriented TCs. The duration of stay in these programmes varies, with a minimum of around six months. Two further concept TCs tackle substance misuse using more cognitive-behavioural strategies: the Ley Prison Programme and the North West Area Therapeutic Community, both of which are around ten months' duration.

Do correctional treatments work?

As was stated at the start of this chapter, meta-analyses of offender treatment outcome studies provide robust information on overall trends. Cognitive-behavioural treatments reduce general and violent recidivism by about 15 to 20 per cent (Dowden and Andrews 2000; Tong and Farrington 2008) and sexual reoffending by about 30 per cent (Hanson *et al.* 2002; Lösel and Schmucker 2005). To put these percentages into perspective, in the general and violent reoffending studies around 52 per cent of those treated reoffended and 62 per cent untreated reoffended, whereas in the sexual reoffending studies around 12 per cent of those treated reoffended and 17 per cent untreated reoffended. Thus the percentage reduction as a proportion of the untreated group reoffending rate (i.e. the base rate of reoffending) is higher for sexual offenders. Concept TCs for substance abusing offenders in prisons show good outcomes, with a meta-analysis showing a 21 per cent reduction in recidivism, i.e. around 44 per cent of those treated reoffended and 56 per cent untreated reoffended (Lipton *et al.* 2002).

These effects are of practical significance when the reduction in reoffending is translated into what really matters: fewer victims of crime, fewer people living in fear of crime, fewer people wasting their lives in prison, less expenditure on criminal justice and more public money to spend on positive matters such as education and health.

Sentence management and throughcare

The process of risk identification, risk management and risk reduction through treatment, education, vocational training and community reintegration needs to be a seamless process for each individual offender. To this end, in 2003 a unitary National Offender Management System (NOMS) was created, joining together the Prison and Probation Services to create the conditions where any offender would be able to benefit from having one person oversee his or her sentence 'end-to-end' from prison into the community (Carter 2003). This is largely based upon a shared structured risk-needs assessment called the Offender Assessment System (OASyS – see Chapter 6). This was designed to promote good sentence management by identifying offending-related needs, resource planning and management, and monitoring outcomes. OASys is computerised and networked, thus enabling information-sharing when moving offenders within and between prisons and communities.

Conclusion

There has been an unprecedented and exceptional rate of development of prison and probation treatment programmes over the past 20 years, and evidence-based treatments for offenders are widely used in the UK today. One issue for the future development of programmes is to meet the needs of specific groups of offenders, for instance youth, women, Black and minority ethnic groups, and learning disabled offenders. Also, research needs not only to evaluate outcome but also the processes by which offenders change in treatment so that treatments can be refined. In an operation as large as the delivery of prison and probation service treatment programmes, constant attention needs to be paid to implementation issues to guard against potential deterioration.

Chapter 8

Treatments in mental health settings

Introduction

Working in those areas where forensic mental health and the law meet is both rewarding and fascinating, but it also gives rise to some ethical dilemmas for forensic practitioners. Within the criminal context, what is at stake is public protection through a determination of the individual's guilt or innocence, whereas for healthcare professionals what is at stake is the patient's best interest. As Adshead and Sarkar (2007) point out:

> Psychiatrists may be experiencing what Erik Erikson summarised as tension between identity and role confusion. On the one hand, they have clear duties to their patients, and mental illness is taken seriously as a medical condition. On the other hand, they apparently have duties to the society, which are both confused and diffuse. Whose agent are they? (p. 422)

In the treatment setting, this role confusion is evident in relation to security. Physical, relational and procedural security measures are all integral to the operation of secure mental health facilities. Inevitably, there will be competing interests between therapy and security. While there has been much debate on how security and therapy can be reconciled in the patient's best interest, security often takes priority over other therapeutic issues. This is particularly so in high-security hospitals (Exworthy and Gunn 2003; Tilt *et al.* 2000).

Risk assessment and risk management also raise ethical issues. Treatment is one way of managing risk. Society sets high expectations on forensic services to protect the public from potential harm caused by mentally disordered individuals, including offering effective treatments. While the best evidence-based treatments may be on offer, there is no absolute guarantee that these will prevent reoffending. There is still much to learn about the factors that explain offending in mentally disordered individuals and how best to target these in treatment. Additionally, there are factors that have a bearing on offending that are beyond the control of forensic mental health professionals, particularly those influences that apply in the community. Because of this, forensic practitioners do not work in isolation from other agencies, but instead work closely with housing services, police, probation services, criminal justice agencies and MAPPA (Multi-Agency Public Protection Arrangements). Successful discharge planning involves inter-agency co-working, communication and information sharing.

While there are complexities in the practice of forensic mental health, these have to be surmounted to deliver treatment. The management of mentally disordered offenders should combine the treatment of mental health issues, the treatment of offending behaviour and risk management. The last two issues have been covered in earlier chapters, and so it is the treatment of mental health issues that is the focus here. Before mentioning specific treatments, however, it is important to know how various inputs from all the professionals involved in a patient's care are coordinated through the Care Programme Approach.

The Care Programme Approach

The Care Programme Approach (CPA) was introduced in 1991 to improve the delivery of care to people with mental disorder by identifying their needs, allocating services and resources appropriately and monitoring the effectiveness of interventions. CPA is underpinned by principles of multidisciplinarity and a patient-centred approach to delivery of care. There are four main components:

- a comprehensive assessment of the patient's health and social care needs;

- a care plan agreed by the patient/carer and professionals involved in the provision of care for the individual. The care plan should address the mental health, social and risk management needs of the patient concerned. It should also contain the contact details of the key individuals involved, a treatment plan, a risk management plan and a contingency plan;

- the appointment of a care coordinator who acts as a point of contact and is responsible for monitoring the delivery of the care plan;

- regular review meetings, held at least once a year and more frequently depending on the patient's needs. It is the responsibility of the care coordinator to arrange these meetings and invite all the professionals involved in the patient's care.

In a typical CPA meeting, every healthcare professional involved in the patient's care is expected to present a report summarising the patient's progress, highlighting areas of need and making recommendations for future treatment. The patient and their carers should be given the opportunity to attend the meeting and express their views on treatment or any other issues relevant to the patient's care. The process may be anxiety provoking for the patient, hence the patient may choose to attend the meeting with a family member or friend, their mental health advocate or a legal representative.

Presentation of reports is usually followed by an open discussion among all the parties involved, covering all aspects of the patient's care and leading to the formulation or amendment of a care plan. A CPA meeting is also a valuable opportunity to update the treatment and risk management plans. Part of the meeting may be dedicated to updating risk assessments, standardised measures of progress (e.g. the Health of Nation Outcomes Scales (HoNOS) – Royal College of Psychiatrists 1996) and work related to safeguarding children. It is worth noting that a CPA review could be held as part of section 117 aftercare (see information about the Mental Health Act in Chapter 1).

Historically, two levels of care programme approach existed – standard and enhanced. The level was decided on an individual basis, depending on patient's needs. Recent policy has abolished this distinction and introduced a single level of CPA, indicating that all patients should receive the same level of care under the CPA (Department of Health 2008).

Treatment of mental health problems

The principles underpinning the treatment of mental disorder, whether in forensic or general mental health settings, are that it is multidisciplinary and targets biological, psychological and social aspects of the disorder. In broad terms, the treatment of mental health issues involves the use of pharmacological treatments (medication), psychological treatments, occupational therapy and social interventions. First, specific treatments for mental health issues will be described in detail. Where available, the guidelines issued by the UK's National Institute for Health and Clinical Excellence (NICE – see http://www.nice.org.uk) will be presented. NICE is an independent organisation responsible for providing national guidance on promoting good health and preventing and treating ill health. The focus here will be on the treatment of those disorders most commonly encountered in forensic mental health settings, namely schizophrenia, bipolar disorder, personality disorder, learning disability and substance misuse disorders.

Schizophrenia

With the advent of chlorpromazine, the first antipsychotic medication, in the 1950s, some predicted that schizophrenia would soon be totally eradicated. Now, more than five decades later, the prevalence of schizophrenia in any given society across the world remains the same at around 1 per cent of the population. This is despite the advent of numerous antipsychotic medications and a range of psychological and social interventions for the treatment of schizophrenia. This is not to say that these interventions are not effective, but to highlight a fact that the current interventions do not provide a 'cure' for schizophrenia which is an enduring, and often disabling, form of mental illness. Therefore the success of treatment should be judged by more realistic outcome measures, such as symptom control and improvement in the functioning or the quality of life of the individual concerned.

As with most mental health treatments, the needs of people with schizophrenia should be comprehensively assessed and addressed, and include medical, psychological, occupational, social, economic, physical and cultural needs. The NICE guidelines for the treatment of schizophrenia are presented in Information Box 8.1.

Antipsychotic medications
The use of antipsychotic medications remains the mainstay of treatment

Information Box 8.1 National Institute of Health and Clinical Excellence guideline for the treatment of schizophrenia (National Institute of Health and Clinical Excellence 2002)

General principles

- Management should address medical, social, psychological, occupational, economic, physical and cultural issues
- Emphasis on service user and carer involvement in decision-making
- Emphasis on consent and advance directives about treatment
- Physical health monitoring

Pharmacological interventions

- Atypical antipsychotics should be used first line for newly diagnosed cases
- Atypical antipsychotics should also be considered if conventional antipsychotics cause intolerable side effects/fail to adequately control symptoms
- If the patient does not respond to a 6–8 week course of two antipsychotics from two different classes, clozapine should be considered
- Antipsychotic treatment should be continued for a year or two after relapse
- Depot antipsychotics to be considered for those who are non-concordant with oral medications

Psychological interventions

- Cognitive behaviour therapy to prevent relapse, reduce symptoms, increase insight and promote adherence to treatment
- Family interventions to be offered to the family of those who have relapsed, or at high risk of relapse, or those with persistent symptoms

Social and occupational interventions

- Assessment of occupational status and potential
- Help the patient to develop employment opportunities
- Assessment of social care needs, accommodation and quality of life

---

of schizophrenia, particularly during the acute phase of illness. These medications can reduce or eliminate the distressing experiences of schizophrenia, for example beliefs about being persecuted or hearing derogatory and abusive voices. When the patient is highly disturbed and distressed, it is difficult for him or her to engage in psychological and social therapies, therefore medication is often essential. As well as treating the acute symptoms of schizophrenia, antispsychotic medications decrease the risk of relapse in the future and thus good compliance with this medication is associated with better long-term outcomes. However, medications are not without their drawbacks, as we shall see.

Antipsychotic medications are available both in oral and injectable forms. Oral preparations are available as ordinary tablets, liquid and dissolvable tablets (i.e. olanzapine velotabs and risperidone quicklets). Injectable preparations are available as short-acting and long-acting injections, the latter called 'depot' injections because the substance injected remains at the site and is absorbed slowly. Broadly speaking, oral preparations are considered first line treatment, although short-acting injections may be considered for rapid tranquillisation in those who are acutely disturbed. Depot antipsychotics may be considered first for those who are non-compliant with oral medication or in those who are known to respond favourably to depot preparations.

Most antipsychotics act through blocking dopamine receptors in the brain. Dopamine is a neurotransmitter, that is a chemical in the brain that carries messages between cells. Dopamine performs many functions relating to attention, thinking and motivation. However, antipsychotics may block a range of other receptors in the brain, including serotenergic, cholinergic, alpha adrenergic and histaminic receptors, giving rise to a wide range of side effects (Taylor *et al.* 2007; see Information Box 8.2).

Antipsychotics are generally thought to fall into two main categories – typical (conventional) and atypical (second generation). This distinction has been made on the basis of their propensity to cause extra-pyramidal side effects. This is where the motor system of the brain is affected, causing problems such as tremor, stiffness and involuntary movements. Some of these side effects are chronic and may not resolve even if the medication is stopped (e.g. the involuntary movements of tardive dyskinesia). Typical antipsychotics are more likely to cause extra-pyramidal side effects than are atypical antipsychotics, although some atypical antipsychotic medications may also do so (particularly risperidone and amisulpiride) (Taylor *et al.* 2007). Moreover, some atypical antipsychotics, especially olanzapine and clozapine, may cause potentially serious side effects such as weight gain and diabetes. Clozapine can cause a severe reduction in the white blood cell count, therefore a patient's blood is tested regularly.

Information Box 8.2 Receptor blockade and side effects of antipsychotic medication (after Puri and Hall, 2004)

Dopamine receptors

- Extra-pyramidal side effects: rigidity, decreased facial expression (mask-like), tremor, shuffling gait, slurred speech, slowness, acute dystonia (involuntary muscle contractions which present as abnormal movements or postures, with or without tremor), akathasia (inability to stay still) and tardive dyskinesia (involuntary movements in the face and neck)
- Hyperprolactinaemia: manifested as menstrual abnormalities, galactorhoea (excessive lactation in women), erectile dysfunction, reduced sperm count

Cholinergic receptors

- Peripheral: dry mouth, constipation, blurred vision, urinary retention
- Central: reduced seizure threshold, fever

Alpha adrenergic receptors

- Postural hypotension
- Sexual dysfunction

Histamine receptors

- Weight gain
- Sedation

Antipsychotic medications are also known to cause a range of other side effects, some very serious, including sexual dysfunction, excessive sedation, cardiac arrhythmias (heart rhythm abnormalities) and, rarely, neuroleptic malignant syndrome, a condition which usually manifests as fever, muscle rigidity, blood pressure lability and fluctuating level of consciousness (see Levenson 1985). The importance of safe prescribing is paramount. This may be achieved by adhering to a number of basic principles of prescribing including:

- when possible, enabling the patient to make informed decisions about their treatment;
- the use of a minimum effective dose;
- regular monitoring of the patient's weight (or preferably the body mass index or waist circumference), blood pressure, blood

glucose, blood cholesterol, liver function, kidney function and heart rhythm.

Psycho-social interventions

A range of psycho-social interventions has been developed for the treatment of schizophrenia. During the acute phase of the illness, nursing interventions are of paramount importance. Nursing staff can provide support, promote compliance with medication and maintain the safety of the patient. Nursing staff may also help to deliver mental health awareness (psycho-education) at a later stage, when the patient's mental state is settled. Occupational therapy plays an important role in the management and rehabilitation of people with schizophrenia, teaching skills for living (e.g. self-care, budgeting, cooking) and interpersonal skills (e.g. communication, problem-solving). Other activities also help to improve functioning and occupational potential, and those typically available in forensic mental health settings are physical fitness and sport, art and craft, woodwork and gardening.

Social interventions involve providing practical help with finance, housing or finding opportunities for leisure and employment. Finding suitable accommodation is not always a straightforward process. Many mentally disordered offenders originate from deprived social backgrounds and neighbourhoods with high crime rates. There are legitimate concerns that discharging patients to where they originally come from may bring them into contact with antisocial peers and illicit substances, hence increasing the risk of relapse and possibly reoffending. On the other hand, accommodating them in a new neighbourhood may deprive them of their social support network (Mullen 2006).

Cognitive-behavioural therapy (CBT) for psychosis

Cognitive-behavioural therapy teaches people the skills for coping with the positive symptoms of schizophrenia (e.g. distraction from hallucinations, reality testing for dealing with hallucinations and cognitive restructuring of delusions). In forensic mental health services, it is particularly important to address hallucinations and delusions that may have previously led to violent behaviour. Negative symptoms are addressed through behavioural activation and social skills training. Relapse prevention techniques are used to identify and control the antecedents to a psychotic episode (e.g. stress, anxiety). A systematic review of 19 trials of cognitive-behavioural therapy for schizophrenia concluded that it was a promising intervention in that it decreased the risk of staying in hospital and improved mental state in the short term (Jones *et al.* 2004).

Family therapy

The influential work of Vaughn and Leff (1976) highlighted the importance of psycho-social stressors in the relapse of schizophrenia. Their work showed that people with schizophrenia who lived in families in which relatives showed high expressed emotions (hostility, over-involvement or criticism) were at an increased risk of relapse to schizophrenia. Therefore it is important that highly expressed emotions are identified and addressed appropriately through family interventions. Family interventions show some positive effects in decreasing relapse and improving compliance with medication (Pharoah *et al.* 2006).

Bipolar affective disorder

Bipolar affective disorder is a cyclical mood condition with depressive and manic/hypomanic episodes. National Institute of Health and Clinical Excellence (2006) has produced guidelines for the treatment of bipolar disorder. Here, the treatment of each of the components of the disorder will be described in turn.

Treatment of depression

As with all mental health conditions, the treatment of depression focuses on medical, psychological and social aspects. The choice of treatment is influenced by a number of factors including the severity of the depressive episode (classified as mild, moderate or severe according to the ICD-10); the pattern of the illness (i.e. whether it is unipolar or part of a bipolar illness); the risks that the patient may pose to him- or herself or to others; and the response to previous treatment. National Institute of Health and Clinical Excellence (2007a) guidelines for the treatment of depression are presented in Information Box 8.3.

Drug treatment

Antidepressant medications are effective in the treatment of moderate to severe depression but are generally not recommended as a first-line treatment for mild depression (National Institute of Health and Clinical Excellence 2007a). A list of commonly used antidepressants and their side effects is presented in Table 8.1.

Information Box 8.3 National Institute of Health and Clinical Excellence guidelines on the treatment of depression (National Institute of Health and Clinical Excellence 2007a)

General principles
- Assessment should include a full assessment of symptoms, risk of suicide, previous treatment history, psycho-social stressors and personality factors
- Assessment should also consider the physical, psychological and social characteristics of the individual concerned
- Patient's preference for treatment to be taken into consideration
- Informed consent to be obtained

Pharmacological therapies
- Antidepressants: SSRIs as first-line treatment
- Mood stabilisers: lithium to be considered in recurrent depression and bipolar disorder
- Antipsychotics combined with antidepressants in cases of depression with psychosis

Psychological therapies
- Counselling
- Couple-focused therapy
- Cognitive-behavioural therapy
- Interpersonal therapy
- Problem-solving therapy
- Short-term psychodynamic psychotherapy

Service level intervention
- Primary care
- Inpatient treatment
- Outpatient treatment
- Day hospital attendance

Stepped care approach

Step 1: Recognition	Assessment of depression
Step 2: Mild depression	Watchful waiting Guided self-help Computerised CBT Psychological interventions
Step 3: Moderate to severe depression	Medication Psycho-social intervention
Step 4: Treatment resistant psychotic depression	Combined treatments (i.e. medication + psychological treatment)
Step 5: Risk to life	Combined treatments Electroconvulsive therapy (ECT)

Table 8.1 Examples of antidepressant medications

Class and Drugs	Licensed indication	Examples of side effects
Tricyclics		
Amitriptyline	Depression	Dry mouth, sedation, constipation, blurred vision, postural hypotension, arrhythmia, tremor, sweating
Lofepramine	Depression	Same as amitriptyline, but less sedating and safer in overdose
SSRIs		
Citalopram	Depression Panic disorder	Nausea, vomiting, diarrhoea, poor appetite, weight loss, sexual dysfunction
Sertraline	Depression OCD PTSD in women	Same as citalopram; also tachycardia, liver failure, pancreatitis, postural hypotension
MAOIs		
Phenelzine	Depression	Postural hypotension, drowsiness, insomnia, dry mouth, constipation, dangerous interaction with food containing tyramine (i.e. mature cheese, meat or yeast extract)
Moclobemide	Depression Social anxiety disorder	Sleep disturbance, dizziness, headache, restlessness, gastro-intestinal problems, less likely to interact with tyramine than phenelzine
SNRIs		
Venlafaxine	Depression Generalised anxiety disorder	Nausea, vomiting, diarrhoea, poor appetite, constipation, palpitation, hypertension, ECG changes, weight changes

NASSA Mirtazapine	Depression	Increased appetite, weight gain, sedation, oedema, sedation, suicidal behaviour
NRIs Reboxetine	Depression	Nausea, dry mouth, constipation, palpitation, headache, postural hypotension
Others Duloxetine	Depression	Nausea, headache, constipation, abdominal pain, diarrhoea, sexual dysfunction

MAOIs: mono-amine oxidase inhibitors
NASSA: noradrenergic and specific serotonin antidepressants
NRIs: noradrenaline re-uptake inhibitors
OCD: obsessive compulsive disorder
PTSD: post-traumatic stress disorder
SNRIs: serotonin-noradrenaline re-uptake inhibitors
SSRIs: selective serotonin re-uptake inhibitors

Antidepressants achieve their therapeutic benefits through acting on certain neurotransmitter systems in the brain. Tricyclic antidepressants were first used in the 1950s and get their name because they consist of three rings of atoms. Tricyclic antidepressants inhibit the re-uptake of the neurotransmitters noradrenaline (norepinephrine) and serotonin after they have performed their function (i.e. a form of recycling neurotransmitters). These two neurotransmitters are key in controlling mood. Tricyclic antidepressants also block cholinergic receptors, causing a range of side effects such as dry mouth, blurred vision, constipation and urinary retention (see Information Box 8.2 and Table 8.1).

Newer forms of antidepressants are more selective than tricyclic antidepressants in their mode of action. Selective serotonin re-uptake inhibitors (SSRIs) maintain the levels of serotonin in the brain. They do not alter levels of noradrenaline and are less likely to block cholinergic receptors and so tend to produce fewer side effects than tricyclic antidepressants. SSRIs have, however, been associated with withdrawal symptoms such as nausea, vomiting, headache, chills, restlessness and anxiety. They should, therefore, be discontinued gradually over a number of weeks. They have also been linked with suicidal behaviour (Gunnell and Ashby 2004).

Antidepressants usually take two weeks or so to show therapeutic benefit. The patient should be made aware of this delay and be advised to report any deterioration in symptoms or emerging side effects. If the patient's depression fails to respond to treatment after 4–6 weeks, switching to another antidepressant, preferably from a different class, should be considered, but before switching medication it is important to check whether the patient has been compliant with treatment. In addition, aggravating factors such as substance misuse and psycho-social stressors should be inquired about and, if possible, appropriately addressed.

Augmentation therapy should be considered when the patient's depression fails to respond to treatment by giving at least two different antidepressants in sufficient doses for an adequate length of time. Augmentation strategies also include combining antidepressant treatment with a mood stabiliser, such as lithium carbonate, sodium valproate or carbamazepine. The mood stabilising drugs and their side effects are listed in Table 8.2. In cases of resistant depression, consideration should be given to combining drug treatment with psychological therapy. In cases of depression with psychotic symptoms, antidepressant treatment may have to be combined with antipsychotic medication.

Table 8.2 Mood stabilisers

Drug	Side effects	Monitoring requirements
Lithium carbonate	Thirst, polyuria, weight gain, tremor, muscular weakness, acne, renal impairment, hypothyroidism	U&E, TFT, lithium levels at baseline and every 6 months thereafter
	Lithium toxicity: course tremor, diarrhoea, vomiting, confusion, fits, coma and death	ECG at baseline and then yearly
Sodium valproate	Sedation, weight gain, nausea, vomiting, hair loss, acne, blood count abnormalities, pancreatitis	FBC, U&E, TFT at baseline and every 6 months thereafter
Carbamazepine	Nausea, ataxia, double vision, drowsiness, hepatitis, skin rash, agranulocytosis, aplastic anaemia	FBC, LFT, TFT at baseline and 3–6 monthly thereafter
	Toxicity: nausea, ataxia, double vision, unsteady gait	
Lamotrigine	Skin rash (rare, but can become life threatening), ataxia, headache, double vision, vomiting	Monitor for skin rash especially during early stages of treatment
Topiramate	Visual disturbance, cognitive decline, nausea, weight loss, abdominal pain	Monitor for visual side effects

ECG: electrocardiograph
FBC: full blood count
LFT: liver function test
TFT: thyroid function test
U&E: urea and electrolytes

Electroconvulsive therapy (ECT)

There is also a place for using ECT in cases of severe depression when there is a significant risk to the life of the individual concerned, for example risk of self-harm, starvation or life threatening dehydration because of the patient's refusal to eat and drink. There are, however, long-standing concerns about the side effects of ECT, in particular memory impairment post-ECT. The use of ECT has been associated with some rare side effects including those due to the risk of having a general anaesthetic. However, the risks of ECT need to be balanced against the risk of untreated severe depression which may include a dangerous deterioration in physical health due to self-neglect and death due to suicide.

Psychological therapies

Existing evidence supports the use of psychological interventions in the treatment of depression. NICE (2007a) recommend the use of a number of psychological therapies, including counselling, problem-solving therapy, cognitive behaviour therapy, couple-focused therapy and interpersonal therapy (see Information Box 8.3). Watchful waiting, computerised cognitive-behavioural therapy or brief psychological interventions are generally recommended as first-line treatment in cases of mild depression. In cases of moderate to severe depression, cognitive behaviour therapy is the psychological treatment of choice, usually in combination with medication.

Mania and hypomania

According to the NICE (2006) guidelines, the treatment of mania and hypomania is generally divided into two phases – the acute phase and long-term treatment. In the acute phase, any antidepressant medication is discontinued and the use of antipsychotics (olanzapine, quetiapine or risperidone) may be considered if the manic symptoms are severe or are associated with marked disturbance of behaviour. Mood stabilisers – lithium carbonate or sodium valproate – may be used if the symptoms are less severe, especially if there has been a previous good response with these drugs. However, sodium valproate should be avoided in women of child-bearing potential because it is known to have adverse effects upon foetal development. If administration of only one type of drug is ineffective, antipsychotics and mood stabilisers may be used in combination. Where the symptoms are severe or life-threatening, electroconvulsive therapy may be used for rapid and short-term improvement. Behavioural techniques aiming at reducing stimuli and daily activities are advisable during manic phases. Long-term treatment of manic conditions involves continued medication and regular physical health monitoring (i.e. weight, blood pressure, full blood count, liver function, kidney function, blood glucose and lipids and electrocardiogram).

Personality disorder

Mental health services have previously often excluded individuals with personality disorders on treatability grounds because of an uncertainty about what treatment could effectively be offered to this group of patients and inadequate provision for people with personality disorder. Only a few specialist personality disorder treatment places have been available in special hospitals and medium-secure units (Duggan and Khalifa 2007). Recently however, a document entitled *Personality Disorder: No Longer a Diagnosis of Exclusion* (National Institute of Mental Health in England 2003) instructed general mental health services not to exclude people with personality disorders from treatment, but rather to develop services for this particular group. Forensic mental health services were also part of the initiative to develop new services for dangerous offenders with severe personality disorders (Department of Health and Home Office 1999). As a result, treatment provision for people with personality disorder has increased substantially.

Psychological interventions for people with personality disorder

Evidence is accumulating that psychological interventions are of benefit in treating personality disorder. The last few decades have witnessed the development of a wide range of psychological interventions, including cognitive behaviour therapies, psychodynamic therapies and therapeutic communities. Meta-analyses of treatment outcomes for personality disorders show a positive effect of treatment for both cognitive-behavioural and psychodynamic approaches (Liechsenring *et al.* 2004; Perry *et al.* 1999).

Information about effective treatments for specific personality disorders is presented in Information Box 8.4. Of all the evaluation studies, most relate to borderline personality disorder (Duggan *et al.* 2007). This is partly due to the fact that individuals with borderline personality disorder frequently present to mental health services, i.e. they are 'treatment seeking' (Tyrer *et al.* 2003). Of particular relevance to forensic mental health populations is antisocial personality disorder. In their systematic review, Duggan *et al.* (2007) identified only two studies which specifically looked at antisocial personality disorder. This is frustrating, given that antisocial personality is at least as common as schizophrenia (which has received considerable attention from researchers and healthcare providers alike) and is associated with a substantial public health burden. However, unlike those with borderline personality disorder, individuals with antisocial personality disorder are 'treatment rejecting' (Tyrer *et al*. 2003).

Dialectical behaviour therapy (DBT) for women with borderline personality disorder is the most widely evaluated psychological treatment for personality disorder. DBT is based on the premise that the borderline personality disorder is typified by a failure to regulate emotions, which has developed as a result of a biologically based emotional vulnerability in combination with an invalidating environment, that is where the child's private experiences are denied, contradicted or punished by significant others (Linehan 1993a, 1993b). DBT is a combination of group and individual therapies lasting about a year and focusing on distress tolerance, emotion regulation, self-acceptance and interpersonal effectiveness. Randomised controlled trials of DBT compared with treatment as usual show DBT to be effective in reducing substance use, preventing treatment drop-out, reducing self-harming behaviours and improving global adjustment (Koons *et al*. 2001; Linehan *et al*. 1999; Verheul *et al*. 2003). DBT has also been used with mentally disordered women offenders in a secure psychiatric hospital, where reduced self-harm, suicidal ideation, depression and dissociative experiences, along with improved survival and coping beliefs were evidenced (Low *et al*. 2001). Women prisoners who received DBT showed improvements in borderline symptoms, improved emotion control, reduced impulsivity and increased internal locus of control (Nee and Farman 2005).

Psychoanalytically oriented partial hospitalisation has also proved effective with patients with borderline personality disorder. Compared with general psychiatric care, therapy of about one and a half years' duration led to patients being less depressed, showing less self-harming behaviours, being in hospital for fewer days and improving their social functioning (Bateman and Fonagy 1999, 2001). The treatment group maintained these gains and showed some further improvement at follow-up 18 months after treatment. Schema-focused therapy (i.e. addressing core beliefs about oneself) has proven effective in retaining borderline personality disordered patients in treatment and reducing the severity of the disorder (Giesen-Bloo *et al*. 2006). Cognitive behaviour therapy, addressing core beliefs and

Information Box 8.4 Psychological treatments for people with personality disorder (Duggan *et al.* 2007)

Interventions that are superior to treatment as usual or waiting list controls
Avoidant personality disorder:

- Cognitive-behavioural therapy (CBT)

Borderline personality disorder:

- Dialectical behavioural therapy (DBT)
- Emotional regulation group intervention (ER)
- Psychoanalytically orientated partial hospitalisation (POPH)

Mixed personality disorder:

- Brief adaptive psychotherapy
- Short dynamic psychotherapy
- Manual-assisted cognitive therapy (MACT)

Interventions compared
Avoidant personality disorder:

- CBT superior to brief dynamic therapy

Borderline personality disorder:

- DBT-oriented treatment superior to client centred therapy
- Schema-focused therapy superior to transference-focused therapy

Antisocial personality disorder + opioid dependency:

- Contingency management superior to standard methadone therapy

Mixed personality disorder:

- DBT superior to community therapy by experts
- Psychoeducation + pharmacotherapy superior to unstructured intervention + pharmacotherapy
- Wellness and lifestyles group superior to creative coping group
- Short psychodynamic supportive psychotherapy + antidepressants superior to antidepressants alone

---

the functions these beliefs have for the individual, has successfully reduced suicidal acts, anxiety and distress in borderline personality disordered patients (Davidson *et al.* 2006).

A recent intervention for a group of people with any of the personality disorders which combined psycho-education (i.e. helping people become aware of their disorder and its likely effects on their functioning) and social problem-solving therapy (i.e. helping people identify problems and tackle them successfully) has been shown to improve social functioning and anger control (Huband *et al.* 2007). This intervention has been used with mentally disordered offenders (McMurran *et al.* 2001) and vulnerable prisoners (Hayward *et al.* 2008).

Therapeutic communities (TCs) aim to address maladaptive interpersonal styles in a democracy where residents confront each other with the impact of their behaviours. In a study of hospitalised personality disordered patients, treatment led to a highly significant reduction in psychological distress (Dolan 1997) and, at three- and five-year follow-ups, fewer TC participants had further convictions or had been hospitalised compared with those assessed but not admitted (Copas *et al.* 1984). However, TCs are not always effective with offenders. Rice *et al.* (1992) carried out a retrospective evaluation of a TC in a maximum security institution for mentally disordered offenders, matching the TC participants with a comparable assessment-only group. Follow-up 10.5 years after discharge showed a modest overall degree of success for the TC in terms of reconviction, revocation of parole or reincarceration, but those in the TC who scored 25 or more on Hare's Psychopathy Checklist showed higher rates of recidivism, particularly violent recidivism, than a comparable non-treated group. That is, treatment in a TC made 'psychopaths' worse than if they had had no treatment at all. This study has, however, been criticised in that the treatment practices within the TC were unusual and not comparable with modern practices. McMurran *et al.* (1998) examined the criminal recidivism of personality disordered offenders discharged from a hospital-based TC after an average of 17 months compared with those who had been assessed only. At a mean follow-up time of almost five years, there was a significant reduction in crime for the whole sample when comparing pre-admission and post-discharge offences, but there were no significant differences between the two groups in terms of reconvictions, suggesting that the TC had no effect on offending.

Pharmacological interventions for people with personality disorder

Several arguments have been put forward to justify the use of medication with people with personality disorder (Tyrer and Bateman 2004). One argument is based on the understanding that personality disorders are associated with neurochemical abnormalities, whether inherited or related to psychological or physical trauma (Skodol *et al.* 2002). For instance, deficits in the neurotransmitter serotonin have been linked to impulsivity and aggression (Linnoila and Virkkunen 1992). Thus it has been argued that the use of medication has the potential to correct deficits in certain neurotransmitter systems in individuals with personality disorder.

Another argument for the use of medication in this population is that medication may help to achieve symptomatic control since it is well established that people with personality disorder experience a range of affective and cognitive symptoms, for example mood swings, anxiety, suspiciousness and paranoia. These symptoms have been categorised under the following symptom domains (Soloff 1998):

- cognitive/perceptual abnormalities (e.g. ideas of reference, magical thinking, paranoid ideation and stress-induced psychotic symptoms);
- affective dysregulation (anger, mood swings, anhedonia);
- anxious-fearful; and
- impulsive/behavioural dyscontrol (e.g. risk-taking behaviour, low frustration tolerance, aggressive behaviour).

Pharmacological treatments for symptom control are presented in Table 8.3.

A review by Soloff (1998) favoured the use of low-dose conventional antipsychotics for cognitive-perceptual symptoms, antidepressants for mood dysregulation and SSRIs for impulsive behavioural dyscontrol. A more recent review concluded that the evidence base for using medication in people with personality disorder is slim, although the results favoured the use of anticonvulsants to reduce aggression and of antipsychotic medication to reduce cognitive-perceptual and mental state disturbance (Duggan *et al.* 2008).

Table 8.3 A symptom-based approach to the use of pharmacological interventions in people with personality disorder

Symptom domains	Drugs
Cognitive-perceptual[1]	
Paranoid ideation	Aripiprazole
Psychoticism	Aripiprazole
Somatisation	Topiramate
Affective dysregulation-mood	
Depression[1,2]	Aripiprazole, fluoxetine, phenelzine
State anger and trait anger[3]	Topiramate, lamotrigine, aripiprazole
Anger in[3] and anger hostility[1]	Topiramate, aripiprazole
Anger out and anger control[3]	Topiramate, lamotrigine, aripiprazole
Anger (general)[4]	Fluoxetine
Hostility (general)[5]	Phenelzine
Affective dysregulation-anxiety	
Anxiety (intropunitiveness)[6]	Phenelzine
Anxiety (general and phobic)[1]	Aripiprazole, topiramate
Anxiety (interpersonal sensitivity)[1]	Divalproex
Insecurity in social contact[1]	Aripiprazole, topiramate
Impulsive behavioural dyscontrol[7]	
Impulsiveness in substance abusers	Nortriptyline
Global functioning	
Overall global functioning[8,9]	Haloperidol, divalproex, phenelzine, risperidone, fluoxetine
Overall symptoms/mental health[1,6]	Haloperidol, topiramate, aripiprazole

1 Symptom Checklist-90 – Revised (Derogatis 1992)
2 Hamilton Depression Scale (Hamilton 1960)
3 Spielberger State-Trait Anger Expression Inventory (Spielberger 1999)
4 Profile of Mood States (McNair *et al.* 1971)
5 Buss Durkee Hostility Inventory (Buss and Durkee 1957)
6 Inpatient Multidimensional Rating Scale (Lorr *et al.* 1966)
7 Self Report Test of Impulse Control (Lazarro et al. 2006)
8 Global Assessment Scale (Endicott *et al.* 1976)
9 Clinical Global Impressions Scale (Guy 1976)

Learning disability

The ordinary healthcare needs of individuals with learning disabilities and the rest of the population are broadly similar (Lindsey 2002), and while they have the same right of access to health services, there are concerns that people with learning disabilities suffer health inequalities (Kerr 2004). Health disparity is likely to result from communication difficulties of learning disabled people and lack of awareness of the healthcare needs of this population, both among their carers and providers of healthcare (Lindsey 2002).

In addition to ordinary healthcare needs, people with learning disabilities may also have special healthcare needs, for example in relation to the treatment of epilepsy, challenging behaviour, developmental disorders (such as autism) and sensory impairment. Therefore the assessment and management of people with learning disabilities should take into consideration genetic, developmental, medical and social perspectives. For instance, Down's syndrome, a well known cause of learning disability in which a person has 47 chromosomes instead of the usual 46, is associated with increased risks of congenital heart diseases, hypothyroidism, hearing impairment, acute leukaemia and dementia of the Alzheimer's type.

Mental health issues

It is well recognised that mental health problems are highly prevalent among people with learning disabilities. The prevalence rates, which lie between 30 and 50 per cent, are much higher than the rate for the general population (Smiley 2005). The principles underpinning the treatment of mental disorder in the learning disabled population remain the same as in other populations. However, precautions should be taken when psychotropic medications are prescribed since people with learning disabilities, particularly those who have epilepsy or neurological abnormalities, are sensitive to side effects such as fits, sedation and extra-pyramidal side effects. Counselling and support should be offered in all cases. Communication difficulties may limit the use of complex psychological interventions in this population, although communication can be facilitated through the use of simple language or visual tools.

Challenging behaviour

Gelder et al. (2006) define challenging behaviours as 'behaviours that are of an intensity or frequency sufficient to impair the physical safety of the learning disabled person, to pose a danger to others, or make difficult participation in the community' (p. 873). Self-injury, aggression and destructiveness are common examples. Challenging behaviours have prevalence rates of 10–20 per cent in people with learning disabilities (Smiley 2005). The rate increases with increasing severity of learning disability. Challenging behaviours may arise out of communication difficulties, pain, discomfort, under-stimulation, disruption of routine and a range of other causes including underlying mental disorder. They may also be caused by genetic or chromosomal disorders, for example Prader-Willi syndrome (a chromosomal condition characterised by learning disability, short stature, excessive sleeping, obesity and immature development of sexual organs) may be associated with self-injurious behaviour. Management of challenging behaviour depends on identifying and treating the underlying cause. They may respond to medication and behavioural management, the latter informed by a functional analysis of the behaviour.

Substance misuse

Substance misuse in mentally disordered individuals has several undesirable consequences including an increased risk of relapse of psychosis (Cantwell and Harrison 1996), increased frequency of hospitalisation (Bartels *et al.* 1993), poor compliance with treatment (Jablensky *et al.* 1992), impairment of integrity of therapeutic regimes in hospitals and increased potential for antisocial behaviour and crime of both an acquisitive and violent nature (Stewart *et al.* 2000). Treatment for substance misuse targets four major domains:

- drug and alcohol use (i.e. quantity and frequency of use, pattern of use, route of administration);
- physical health (e.g. blood-borne infections, risk behaviours, liver disease, abscesses, overdose, enduring or severe physical disabilities) and psychological health (e.g. self-harm, history of abuse, trauma, depression, psychiatric co-morbidity);
- social functioning (e.g. childcare issues, domestic violence, family, housing, employment, benefits, financial problems); and
- criminal involvement (National Treatment Agency for Substance Misuse 2002).

Treatment is offered in four tiers:

Information Box 8.5 Substance withdrawal state

Alcohol withdrawal state
Tremor of the tongue, eyelids or outstretched hands, sweating, nausea or vomiting, tachycardia or hypertension, psychomotor agitation, seizures, restlessness, anxiety, poor sleep, loss of appetite, transient visual, tactile or auditory hallucinations

Opioid withdrawal state
Craving for an opioid drug, yawning, sweating, lacrimation, rhinorrhea, nausea or vomiting, restlessness, insomnia, dilated pupils, piloerection, chills, tachycardia, hypertension, nausea/vomiting, abdominal cramps, diarrhoea, and muscle aches and pains

Sedative or hypnotic withdrawal state
Tremor of the tongue, eyelids or outstretched hands, nausea or vomiting, tachycardia or hypertension, psychomotor agitation, insomnia, headache, weakness, paranoia, transient visual, tactile or auditory hallucinations

Withdrawal state from stimulant drugs
Lethargy, fatigue, psychomotor retardation or agitation, increased appetite, bizarre dreams, insomnia or excessive sleep

---

- screening and referral;
- advice and support (e.g. harm reduction);
- specialist services (e.g. psychological therapy, methadone maintenance); and
- residential treatment (e.g. detoxification, therapeutic community treatment).

In forensic mental health services, patients have usually detoxified from alcohol and drugs, where necessary, in prison, under the care of the prison health service. Detoxification is aimed at suppressing withdrawal features (see Information Box 8.5), and pharmacological agents can be prescribed to aid this process. For alcohol detoxification, benzodiazepines such as lorazepam, oxazepam, diazepam or chlordiazepoxide are used to suppress withdrawal symptoms. Individuals undergoing alcohol detoxification should also receive thiamine (vitamin B1) supplements to prevent Wernicke's encephalopathy. This is a neurological condition that is caused by a thiamine deficiency and presents with a triad of ataxia (disorders of movement), confusion and ophthalmoplagia and nystagmus (eye movement disorders). Symptomatic treatment involves maintaining adequate fluid intake and symptomatic control (e.g. paracetamol for pain control). The preferred medications used for detoxification from opioids are methadone and buprenorphine (NICE 2007b). Both of these are opioid drugs themselves and so stop withdrawal symptoms.

Screening for substance misuse in mentally disordered individuals is the first step in the management of substance misuse disorders. Screening methods include history taking, the use of questionnaires or rating scales, structured or semi-structured interviews and the use of biological markers of illicit drug misuse (Crome *et al*. 2006; Wolff *et al*. 1999). In forensic settings, the use of biological tests may have a clinical and a security function. These biological screening methods are listed in Table 8.4. The process of screening may provide opportunities for advice (e.g., on the adverse consequences of substance misuse), enhancing motivation to change, or referral for treatment.

Techniques of motivational interviewing may help to enhance the patient's motivation to change their substance-taking behaviour (Miller and Rollnick 2002), although a review of the application of motivational interviewing with offenders shows that its primary value is in engaging and retaining substance users in treatment (McMurran, in press). Abstinence is not always an acceptable goal, and so harm reduction may therefore be a more realistic option for some people. Harm reduction strategies include providing sterile injection equipment to minimise the chance of sharing contaminated needles among users, thereby reducing the risks of HIV and hepatitis B or C viral infections.

Psychological components of treatment include:

- *behavioural self-control training*, which teaches people to recognise and cope with triggers for drinking or drug use;

- *enhancing cognitive coping skills*, equipping people to cope with cravings, change their expected outcomes from substance use and avoid relapse;

- *improving problem-solving skills*, so that people can cope better with interpersonal and emotional difficulties;

- *improving interpersonal skills*, so that people can resist peer pressure, change antisocial peer networks and be resilient to the saboteurs who may undermine change attempts;

Table 8.4 Drug detection strategies: the use of biological markers

Method	Advantages	Disadvantages
Urine analysis	Urine is available in sufficient quantity Urine is easy to collect Drugs tend to be present in urine in high concentration	Short duration of detectability* Easily adulterated with chemicals** or diluted to produce false results
Hair analysis	Easily obtained under close supervision Not subject to adulteration or substitution A second sample can be collected in disputed cases Has long detection window (up to three months) Hair sample can be matched to the individual	Relatively expensive Hair doesn't grow out of the follicle sufficiently to be clipped for about a week
Saliva testing	Easy to obtain Can be carried out by untrained personnel High correlation between saliva and plasma concentrations for many drugs	Relatively more expensive than urine analysis

* With the exception of cannabis and benzodiazepines
** Such as bleach, vinegar, liquid soap
After Wolff *et al.* (1999).

- *relapse prevention*, which helps identify and cope with relapse risk factors; and

- *lifestyle change*, where a non-substance using, non-criminal life is sustained through new accommodation, work, leisure activities, social networks and close relationships (McMurran 2006).

Psychological interventions can be implemented alongside medical treatments such as methadone maintenance. Methadone is a synthetic opioid that stops the withdrawal but without giving the buzz of natural opioids. Because of this, it is also used as a substitute drug in long-term maintenance treatment. Upon discharge, a patient may be referred to a specialist inpatient alcohol or drug treatment unit if there is a need for more intensive treatment.

Conclusion

The treatment of mentally disordered offenders requires expertise in the application of effective medical and psychosocial interventions for a range of distinct problems. These interventions are conducted with reference to the patient's offending behaviour and are often conducted in secure settings. The constraints imposed by these secure settings often create difficulties in assessing change. Will the patient continue to take medication in the community? Will the patient be able to use newly acquired skills, such as emotion regulation, problem-solving and conflict resolution? Will he or she be able to abstain from illicit drugs? Obviously, a certain level of risk must be accepted by mental health professionals, patients and members of the community if patients are to be given the opportunity to progress out of forensic mental health services. Forensic mental health professionals, in conjunction with other agencies, act to ensure that these risks are minimised. How a patient leaves the system is the subject of the final chapter.

Chapter 9

Leaving the system, patients' rights and advocacy

Introduction

Legal decision-making has a major influence on how long a person spends in secure care and when (or if) the person is released into the community. The main bodies involved in this decision-making are Mental Health Review Tribunals (MHRTs) and Parole Boards. The initial part of this chapter will describe the functioning of these bodies before moving onto discuss how the Multi-Agency Public Protection Arrangements (MAPPA) are used to enhance the management of offenders in the community. Finally, this chapter will conclude by outlining the systems that are in place to protect patients' rights and advocate on their behalf.

Mental Health Review Tribunals

History and role of the tribunal

Mental Health Review Tribunals (MHRTs) are independent judicial bodies whose primary function is to determine if the statutory criteria for compulsory detention under the Mental Health Act (MHA) are still met. If they are not met, then the patient is discharged. First introduced under the MHA 1959, their operation was substantially amended by the MHA 1983 and the Mental Health Review Tribunal Rules 1983. More recently, their functioning has been amended in light of case law and the need to ensure compliance with European Court of Human Rights (ECHR) legislation.

Application to and powers of the Mental Health Review Tribunal

The exact powers of and the rules regarding when a patient can apply for an MHRT differ slightly depending upon which section of the MHA a patient is detained under (Jones 2008). Broadly speaking, patients detained under the MHA are entitled to apply for an MHRT hearing within the first six months of their detention and can then apply once each time the section is renewed (i.e. for patients detained under sections 3 or 37 of the MHA, this is at six months, then 12 months and annually thereafter). If a patient chooses not to apply for an MHRT hearing after a period of three years, there will be an automatic referral to a Tribunal regardless of the patient's wishes.

The MHRT's main function is to decide if the essential criteria for continued detention under the MHA are met. Although criteria vary slightly depending upon which section the patient is detained under, generally the MHRT must discharge the patient if they are satisfied that:

- he/she is *not* suffering from a mental disorder of a nature or degree which makes hospital treatment appropriate; or
- his/her detention is *not* justified in the interests of his/her health and safety or the protection of others.

It has been established by recent case law that it is for the detaining authority to establish on the balance of probabilities (i.e. the civil law standard of proof) that these criteria are met. Thus it is for the hospital to demonstrate to the MHRT that the patient is suffering from a mental disorder which requires treatment in hospital and that this is justified in the interests of his or her health and safety or for the protection of others. It is not the patient's duty to prove that he or she is well and does not need to be in hospital. MHRTs may decide to grant a *deferred discharge*, that is where discharge is delayed for a specified period in order to give local community services sufficient time to prepare an adequate care package. Patients detained under a restriction order (section 41 of the MHA) are usually discharged by way of a *conditional discharge*. This gives the MHRT and the Ministry of Justice the power to impose a set of conditions which the patient must meet when in the community (e.g. to attend regular outpatient appointments, abstinence from illicit drugs, conditions of residency). When in the community, a conditionally discharged patient remains liable to *recall to hospital* if it is thought that his or her mental health is deteriorating or there is evidence of increased risk to others (see Chapter 1).

In addition to the mandatory requirement to discharge if the criteria for detention are no longer met, the MHRT also has the discretion to discharge patients (except for those subject to restrictions under sections 41 or 49) if they feel that this is appropriate – even where the statutory criteria for detention are met. When exercising this discretionary power, the MHRT is also required to consider the likelihood of medical treatment alleviating or preventing a deterioration of the patient's condition. Patients subject to a section 41 restriction order may be either absolutely discharged or conditionally discharged by the MHRT with the criterion for absolute discharge being that it is not appropriate for the patient to remain liable to be recalled to hospital for treatment.

MHRTs may also recommend transfer to another hospital, for instance a less secure hospital, or section 17 leave of absence, for example to aid rehabilitation. Although an MHRT recommendation for transfer or leave of absence is not binding upon the patient's care team, the Tribunal is entitled to reconvene and reconsider discharge if these recommendations are not followed. Once again the MHRT's powers in this respect are limited for restricted patients (i.e. those subject to sections 41 or 49 of the MHA 1983) and the Tribunal cannot make such recommendations but can only make suggestions to the Ministry of Justice.

Structure and proceedings of the MHRT

The Tribunals service is organised into five geographical regions for England and Wales. Appointments to the panels for each region are made by the Lord Chancellor, but in the case of non-legal (i.e. medical and lay) members, the Secretary of State for Health (and in Wales, the Secretary of State for Wales) is also consulted. For each individual hearing, the Regional Chairperson appoints the regional members to sit at a particular Tribunal. Each Tribunal panel sits with three members: a medical member (usually a consultant psychiatrist), a legal member and a lay member. For most Tribunals, the legal member will be a senior lawyer but for Tribunals involving restricted patients the legal member must be a senior judge.

The legal member of the Tribunal acts as its chairperson and is responsible for ensuring that the hearing is conducted in a fair manner and for producing a written statement explaining the reasons for the Tribunal's eventual decision. He or she will also advise the other members on points of law if necessary. The medical member has a dual role in that he or she is required personally to examine and form a clinical opinion on the patient prior to the Tribunal sitting. This member then also sits as part of the Tribunal. The lay member usually has a background in social work, nursing or psychology and helps to provide a balance between the legal and medical perspectives. While recognising the specialist experience of the legal and medical members of the MHRT, each member should have an equal voice on all matters.

Prior to the MHRT hearing, written reports must be provided to the Tribunal office from the clinician in charge of the patient's treatment and a social worker involved in the case. The clinician in charge is usually a consultant psychiatrist, known in this role as the Responsible Medical Officer or Responsible Clinician. The patient's local social services department will also be asked to produce a report detailing what support and accommodation would be available to the patient if discharged. The patient is also entitled to present any independent psychiatric reports which he or she believes will aid his or her case.

Typically, the Tribunal will meet approximately 30 minutes before the hearing to discuss the written reports and the medical member will also use this opportunity to make the other members aware of any issues considered relevant at this stage. Following this discussion, the hearing proper will begin. MHRT rules emphasise that the Tribunal should proceed in an informal manner and as directed by the chairperson. However, it must be remembered that the Tribunal is essentially a court hearing and should be treated with appropriate respect. Most Tribunals are held in private, at the hospital in which the patient is detained, but the patient can apply to the chairperson for it to be held in public. In this rare case the chairperson must agree that it would not be detrimental to the patient's mental health to do so. The patient is usually legally represented by his or her solicitor. In cases where there is great concern, the detaining authority (i.e. the hospital) and the Ministry of Justice (for restricted cases only) may also be legally represented.

The order in which those in attendance are asked to speak varies from Tribunal to Tribunal depending upon the patient and the Tribunal's need. Generally, each member of the panel is given the opportunity to ask questions of all the witnesses but questioning is led by the legal chairperson. The patient and his or her representative are also able to ask questions of the witnesses. This process of hearing evidence usually lasts between one and three hours, but some complicated cases may take place over several days. Rarely, the Tribunal may decide to adjourn in order to allow further evidence, for example the production of independent reports. Although rarely used, MHRTs have the power to subpoena witnesses and to initiate contempt of court proceedings.

All the evidence to be considered by the Tribunal must be presented to the patient's representative, the detaining authority and, for restricted patients, the Ministry of Justice. If there is information which it is not thought to be appropriate to be disclosed to the patient, for example confidential third-party information or information which may be very distressing to the patient, this evidence must be disclosed to the Tribunal who will then rule on whether or not it may be disclosed to the patient (although it must always be disclosed to his or her legal representative who is bound not to disclose it if the Tribunal decides this).

After hearing all the evidence, the Tribunal members discuss the case in private and decide upon whether the patient should be liable to detention under the Mental Health Act. If there is disagreement between the members, the majority view prevails. The Tribunal must then orally present its decision to the patient or the patient's representative. A written decision and the reasons for this must also be produced by the Tribunal.

Criticisms of the Tribunal system

The operation of MHRTs has been criticised as giving too much weight to the views of mental health professionals (in particular the Responsible Medical Officer/Responsible Clinician) rather than to the views of the patient (Myers 1997; Peay 1989). Other criticisms are that MHRTs are inflexible, slow to react and more mindful of risk issues than patient liberty. MHRTs may also create an unnecessarily adversarial process in which the patient and his or her legal advocate are pitted against the clinical team rather than working together constructively. However, it must be recognised that the MHRT acts as an essential safeguard to protect individual liberty and it is vital that the decision to detain an individual against his or her will is regularly reviewed and open to potential challenge. This reflects the view of the psychiatrist Birley (1991), who said that 'Every citizen should have the right to be admitted against his or her will, to be treated without loss of dignity, in a first class psychiatric service' (p. 1).

The Parole Board

Role and function

The Parole Board was established in 1968 under the Criminal Justice Act (CJA) 1967 as an independent executive body now sponsored by the Ministry of Justice. The Board defines it purpose as follows:

> The Parole Board is an independent body that works with its criminal justice partners to protect the public by risk assessing prisoners to decide whether they can safely be released into the community. (Parole Board 2007: 2)

The parole system is a system whereby prisoners who are serving determinate (fixed) sentences are released part way through their sentence. This system also decides when prisoners serving indeterminate sentences (see Information Box 9.1) should be released. It is the Board's job to decide which prisoners are suitable for release. When it was first established, the Board had only an advisory capacity, giving advice to the Home Secretary on which prisoners were suitable for early release. More recently it has become a quasi-judicial body that directly decides when the most dangerous prisoners should be released.

Prior to the CJA 2003, all determinate (fixed) sentence prisoners serving between 4 and 15 years were eligible for parole after serving between half and two-thirds of their sentence. The CJA made release at the halfway point automatic for all determinate sentence prisoners serving over twelve months, with probation supervision in the community until the end of their sentence. This means that the Parole Board no longer has a role in decision-making for determinate sentenced prisoners who were sentenced before April 2005. However, for the remaining cohort of determinate sentence prisoners sentenced before this date, the Parole Board still decides upon parole eligibility.

Instead, the Parole Board now concentrates upon the most dangerous prisoners, convicted of violent and sexual offences, who have been given either indeterminate or extended sentences. These changes were brought into being by the CJA 2003. In addition to its main role in making release decisions, the Parole Board also considers recall decisions made by the Probation Service.

Currently the Parole Board has approximately 180 members: 1 chairman, 2 salaried members, 3 high court judges, 50 judges, 21

Information Box 9.1 Types of custodial sentence

Determinate sentence
Fixed length sentence at the expiry of which the prisoner must be released. Most prisoners subject to determinate sentences will be automatically given parole at the halfway point of their determinate sentence, although they are still subject to probation supervision and are liable to recall to prison if they break the conditions of their release.

Indeterminate sentence
Prisoner can be kept in custody indefinitely until he is no longer thought to pose a risk to others. Indeterminate sentence prisoners are given a tariff which is the minimum period they must serve in prison before they can apply for parole. After serving their tariff the prisoner can apply to the Parole Board for release but will only be released if the Board thinks it safe to do so. There are four types of indeterminate sentence:

1 *Mandatory life sentence* – must be imposed for those over the age of 21 years convicted of murder.
2 *Discretionary life sentence* – may be imposed for certain violent and sexual offences (e.g. rape, manslaughter, arson).
3 *Automatic life sentence* – previously meant that those convicted of a serious sexual or violent offence who had a previous conviction for such an offence had to be given a life sentence. Now abolished by CJA 2003.
4 *Imprisonment for public protection (IPP)* – sentence imposed under the CJA 2003 on conviction for a serious offence, which does not carry a maximum of life imprisonment (i.e. discretionary life sentence not available), where the court believes that the offender poses a significant risk of serious harm to others.

Extended sentence
Type of determinate sentence that can be imposed for persistent, sexual or violent offenders. The prisoner can apply for parole at the midway point of his sentence but if unsuccessful must be released at the end of their determinate sentence (unlike other determinate sentence prisoners who are automatically granted parole at this point). If successful the prisoner remains subject to supervision by the probation service and is liable to recall to prison if he breaks the conditions of his release. When in the community, the released prisoner will remain under the care of the probation service and is liable to recall to prison for an extended period past the expiry of his custodial sentence.

psychiatrists, 4 psychologists, 4 criminologists, 14 probation service members and 83 independent members (Parole Board 2008).

How the Parole Board operates

The Parole Board has three types of decision-making body: paper panels, oral hearings and recall panels. In the year 2006–7, the Parole Board of England and Wales dealt with a total of 25,436 cases. This included 7,857 paper panels, 2,505 oral hearings and 14,669 recall cases (Parole Board 2007).

When making a decision, the Board's priority is public protection and thus it will not order the release of a prisoner until it decides that he or she no longer presents a significant risk to others. Information Box 9.2 shows some of the factors which the Parole Board takes into account when making its decisions. If declined for release, the Board must give the prisoner written reasons for its decision. The prisoner may make an application for parole or release on licence once they have passed a certain point in their sentence (determined by type and length of sentence) and if unsuccessful may reapply at regular intervals

Paper panels

The vast majority of current parole decisions are made by way of so-called paper panels which deal with prisoners serving determinate and, more rarely, extended sentences. A paper panel consists of three members who sit for the whole day and consider 24 parole

Information Box 9.2 Factors which may be considered by the Parole Board when making decisions to release a prisoner

* Nature, circumstances and pattern of previous offending and index offence
* Actuarial risk assessment and current risk assessments
* Reports from the trial (including the judge's sentencing remarks)
* Prison behaviour and results of illicit drug testing
* Medical, psychiatric and psychological reports
* Prisoner's current insight into their offending behaviour and the impact it has had upon others
* Likelihood of the prisoner complying with supervision and licence conditions
* Victim's representations – but only where they relate to current risk
* Any other issues the Board thinks of relevance

applications in a session. Each member takes it in turn to prepare the paperwork over the preceding four weeks and present the case to the other panel members. All three members then discuss the case and decide if the prisoner should be released.

In the case dossier may be reports from the prisoner's original trial, probation reports, offending behaviour treatment reports, psychiatric reports, medical reports, psychological reports, risk assessments and records of behaviour while in prison. The dossier may also contain a Victim Personal Statement (a written statement from either the victim of the offence or a relative of the victim describing the effect that the offence has had upon their life and the impact that the prisoner's release may have upon them).

Over 200 paper case decisions are taken each week at the Parole Board's headquarters in London. While these cases currently make up the majority of Board decisions, they will gradually decrease due to the effect of the CJA 2003 which gives automatic parole for determinate sentence prisoners.

Oral hearings

These hearings are used to take the most crucial decisions about the release and recall of prisoners serving indeterminate sentences (i.e. mandatory life sentence, discretionary life sentence and imprisonment for public protection (IPP)). Prisoners serving indeterminate sentences must serve a certain period set by the trial judge (known as the tariff) and once past this period they can apply to the Parole Board but will only be released if it is thought safe to do so. For prisoners serving a life sentence, the Board can also make recommendations about transfer to an open (Category D) prison.

Oral hearings usually take place in the prison in which the prisoner is being held, and recently some hearings have begun to be held using videoconferencing technology. The panel sits with three members and is chaired by a judge. Professional witnesses (e.g. probation and prison staff, psychologists and psychiatrists) may be called to give evidence. The prisoner has legal representation and can also speak if he or she chooses. A Victim Personal Statement may be provided in written form or as oral evidence presented by a Public Protection Advocate (a member of the National Offender Management Service whose role is to represent the victim's views to the Board). While the Secretary of State for Justice has the right to be represented and give the panel directions, a recent Court of Appeal judgement (Girling v. Parole Board 2007) confirmed that the Parole Board is not obliged to follow these directions.

If the Board is minded to release a prisoner, it can then specify a number of licence conditions, such as directing that the prisoner reside in a certain area, abstain from illicit drugs and alcohol, comply with psychiatric treatment and maintain regular contact with the probation service. The prisoner must obey these conditions upon release into the community. Of the oral hearings which took place for life sentenced prisoners in 2007, only 15 per cent resulted in a recommendation for release being made (Parole Board 2007).

Recall cases

Recall panels consider every case in which a prisoner who was on licence or parole in the community is recalled to prison. Prisoners on licence or parole can be recalled due to alleged reoffending, failure to comply with licence conditions or concern that their risk to others has increased. A recall panel consists of two members who, after reviewing the case paperwork (including reasons for recall), can recommend re-release or further review or can send the case to an oral hearing. Following a House of Lords decision in 2005, the Board must proceed to an oral hearing if there is a dispute as to the facts, unless they have already recommended re-release or the prisoner declines.

The Parole Board and prisoners transferred to psychiatric hospital

For serving prisoners who are transferred from prison to a psychiatric hospital under sections 47/49 of the MHA 1983, time spent in hospital is counted as part of the sentence served. Thus, while they are in hospital they may become eligible for release on parole or licence. However, apart from under exceptional circumstances, the prisoner cannot be considered for release from his sentence unless he returns to prison and applies to the Parole Board from there. Thus a prisoner-patient must first obtain his transfer back to prison (by agreement of his treating psychiatric team and the Ministry of Justice or an MHRT) and, once back in prison, the application for parole can be made.

This process can be lengthy as the prisoner may need to be back in prison for a substantial amount of time to allow the appropriate prison reports to be produced for the Board. Another potential difficulty is that some of the treatments which may have been completed in hospital (such as a sex offender treatment programme or an anger intervention) may not be recognised by the Prison Service and thus the Board may require the prisoner to repeat the accredited prison versions of these programmes. The effect of this can significantly delay the prisoner's progress back into the community. It should also be borne in mind that the strain of this prolonged period may have an adverse effect upon the prisoner's mental state with risk of relapse of their mental disorder.

The future of the Parole Board

Due to the changes introduced by the CJA 2003, the number of life sentenced and IPP prisoners will increase while the number of determinate sentence cases heard by the Board will fall. Once all the determinate sentence prisoners who were sentenced prior to April 2005 have been released, the Board will no longer have any role for determinate sentences, other than for those who receive an extended sentence. However, the number of extended sentence cases is also likely to fall as such cases are now more likely to receive an IPP sentence.

The net result of this is that over the next few years the Board will complete its transition into a judicial body, sitting as a three-member oral hearing to determine when indeterminate sentence prisoners can safely be released and reviewing the recall to prison of such prisoners.

Multi-agency Public Protection Arrangements

There has been increasing concern about how those convicted of serious sexual or violent offences are managed in the community when they are released from prison or secure hospitals. Of particular concern was the difficulty in ensuring effective cooperation and information sharing between the different agencies that were involved in a released offender's care in the community (such as the probation service, police, mental health trusts, housing and social services). In order to address this need, Multi-Agency Public Protection Arrangements (MAPPA) were established by the Criminal Justice and Court Services Act 2000. The probation, police and prison services are the lead agencies in managing the MAPPA process in each of the 42 administrative police and probation areas. In 2003, the CJA imposed a duty upon healthcare services and other agencies that are not part of the formal criminal justice system to 'cooperate' with MAPPA.

The aim of the MAPPA is to reduce serious reoffending by convicted sexual and violent offenders after their release into the community by effective multi-agency risk management. In a review of good practice, Kemshall (2003) outlined that public protection by MAPPA was dependent upon: defensible decision-making, rigorous risk assessment, the delivery of risk management plans that match the identified public protection need and the evaluation of performance. MAPPA are not statutory bodies but instead act as administrative arrangements that help to manage risk by coordinating multi-agency risk management plans and ensuring that such plans are efficiently implemented and reviewed.

While the arrangements principally concern those being released from prison after serving sentences for sexual or violent offences, they also encompass those being released from psychiatric hospitals who were convicted of sexual and violent offences and made the subject of a hospital order under the MHA or found to be unfit to plead or not guilty by reason of insanity (see Chapter 3). Those who have not been convicted of a sexual or violent offence cannot be made the subject of MAPPA regardless of the potential risk that they are thought to pose. The following three categories of offender have been identified as falling within the remit of MAPPA (Home Office 2003): Category 1: registered sex offenders under statutory supervision by the probation service; Category 2: violent offenders and sex offenders under statutory supervision by the probation service (i.e. sex offenders who are not subject to a sex offender registration order); and Category 3: other offenders.

Category 3 offenders are those offenders who are not in either Category 1 or 2 but who are thought to pose a serious risk of harm to the public and have a conviction for an offence that indicates they may cause serious harm to others. This conviction may have been given by a court outside the United Kingdom. Offenders who are in Category 1 or 2 but who are judged still to pose a high risk to others at the end of their period of probation service statutory supervision may also be included in Category 3 to allow their case to continue to be managed under the MAPPA. In 2005–6, approximately 48,000 offenders were the subject of MAPPA. This consisted of 29,973 Category 1 offenders, 14,317 Category 2 offenders and 3,363 Category 3 offenders (Home Office and Probation Service 2006).

Offenders who are subject to the MAPPA are risk assessed using the OASys risk assessment tool that is used by the prison and probation services (see Chapter 6). Sexual offenders are also risk assessed using the Risk Matrix 2000. In addition to this, other risk assessment methods may be used if thought appropriate. The offender's case will be allocated to one of three levels (Information Box 9.3) depending upon the outcome of these risk assessments and complexity of the risk management plans that are required to safely contain this risk. As risk is dynamic, cases may move between levels in response to significant changes in the offender's risk assessment or management plans. Overall, 71 per cent of MAPPA offenders are managed at Level 1, 26 per cent at Level 2 and 3 per cent (some 1,278 offenders) at Level 3 (Home Office and Probation Service 2006).

Level 3 management is reserved for the so-called 'critical few' and is prioritised for intensive input under the Multi-Agency Public Protection Panel (MAPPP). MAPPP hold regular meetings to review the care of this group of offenders. Given the complexity and risks presented by MAPPA Level 3 offenders, the MAPP is comprised of senior representatives from each involved agency who have the authority to make decisions concerning their agency's involvement and to commit significant resources if necessary. In addition to regular

Information Box 9.3 Levels of MAPPA management (Home Office 2003)

Level 1 – Ordinary risk management
- Risk from the offender can be managed by a single agency without the need for the active involvement of other agencies.
- These offenders are generally assessed as presenting low or medium risk to others.
- Large proportion of MAPPA offenders are managed at this level.

Level 2 – Local inter-agency risk management
- Active involvement of more than one agency is required but the level of risk or complexity of risk management plans does not require Level 3.

Level 3 – Multi-Agency Public Protection Panels (MAPPP)
- Assessed as being high or very high risk and those risks that can only be managed by a plan that requires close cooperation at a senior level due to its complexity or intensive resource requirements.

Or

- Although not assessed as high risk the case is of particular importance and is exceptional because of high public/media interest and there is a need to ensure public confidence in the criminal justice system is sustained.

---

meetings, for which written reports will be prepared in advance, the MAPPP may also meet at short notice in emergency meetings should the need arise.

Although mental health professionals have a duty to cooperate with the MAPPA process, this does not mean that the usual rules of professional confidentiality no longer apply. While different professionals have their own codes of confidentiality, generally information about a patient should not be shared with others if the patient has not given informed consent to this. Requests for disclosure of confidential clinical information to MAPPA should be considered on a case-by-case basis, the test being whether the release of such information to protect others from harm justifies breaching confidentiality. In this situation the risks of non-disclosure must be considered as well as the benefits of disclosure. Only that information which immediately relates to risk should be shared. Detailed guidance on this complex issue has been produced by the Royal College of Psychiatrists (2006). MAPPA guidance also states that, while information sharing is one of the key principles of the MAPPA, such information sharing should: have lawful authority, be necessary, be proportionate, be done in ways that ensure the safety and security of the information shared and be accountable (Home Office 2003).

Legal representation

Within the English jurisdiction, legal representation can be made by two types of lawyers: solicitors and barristers. Generally speaking, solicitors have more direct contact with clients than barristers and, while they do not conduct proceedings in courts they deal with all other legal issues. They may also represent clients in minor cases tried in Magistrates' Courts. In contrast, barristers have 'rights of audience' in the higher courts. They rarely take direct instructions from clients and are usually instructed by solicitors on behalf of the clients. For many years, barristers had a 'monopoly' on the right to represent people in the higher courts (Bar Council 2008b). However, the strict distinction between the roles of solicitors and barristers is beginning to blur, allowing more cross-professional work to be undertaken. For example, 'advocate-solicitors' increasingly represent clients in both lower and higher courts. Furthermore, barristers are now allowed to take direct instructions from clients, albeit with some limitations on the type of work they can undertake. Despite this overlap between the roles of solicitors and barristers, there remain some fundamental differences in their training and expertise which we will discuss in this section.

Solicitors

Becoming a solicitor requires the completion of two key stages of training: academic and vocational. The academic stage can be completed by achieving any of the following: (1) obtaining an undergraduate law degree or an exempting law degree; (2) passing a common professional examination; (3) gaining a diploma in law; or (4) completing an integrated course (Solicitors Regulation Authority 2008). Thereafter, the person must obtain a certificate of completion of the academic stage which is issued by the Law Society. This allows the person to proceed to the vocational stage of training. This entails completing a legal practice course, or an integrated course, or obtaining an exempting law degree, followed by serving under a training contract during which the trainee solicitor must complete the professional skills course (Solicitors Regulation Authority 2008). Upon successful completion of the academic and vocational stages of training the person becomes a solicitor and is admitted to the 'roll' (register) of solicitors. The Solicitors Regulation Authority administers the roll and keeps it on behalf of the head of the Court of Appeal of England and Wales who is also 'Master of the Rolls'.

The Law Society is the professional body for solicitors in England and Wales. It has the authority to issue practising certificates as set out in the Solicitors Act 1974 (Ministry of Justice 2008). The Solicitors Regulation Authority (a branch of the Law Society) deals with all regulatory and disciplinary matters for solicitors across England and Wales. Solicitors who are being disciplined by the Solicitors Regulation Authority can be suspended from or even struck off the register, which prevents them practising as a solicitor.

Solicitors usually operate from solicitor firms that are often referred to as partnerships. Solicitors act as legal advocates for their clients. In other words they can initiate legal proceedings (litigations) and write letters to courts or clients' opponents. They can instruct a barrister to give advice on points of law or when legal representation is required before the courts. In the context of mental healthcare, solicitors may act on behalf of patients in various matters. They often represent patients (detained under the Mental Health Act) in Mental Health Review Tribunals (see above). MHRTs are adversarial in nature and the patient has the right to be represented by a solicitor, although some patients choose to represent themselves. In addition to representation in Tribunals, patients may engage solicitors in relation to the care they receive from mental health services. For instance, it is nowadays not uncommon for patients detained in secure hospitals to ask their solicitors to attend Care Programme Approach meetings. There are, however, mixed views on this issue. While some professionals welcome the presence of solicitors in such meetings, others are concerned that it may distort an essentially clinical meeting into a legal one. Some also argue that the presence of a solicitor may also imply a lack of trust between the patient and mental health professionals and act as a barrier to effective collaboration between the patient and care professionals.

Barristers

Becoming a barrister requires the completion of three stages of training: academic, vocational and pupillage (Bar Council 2008a). The academic stage is similar to that of solicitors (see above). The person is then required to join one of the four Inns of Court (Lincoln's Inn, Inner Temple, Middle Temple and Gray's Inn) before commencing the vocational stage of training. This stage, in turn, requires completion of the Bar Vocational Course and undertaking twelve qualifying sessions before the person is called to the Bar by their Inn. Pupillage, which is the final stage of training, involves spending one year (split into periods of six months non-practising and six months practising) in an authorised pupillage training organisation.

The Bar Council is the professional body for barristers in England and Wales. It was established in 1894 to represent the interests of barristers. Its role is to 'promote and improve the services and functions of the Bar, and to represent the interests of the Bar on all matters relating to the profession, whether trade union, disciplinary, public interest or in any way affecting the administration of justice' (Bar Council 2008b). Barristers in England and Wales are regulated by the Bar Standards Board, which was established in January 2006. The Board works independently and has a separate membership from the Bar Council.

Barristers operate as sole practitioners and are not allowed to form firms or partnerships. However, they are allowed to operate in chambers and within solicitors' firms where they may act as legal advisors. In the context of forensic mental health, barristers usually represent mentally disordered offenders appearing before courts and in exceptional circumstance in Mental Health Review Tribunals.

The Mental Health Act Commission

The Mental Health Act 1983, alongside its powers to treat patients under compulsion, has introduced a number of safeguards for people detained in hospital under the provisions of the Act. The Mental Health Act Commission (MHAC), which was established in September 1983, is an example. The Commission is a special health authority which is responsible for monitoring the operation of the Mental Health Act in England and Wales. Its prime responsibility is to monitor the legality of detention and the protection of individuals' human rights (see http://www.mhac.org for further information). In practice, this responsibility is fulfilled through a number of functions (see Information Box 9.4).

Organisation

The Mental Health Act Commission is managed by a Commission Board, whose members are a chairman, vice chairman, chief executive, director of finance and non-executive members. The Commission also employs a number of commissioners and administrative staff. In addition, it has a panel of consultant psychiatrists who provide the second opinion doctor service and another group which considers requests for neurosurgery for mental disorder. Commissioners, who are part-time, work within four regional teams, each covering a defined geographical area. They come from a wide range of professional

Information Box 9.4 Functions of Mental Health Act Commission (after MHAC 2007)

- To monitor the operation of the MHA in relation to patients detained or liable to be detained under its provisions.
- To conduct visits to mental health facilities and nursing homes where patients may be detained under the MHA.
- To investigate complaints which fall within the remit of the Commission.
- To review decisions to withhold the mail of patients detained in the high-security hospitals.
- To publish a biennial report on its activities for Parliament.
- To provide a second opinion appointed doctor (SOAD) service.
- To monitor the implementation of the MHA Code of Practice.

---

backgrounds including lawyers, doctors, nurses, social workers, psychologists, academics and laypeople (Curran and Bingley 1994).

Visits to mental health facilities

Commissioners also have a responsibility to conduct visits to mental health facilities where patients are detained under the Mental Health Act. The purpose of these visits, which are often unannounced, is to ensure compliance with the Act and Code of Practice. This may involve interviewing detained patients in private, examining psychiatric records and any other issues related to their care whilst detained under the provisions of the Mental Health Act. While the aim of these visits is a laudable one, some commentators argue that they may cause fear and anxiety among both the patients and service providers (Tyrer *et al.* 1998).

Second Opinion Appointed Doctor service

This is an important safeguard provided under sections 57 and 58 of the Mental Health Act. Section 57 concerns neurosurgery for mental disorder and surgical implantation of anti-libidinal hormones. Such treatments are deemed potentially so hazardous that they cannot be given to non-consenting individuals. Requests for such treatments are considered by a panel of three people, one of whom must be a doctor. The role of the panel is to establish that the person concerned has a capacity to consent for the proposed treatment (neurosurgery or hormone implantation). In contrast, section 58 concerns patients who either lack capacity to consent or refuse to consent for certain treatments including medication and electroconvulsive therapy (ECT).

Psychotropic medication (i.e. those drugs which act upon the brain and are used to treat mental disorder – see Chapter 8) can be administered, irrespective of consent, for three months. Thereafter the patient's capacity to take medication has to be established before any further treatment can be given under the provisions of the Act. For those who have the capacity and are willing to give consent, treatment can be provided under section 58(a) and a second opinion is not required. However, for those who lack capacity to consent or refuse to consent, the Mental Health Act Commission should be approached to provide a Second Opinion Appointed Doctor (SOAD). The SOAD is an experienced independent consultant psychiatrist appointed by the Commission. The SOAD will then visit the hospital and examine the patient's clinical records, interview the patient and discuss their case with members of the patient's care team. If the SOAD agrees that the proposed treatment is reasonable given the circumstances, and that the patient either lacks capacity to consent or has capacity but is refusing, then treatment can then be given against the patient's wishes under the provisions of section 58(b). In the case of ECT, the SOAD service is required at any stage following detention for non-consenting patients (i.e. unlike medication, ECT cannot be given to an unwilling patient under the three-month rule).

Investigation of complaints

The Commission also has a duty to investigate complaints made by detained patients in relation to issues that have occurred during the detention period, and which have not been dealt with satisfactorily through the initial stages of the NHS complaint procedure, namely local resolution and independent review. In addition, the Commission may offer detained patients advice and information about their rights and the complaint procedures open to them.

Other roles

The Commission is a member of the Forum for Preventing Death in Custody, a group comprised of a number of healthcare and criminal justice agencies (see http://www.preventingcustodydeaths.org.uk). The Commission has a duty to record and review all deaths of detained patients who die during the detention period. The aim of this exercise is to ensure that the Code of Practice has been adhered to and to learn lessons for future practice. The detaining authority is required to inform the Commission of such deaths within three working days.

Mental health advocacy

It is often argued that people with mental health problems may find it difficult to communicate their views and evaluate information about their rights and the services available to them. Moreover, the days of 'medical paternalism' have gone (Thomas and Bracken 1999). The patient's choice and control are now central to the government's healthcare reform agenda. Hence, mental health advocacy is becoming increasingly important.

To advocate is to speak on behalf of someone. In the context of mental healthcare advocacy has a broader meaning. It entails helping people to be heard and ensuring that what they say influences the decisions of clinical staff (Royal College of Psychiatrists 1999). In practice, the process of advocacy involves enabling the individual to express their views, to access relevant information (e.g. on their mental health condition, legal rights and services available) and to stand up for their rights and explore their choices. While mental health, social and legal professionals may assist the individual in some of these issues, there may be a conflict of interest and hence they are not deemed independent. Therefore the importance of independence is paramount. This is particularly so in secure forensic hospitals where almost all the patients are detained under either mental health or criminal legislation.

Models of advocacy

There currently exist various types of mental health advocacy (see Information Box 9.5), although the principles underpinning them are

Information Box 9.5 Models of advocacy (after Mind 2006)

Self-advocacy
Speaking up for one's own views and wishes. It can be further enhanced by assertiveness training and/or the use of crisis cards and advanced directives.

Group advocacy
A group of individuals with similar views advocate for shared views and interests. Can operate at both local and national levels.

Peer advocacy
Support from an individual with experience of using mental health services.

Professional advocacy
Provided by voluntary organisations that train and often pay advocates to work with those using their services. The focus of support is short term (e.g. at times of crisis).

Citizen advocacy
Entails matching people with 'partners' who are members of their local community to provide long-term support. Provided by trained volunteers operating within a citizen advocacy scheme.

---

similar and most advocates work to a code of practice based on the recommendations of the Durham Report (Barnes and Brandon 2002). Most mental health advocacy services are run by volunteers who have received some form of training (Mind 2006). Within secure mental health services, advocates are often paid workers with experience of working in mental health. Advocacy services are often funded by central government or mental health charities. NHS Trusts may also commission or fund such services although it is well established that advocacy services must remain autonomous and independent of healthcare providers regardless of who funds them.

Advocacy and the Mental Health Act

The role of mental health advocates in safeguarding the rights of patients has been endorsed within the Mental Health Act 2007. The Act places a duty on the appropriate national authority to arrange access to independent mental health advocates. Section 30 of the Act gives certain patients access to independent mental health advocates including those who:

- are detained or liable to be detained under the Act;
- are subject to guardianship and community treatment orders;
- discuss with their doctor or approved clinician the possibility of treatment that requires consent and a second opinion such as psychosurgery;
- are under the age of 18 and discuss with their doctor or approved clinician the possibility of treatment that requires a second opinion such as ECT or psychosurgery.

Voluntary Groups

A large number of voluntary organisations provide information, help and support for people with mental health problems and their carers. Some of them also provide advocacy services. The Mental Health Foundation website (http://www.mentalhealth.org.uk) maintains an extensive list of such organisations. The contact details for some of the leading voluntary organisations in the United Kingdom are provided in Information Box 9.6.

Information Box 9.6 Mental health charities in the UK

The King's Fund (http://www.kingsfund.org.uk)
11–13 Cavendish Square, London W1G 0AN
Tel: 020 7307 2400

Mind (http://www.mind.org.uk)
15–19 Broadway, London E15 4BQ
Tel: 020 8519 2122

Rethink (http://www.rethink.org)
Royal London House, 22–25 Finsbury Square, London EC2A 1DX
Tel: 0845 456 0455

Samaritans (http://www.samaritans.org.uk)
Chris, PO Box 9090, Stirling FK8 2SA
Tel: 08457 90 90 90

Turning point (http://www.turning-point.co.uk)
Standon House, 21 Mansell Street, London E1 8AA
Tel: 020 7481 7600

Alcoholics Anonymous (http://www.alcoholics-anonymous.org.uk)
PO Box 1, 10 Toft Green, York YO1 7ND
Tel: 01904 644026

Sainsbury Centre for Mental Health (http://www.scmh.org.uk)
134–138 Borough High Street, London SE1 1LB
Tel: 020 7827 8300

SANE (http://www.sane.org.uk)
First floor, Cityside House, 40 Adler Street, London E1 1EE
Tel: 020 7375 1002

Conclusion

People with mental health problems have a right to humane and good quality mental healthcare, regardless of their offending background. They also have the right to be managed in the community when it is safe to do so. However, the public also has the right to be protected from those that may pose a risk to them. Balancing these often competing rights is one of the key tasks of forensic mental health professionals. This chapter has shown how various statutory and non-statutory bodies help to balance these competing demands to ensure that mentally disordered offenders receive the care that is appropriate to both their clinical need and to the risks they may present.

Afterword

As we mentioned at the outset, this book is intended for the newcomer to the topic of forensic mental health, and our aim was to give this newcomer a clear and succinct overview of the contexts in which forensic mental health professionals work and the kinds of services and treatments that they provide. We hope we have achieved this aim. Shortly before we finished writing this book, Willan published a comprehensive *Handbook of Forensic Mental Health*, edited by Keith Soothill, Paul Rogers and Mairead Dolan (2008). Contributors to the *Handbook* are eminent academics, researchers and practitioners who have written in depth about topics on which they are expert. Our introductory text may be a primer, and those who wish to access more detailed information on the topics covered here may graduate on to reading the *Handbook*.

The contents of this book reflect the state of play at the time of writing in the first half of 2008. We hope that the book has stood the test of time by at least being correct at the time of publication! However, the new Mental Health Act 2007 is due to come into force fully in November 2008, well after the preparation of the manuscript for this book. In the months and years after the implementation of the Mental Health Act 2007, there will be practice developments to report. So, even before this book is published, we aspire to writing a second edition updating this text!

If we ever do write a second edition, we hope we can once again call upon the patience of our partners and families, who have been supportive of our time-consuming writing endeavours. We would also wish again for the support of our colleagues. This book benefited specifically from the advice of Sam Verity, medical records manager, and Maxine Whale, independent patient advocate, both at Arnold Lodge medium-secure unit in Leicester. We would like to thank Professor Conor Duggan, Head of the Section of Forensic Mental Health in the Division of Psychiatry, University of Nottingham for supporting our academic, research and clinical work over the years. His contribution to forensic mental health practice has been significant and substantial, and we consider ourselves highly fortunate to work with him. Finally, we acknowledge all the members of the multidisciplinary teams and all the patients with whom we have worked. Reading about it in a book is one thing, but putting it into practice with other professionals and patients is the real business. We wish readers of this book every success in their forensic mental health practice.

References

Adshead, G. and Sarkar, S. (2007) 'Ethical issues in forensic psychiatry', *Psychiatry*, 6: 420–3.

American Psychiatric Association (1994) *Diagnostic and Statistical Manual of Mental Disorders*, 4th edn. Washington, DC: APA.

Andrews, D. A. and Bonta, J. (1995) *The Level of Service Inventory – Revised Manual*. Toronto: Multi-Health Systems.

Andrews, D. A. and Bonta, J. (2003) *The Psychology of Criminal Conduct*. Cincinnati, OH: Anderson.

Andrews, D. A., Bonta, J. and Wormith, J. S. (2004) *The Level of Service/Case Management Inventory (LS/CMI)*. Toronto: Multi-Health Systems.

Andrews, D.A., Bonta, J. and Wormith, J. S. (2006) 'The recent past and near future of risk and/or need assessment', *Crime and Delinquency*, 52: 7–27.

Antonowicz, D. H. (2005) 'The Reasoning and Rehabilitation Program: outcome evaluations with offenders', in M. McMurran and J. McGuire (eds), *Social Problem Solving and Offending*: *Evidence, Evaluation, and Evolution*. Chichester: Wiley.

Arseneault, L., Moffitt, T. E., Caspi, A., Taylor, P. J. and Silva, P. A. (2000) 'Mental disorders and violence in a total birth cohort – results from the Dunedin study', *Archives of General Psychiatry*, 57: 979–86.

Badger, D., Nursten, J., Williams, P. and Woodward, M. (1999) *Systematic Review of the International Literature on the Epidemiology of Mentally Disordered Offenders*. York: NHS Centre for Reviews and Dissemination.

Bailey, J. and MacCulloch, M. (1992) 'Characteristics of 112 cases discharged directly to the community from a new special hospital and some comparisons of performance', *Journal of Forensic Psychiatry*, 3: 91–112.

Bar Council (2008a) *Qualifying as a Barrister*. Retrieved 6 March 2008 from http://www.barcouncil.org.uk/trainingand education/howtobecomeabarrister.

Bar Council (2008b) *About the Bar Council*. Retrieved 6 March 2008 from http://www.barcouncil.org.ukaboutthebarcouncil.

Barnes, D. and Brandon, T. (2002) *Independent Specialist Advocacy in England and Wales: Recommendations for Good Practice, Evidence and Examples*. Department of Health, London. Retrieved 10 June 2008 from http://www.dh.gov.uk/en/consultations/Closedconsultations/DH_4017090.

Bartels, S. J., Teague, G. B. and Drake, R. E. (1993) 'Substance misuse in schizophrenia: service utilization and costs', *Journal of Nervous and Mental Disease*, 181: 227–32.

Bartlett, A. and Hasell, Y. (2001) 'Do women need special secure services?', *Advances in Psychiatric Treatment*, 7: 302–9.

Bateman, A. and Fonagy, P. (1999) 'Effectiveness of partial hospitalization in the treatment of borderline personality disorder: a randomized controlled trial', *American Journal of Psychiatry*, 156: 1563–9.

Bateman, A. and Fonagy, P. (2001) 'Treatment of borderline personality disorder with psychoanalytically oriented partial hospitalization: an 18-month follow-up', *American Journal of Psychiatry*, 158: 36–42.

Baumeister, R. F., Heatherton, T. F. and Tice, D. M. (1994) *Losing Control: How and Why People Fail at Self Regulation*. San Diego, CA: Academic Press.

Bhui, K. and Sashidharan, S. (2003) 'Should there be separate psychiatric services for ethnic minority groups?', *British Journal of Psychiatry*, 182: 10–12.

Bhui, K., Stansfeld, S., Hull, S., Priebe, S., Mole, F. and Feder, G. (2003) 'Ethnic variations in pathways to and use of specialist mental health services in the UK: systematic review', *British Journal of Psychiatry*, 182: 105–16.

Birley, J. L. T. (1991) 'Psychiatrists and citizens', *British Journal of Psychiatry*, 159: 1–6.

Birmingham, L. (2000) 'Diversion from custody', *Advances in Psychiatric Treatment*, 7: 198–207.

Birmingham, L. (2003) 'The mental health of prisoners', *Advances in Psychiatric Treatment*, 9: 191–201.

Blackburn, R. (1988) 'On moral judgements and personality disorders: the myth of psychopathic personality disorder revisited', *British Journal of Psychiatry*, 153: 505–12.

Boer, D. P., Hart, S. D., Kropp, P. R. and Webster, C. D. (1998) *Manual for the Sexual Violence Risk-20: Professional Guidelines for Assessing Risk of Sexual Violence*. Burnaby, BC: Simon Fraser University.

Bonta, J. and Andrews, D. A. (2003) 'A commentary on Ward and Stewart's model of human needs', *Psychology, Crime, and Law*, 9: 215–18.

Bonta, J., Law, M. and Hanson, K. (1998) 'The prediction of criminal and violent recidivism among mentally disordered offenders: a meta-analysis', *Psychological Bulletin*, 123: 123–42.

Bowen, P. (2008) *Blackstone's Guide to the Mental Health Act*. Oxford: Oxford University Press.

Bowring-Lossock, E. (2006) 'The forensic mental health nurse – a literature review', *Journal of Psychiatric and Mental Health Nursing*, 13: 780–5.

Brennan, P. A., Mednick, S. A. and Hodgins, S. (2000) 'Major mental disorders and criminal violence in a Danish birth cohort', *Archives of General Psychiatry*, 57: 494–500.

British Psychological Society (2006a) *Core Competencies – Clinical Psychology: A Guide.* Leicester: British Psychological Society.

British Psychological Society (2006b) *Core Competencies – Forensic Psychology: A Guide.* Leicester: British Psychological Society.

Buchanan, A. (1998) 'Criminal conviction after discharge from special (high security) hospital: incidence in the first 10 years', *British Journal of Psychiatry*, 172: 472–6.

Buss, A. H. and Durkee, A. (1957) 'An inventory for assessing different kinds of hostility', *Journal of Consulting Psychology*, 21: 343–9.

Cantwell, R. and Harrison, G. (1996) 'Substance misuse in the severely mentally ill', *Advances in Psychiatric Treatment*, 2: 117–24.

Care Services Improvement Partnership and the National Institute for Mental Health in England (2007) *New Ways of Working for Everyone: A Best Practice Implementation Guide.* York: CSIP/NIMHE.

Carter, P. (2003) *Managing Offenders, Reducing Crime: A New Approach.* London: Cabinet Office Strategy Unit.

Clark, D. (2000) *Theory Manual for Enhanced Thinking Skills.* London: Home Office.

Cleckley, H. (1941) *The Mask of Sanity*, 5th edn. St Louis, MO: Mosby.

Coid, J., Hickey, N. and Yang, M. (2007) 'Comparison of outcomes following after-care from forensic and general adult psychiatric services', *British Journal of Psychiatry*, 190: 509–14.

Coid, J., Kahtan, N., Gault, S. and Jarman, B. (1999) 'Patients with personality disorder admitted to secure forensic psychiatry services', *British Journal of Psychiatry*, 175: 528–36.

Coid, J., Kahtan, N., Gault, S. and Jarman, B. (2000) 'Ethnic differences in admissions to secure psychiatric services', *British Journal of Psychiatry*, 177: 241–7.

Coid, J., Kahtan, N., Gault, S., Cook, A. and Jarman, B. (2001) 'Medium secure forensic psychiatry services, comparison of seven English health regions', *British Journal of Psychiatry*, 178: 55–61.

Coid, J., Yang, M., Roberts, A., Ullrich, S., Moran, P., Bebbington, P., Brugha, T., Jenkins, R., Farrell, M., Lewis, G. and Singleton, N. (2006a) 'Violence and psychiatric morbidity in the national household population of Britain: public health implications', *British Journal of Psychiatry*, 189: 12–19.

Coid, J., Yang, M., Roberts, A., Ullrich, S., Moran, P., Bebbington, P., Brugha, T., Jenkins, R., Farrell, M., Lewis, G. and Singleton, N. (2006b) 'Violence and psychiatric morbidity in a national household population: a report from the British household survey', *American Journal of Epidemiology*, 164: 1199–208.

Commission for Healthcare Audit and Inspection (2006) *Count Me In: Results of the 2006 National Census of Inpatients in Mental Health and Learning Disability Services in England and Wales*. Retrieved 17 June 2008 from: http://healthcarecommission.org.uk_db/_documents/count_me_in_1006.pdf.

Conroy, M. A. and Murrie, D. C. (2007) *Forensic Assessment of Violence Risk: A Guide for Risk Assessment and Risk Management*. Chichester: Wiley.

Cooke, D. J. (1995) 'Psychopathic disturbance in the Scottish prison population: the cross-cultural generalisability of the Hare Psychopathy Checklist', *Psychology, Crime and Law*, 2: 101–8.

Cooke, D. J., Michie, C. and Skeem, J. (2007) 'Understanding the structure of the Psychopathy Checklist – Revised', *British Journal of Psychiatry*, 190 (suppl. 49): s39–s50.

Copas, J. and Marshall, P. (1998) 'The Offender Group Reconviction Scale: a statistical reconviction score for use by probation officers', *Applied Statistics*, 47: 159–71.

Copas, J., O'Brien, M., Roberts, J. and Whiteley, S. (1984) 'Treatment outcome in personality disorder', *Personality and Individual Differences*, 5: 565–73.

Correctional Services Accreditation Panel (2003) *Programme Accreditation Criteria*. London: Home Office.

Correctional Services Accreditation Panel (2005–6) *The Correctional Services Accreditation Panel Report, 2005–2006*. London: Home Office.

Crome, I. B., Bloor, R. and Thom, B. (2006) 'Screening for illicit drug use in psychiatric hospitals: whose job is it?', *Advances in Psychiatric Treatment*, 12: 375–83.

Cullen, E., Jones, L. and Woodward, R. (eds) (1997) *Therapeutic Communities for Offenders*. Chichester: Wiley.

Curran, C. and Bingley, W. (1994) 'The Mental Health Act Commission', *Psychiatric Bulletin*, 18: 328–32.

Davidson, K. M., Norrie, J., Tyrer, P., Gumley, A., Tata, P., Murray, H. and Palmer, S. (2006) 'The effectiveness of cognitive behaviour therapy for borderline personality disorder: results from the borderline personality disorder study of cognitive therapy (BOSCOT) trial', *Journal of Personality Disorders*, 20: 450–65.

Davies, S., Clarke, M., Hollin, C. and Duggan, C. (2007) 'Long-term outcomes after discharge from medium secure care: a cause for concern', *British Journal of Psychiatry*, 191: 70–4.

de Silva, N., Cowell, P. Chow, T. and Worthington, P. (2006) *Prison Population Projections, 2006–2013, England and Wales*, Home Office Statistical Bulletin, 11/06. London: Home Office Research, Development and Statistics Directorate.

de Vogel, V., de Ruiter, C., van Beek, D. and Mead, G. (2004) 'Predictive validity of the SVR-20 and Static-99 in a Dutch sample of treated sex offenders', *Law and Human Behavior*, 28: 235–51.

Department of Health (2001) *Valuing People – A New Strategy for Learning Disability for the 21st Century*. London: Department of Health.

Department of Health (2002a) *Women's Mental Health: Into the Mainstream*. Retrieved 5 January 2008 from http://www.doh.gov.uk.

Department of Health (2002b) *A Sign of the Times: Modernising Mental Health Services for People Who Are Deaf*. London: Department of Health.

Department of Health (2002c) *Requirements for Social Work Training*. London: Department of Health.

Department of Health (2003a) *Mainstreaming Gender and Women's Mental Health*. Retrieved 4 January 2007 from http://www.doh.gov.uk.

Department of Health (2003b) *The NHS Knowledge and Skills Framework (NHS KSF) and Development Review Guidance*. Leeds: Department of Health Pay Modernisation Unit.

Department of Health (2004a) *The Ten Essential Shared Capabilities: A Framework for the Whole of the Mental Health Workforce*. London: NIMHE/SCMH Joint Workforce Support Unit.

Department of Health (2004b) *Modernising Medical Careers*. London: Department of Health. Accessed 18 June 2008 from http://www.dh.gov.uk/prod_consum_dh/groups/dh_digitalassets/@dh/@en/documents/digitalasset/dh_4079532.pdf.

Department of Health (2005) *Delivering Race Equality in Mental Health Care: An Action Plan for Reform Inside and Outside Services and the Government's Response to the Independent Inquiry into the Death of David Bennett*. Retrieved 10 January 2008 from http://www.doh.gov.uk/en/Publicationsandstatistics/Publications/PublicationsPolicyAndGuidance/DH_4100773.

Department of Health (2006) *Best Practice Competencies and Capabilities for Pre-registration Mental Health Nurses in England: The Chief Nursing Officer's Review of Mental Health Nursing*. London: Department of Health.

Department of Health (2007) *Best Practice Guidance: Specifications for Adult Medium Secure Services*. London: Department of Health.

Department of Health (2008) *Refocusing the Care Programme Approach: Policy and Positive Practice Guidance*. Retrieved on 23 May 2008 from http://www.doh.gov.uk/en/Publicationsandstatistics/Publications/PublicationsPolicyAndGuidance/DH_083647.

Department of Health and Home Office (1992) *Review of Health and Social Services for Mentally Disordered Offenders and Others Requiring Similar Services* (Reed Report). London: HMSO.

Department of Health and Home Office (1999) *Managing Dangerous People with Severe Personality Disorder*. London: Department of Health.

Department of Health and Social Security (1974) *Security in NHS Hospitals for the Mentally Ill and the Mentally Handicapped* (Glancy Report). London: DHSS.

Department of Health, Home Office and HM Prison Service (2004) *Dangerous and Severe Personality Disorder (DSPD) High Security Services: Planning and Delivery Guide*. London: Home Office.

Derogatis, L. R. (1992) *SCL-90-R: Administration, Scoring and Procedures Manual – II*. Baltimore, MD: Clinical Psychometric Research.

Dolan, B. (1997) 'A community based TC: The Henderson Hospital', in E. Cullen, L. Jones, and R. Woodward (eds), *Therapeutic Communities for Offenders*. Chichester: Wiley.

Douglas, K. S., Guy, L. S. and Weir, J. (2006) *HCR-20 Violence Risk Assessment Scheme: Overview and Annotated Bibliography*. Retrieved 3 December 2007 from http://www.sfu.ca/psych/faculty/hart/HCR-20%20Annotated%20Bibliograph,%202006.pdf.

Dowden, C. and Andrews, D. A. (2000) 'Effective correctional treatment and violent reoffending', *Canadian Journal of Criminology*, 42: 449–67.

Dowsett, J. and Craissati, J. (2007) *Managing Personality Disordered Offenders in the Community: A Psychological Approach*. London: Routledge.

Duggan, C. and Gibbon, S. (2008) 'The assessment of personality disorder', *Psychiatry*, 7: 99–101.

Duggan, C. and Howard, R. C. (in press) 'The "functional link" between personality disorder and violence: a critical appraisal', in M. McMurran and R. C. Howard (eds), *Personality, Personality Disorder and Violence*. Chichester: Wiley.

Duggan, C. and Khalifa, N. (2007) 'Community treatment for offenders with personality disorder', *Psychiatry*, 6: 470–3.

Duggan, C., Huband, N., Smailagic, N., Ferriter, M. and Adams, C. (2007) 'The use of psychological treatments for people with personality disorders: a systematic review of randomised controlled trials', *Personality and Mental Health*, 1: 95–125.

Duggan, C., Huband, N., Smailagic, N., Ferriter, M. and Adams, C. (2008) 'The use of pharmacological treatments for people with personality disorders: a systematic review of randomised controlled trials', *Personality and Mental Health*, 2: 119–70.

Edwards, J., Steed, P. and Murray, K. (2002) 'Clinical and forensic outcomes 2 years and 5 years after admission to a medium secure unit', *Journal of Forensic Psychiatry*, 13: 68–87.

Endicott, J., Spitzer, R. L., Fleiss, J. L. and Cohen, J. (1976) 'The Global Assessment Scale: a procedure for measuring overall severity of psychiatric disturbance', *Archives of General Psychiatry*, 33: 766–71.

Eronen, M., Hakola, P. and Tiihonen, J. (1996) 'Mental disorders and homicidal behaviour in Finland', *Archives of General Psychiatry*, 53: 497–501.

Exworthy, T. and Gunn, J. (2003) 'Taking another tilt at high secure hospitals: the Tilt Report and its consequences for secure psychiatric services', *British Journal of Psychiatry*, 182: 469–71.

Falla, S., Sugarman, P. and Roberts, L. (2000) 'Reconviction after discharge from a regional secure unit', *Medicine Science and the Law*, 40: 156–7.

Fallon, P., Bluglass, R., Edwards, B. and Daniels, G. (1999) *Report of the Committee of Inquiry into the Personality Disorder Unit, Ashworth Special Hospital*. London: Stationery Office.

Farrington, D. (1995) 'The development of offending and antisocial behaviour from childhood: key findings from the Cambridge study in delinquent development', *Journal of Child Psychology and Psychiatry*, 360: 929–64.

Farrington, D. P. (2005) 'Childhood origins of antisocial behaviour', *Clinical Psychology and Psychotherapy*, 12: 177–90.

Fazel, S. and Danesh, J. (2002) 'Serious mental disorder in 23,000 prisoners: a systematic review of 62 surveys', *The Lancet*, 359: 545–50.

Feeney, A. (2003) 'Dangerous severe personality disorder', *Advances in Psychiatric Treatment*, 9: 349–58.

Gall, J. A. and Freckelton, I. (1999) 'Fitness for interview: current trends, views and an approach to the assessment procedure', *Journal of Clinical Forensic Medicine*, 6: 213–23.

Gelder, M. C., Cowen, P. and Harrison, P (2006) *Shorter Oxford Textbook of Psychiatry*. Oxford: Oxford University Press.

Gelder, M. C., Lopez-Ibor, J. J. and Andreasen, N. C. (eds) (2003) *New Oxford Textbook of Psychiatry*. Oxford: Oxford University Press.

General Medical Council (2006) *Good Medical Practice: The Duties of a Doctor Registered with the General Medical Council*. London: General Medical Council.

Gibbon, S., Duggan, C., Langley, M. and Khalifa, N. (2008) 'Careers in academic forensic psychiatry', *British Medical Journal Careers*, 5 January, 3–4.

Giesen-Bloo, J., van Dyck, R., Spinhoven, P., van Tilburg, W., Dirksen, C., van Asselt, T., Kremers, I., Nadort, M. and Arntz, A. (2006) 'Outpatient psychotherapy for borderline personality disorder: randomized trial of schema-focused therapy vs transference-focused therapy', *Archives of General Psychiatry*, 63: 649–59.

Goldstein, A. P., Nensén, R., Daleflod, B. and Kalt, M. (2004) *New Perspectives in Aggression Replacement Training*. Chichester: Wiley.

Grounds, A., Melzer, D., Fryers, T. and Brugha, T. (2004) 'What determines admission to medium secure psychiatric provision?', *Journal of Forensic Psychiatry and Psychology*, 15: 1–6.

Grubin, D. H. (1991) 'Unfit to plead in England and Wales, 1976–1988: a survey', *British Journal of Psychiatry*, 158: 540–8.

Grubin, D., Carson, D. and Parsons, S. (2002) *Report on New Reception Health Screening Arrangements: The Result of a Pilot Study in 10 Prisons*. London: Department of Health.

Gudjonsson, G. H. (1995) '"Fitness for interview" during police detention: a conceptual framework for forensic assessment', *Journal of Forensic Psychiatry*, 6: 185–97.

Gudjonsson, G., Clare, I., Rutter, S. and Pears, J. (1993) *Persons at Risk During Interviews in Police Custody: The Identification of Vulnerabilities*, Royal

Commission on Criminal Justice. London: HMSO.

Gudjonsson, G. H., Hayes, G. D. and Rowlands, P. (2000) 'Fitness to be interviewed and psychological vulnerability: the views of doctors, lawyers and police officers', *Journal of Forensic Psychiatry*, 11: 74–92.

Gunn, J., Maden, A. and Swinton, M. (1991) *Mentally Disordered Prisoners.* London: Home Office.

Gunnell, D. and Ashby, D. (2004) 'Antidepressants and suicide: what is the balance of benefit and harm?', *British Medical Journal*, 329: 34–8.

Guy, W. (ed.) (1976) *ECDEU Assessment Manual for Psychopharmacology.* Rockville, MD: US Department of Heath, Education, and Welfare Public Health Service Alcohol, Drug Abuse, and Mental Health Administration.

Hamilton, M. (1960) 'A rating scale for depression', *Journal of Neurology, Neurosurgery and Psychiatry*, 23: 56–62.

Hanson, R. K. (1997) *The Development of a Brief Actuarial Risk Scale for Sexual Offence Recidivism.* Ottawa: Department of the Solicitor General of Canada.

Hanson, R. K. and Bussière, M. T. (1998) 'Predicting relapse: a meta-analysis of sexual offender recidivism studies', *Journal of Consulting and Clinical Psychology*, 66: 348–62.

Hanson, R. K. and Thornton, D. M. (1999) *Static 99: Improving Actuarial Risk Assessments for Sex Offenders.* Ottawa: Public Works and Government Services Canada.

Hanson, R. K., Gordon, A., Harris, A. J. R., Marques, J., Murphy, W., Quinsey, V. L. and Seto, M. C. (2002) 'First report of the collaborative outcome data project on the effectiveness of psychological treatment for sex offenders', *Sexual Abuse: A Journal of Research and Treatment*, 14: 169–94.

Haque, Q. and Cumming, I. (2003) 'Intoxication and legal defences', *Advances in Psychiatric Treatment*, 9: 144–51.

Hare, R. D. (1991) *The Hare Psychopathy Checklist – Revised.* North Tonawanda, NY: Multi-Health Systems.

Hare, R. D. (1996) 'Psychopathy and antisocial personality disorder: a case of diagnostic confusion', *Psychiatric Times*, 13. Retrieved 10 June 2008 from http://www.psychiatrictimes.com/display/article/10168/51816.

Hare, R. D. (2003) *The Hare Psychopathy Checklist – Revised*, 2nd edn. North Tonawanda, NY: Multi-Health Systems.

Hare, R. D., Clark, D., Grann, M. and Thornton, D. (2000) 'Psychopathy and the predictive validity of the PCL-R: an international perspective', *Behavioral Sciences and the Law*, 18: 623–45.

Hare, R. D., Harpur, T. J., Hakstian, A. R., Forth, A. E., Hart, S. D. and Newman, J. P. (1990) 'The Revised Psychopathy Checklist: reliability and factor structure', *Psychological Assessment*, 2: 338–41.

Harris, A. and Lurigio, A. J. (2007) 'Mental illness and violence: a brief review of research and assessment strategies', *Aggression and Violent Behavior*, 12: 542–51.

Harris, E. C. and Barraclough, B. (1998) 'Excess mortality of mental disorder', *British Journal of Psychiatry*, 173: 11–53.

Harris, F., Hek, G. and Condon, L. (2007) 'Health needs of prisoners in England and Wales: the implications for prison healthcare of gender, age and ethnicity', *Health and Social Care in the Community*, 15: 56–66.

Harris, G. T., Rice, M. T. and Cormier, C. A. (1991) 'Psychopathy and violent recidivism', *Law and Human Behaviour*, 15: 625–37.

Hart, S. D. (1998) 'Psychopathy and risk for violence', in D. Cooke, A. E. Forth and R. Hare (eds), *Psychopathy: Theory, Research and Implications for Society*. Dordrecht: Kluwer.

Hart, S. D., Kropp, P. R., Laws, D. R., Klaver, J., Logan, C. and Watt, K. A. (2003) *The Risk for Sexual Violence Protocol (RSVP): Structured Professional Guidelines for Assessing Risk of Sexual Violence*. Burnaby, BC: Simon Fraser University.

Hayward, J., McMurran, M. and Sellen, J. (2008) 'Social problem solving in vulnerable adult prisoners: profile and intervention', *Journal of Forensic Psychiatry and Psychology*, 19: 243–8.

Health Advisory Committee for the Prison Service (1997) *The Provision of Mental Health Care in Prisons*. London: HM Prison Service.

Health Professions Council (2007a) *Standards of Proficiency: Occupational Therapists*. London: Health Professions Council.

Health Professions Council (2007b) *Standards of Proficiency: Arts Therapists*. London: Health Professions Council.

Hemphill, J. F., Hare, R. D. and Wong, S. (1998) 'Psychopathy and recidivism: a review', *Legal and Criminological Psychology*, 3: 139–70.

Her Majesty's Inspectorate of Prisons (1996) *Patient or Prisoner? A New Strategy for Health Care in Prisons*. London: Home Office.

Hiscoke, U. L., Långström, N., Ottosson, H. and Grann, M. (2003) 'Self-reported personality traits and disorders (DSM-IV) and risk of criminal recidivism: a prospective study', *Journal of Personality Disorders*, 17: 293–305.

Hollin, C. R. (2002) 'Risk-needs assessment and allocation to offender programmes', in J. McGuire (ed.), *Offender Rehabilitation and Treatment: Effective Programmes and Policies to Reduce Reoffending*. Chichester: Wiley.

Home Office (1975) *Report of the Committee on Mentally Abnormal Offenders* (Butler Report). London: HMSO.

Home Office (2003) *Multi Agency Public Protection Arrangements (MAPPA) Guidance*. London: Home Office. Retrieved 11 June 2008 from http://www.probation.homeoffice.gov.uk/files/pdf/MAPPA%20Guidance.pdf.

Home Office (2007) *The Home Office Statistical Bulletin 2006–2007*. London: HMSO.

Home Office and Department of Health (1999) *Managing People with Severe Personality Disorder*. London: Home Office.

Home Office and Department of Health (2001) *DSPD Programme: Dangerous People with Severe Personality Disorder Initiative: Progress Report*. London: Home Office.

Home Office and Probation Service (2006) *MAPPA Nottinghamshire Annual Report 2005–2006*. London: Home Office. Retrieved 11 June 2008 from http://www.probation.homeoffice.gov.uk/files/pdf/Nottinghamshire%20 2006%Report.pdf.

Home Office Police (2008) *Police and Criminal Evidence Act 1984 (PACE) and accompanying Codes of Practice*. Retrieved 23 June 2008 from http://police. homeoffice.gov.uk/operational-policing/powers-pace-codes/pace-code-intro.

Howard, P., Clark, D. and Garnham, N. (1999) *An Evaluation of the Offender Assessment System in Three Pilots, 1999–2001*. Retrieved 4 December 2007 from http://noms.justice.gov.uk/news-publications/strategy/oasys-report?view=Binary.

Huband, N., McMurran, M., Evans, C. and Duggan, C. (2007) 'Social problem solving plus psychoeducation for adults with personality disorder: a pragmatic randomised controlled trial', *British Journal of Psychiatry*, 190: 307–13.

Izycky, A., Gibbon, S., Baker, K. and Gahir, M. (2007) 'Application of therapeutic community principles to a high secure deaf service', *Therapeutic Communities*, 28: 372–89.

Jablensky, A., Sartorius, N., Emberg, C., Anker, M., Korten, A., Cooper, J. E., Day, R. and Bertelsen, A. (1992) 'Schizophrenia: manifestations, incidence and course in different cultures. A World Health Organization ten-country study', *Psychological Medicine*, Suppl. 20: 1–97.

James, D. (1999) 'Court diversion at 10 years. Can it work, does it work, and has it a future?', *Journal of Forensic Psychiatry*, 10: 507–24.

James, D. (2000) Police diversion schemes: role and efficacy in central London', *Journal of Forensic Psychiatry*, 11, 532–55.

Jamieson, L. and Taylor, P. J. (2004) 'A reconviction study of special (high security) hospital patients', *British Journal of Criminology*, 44: 783–802.

Jethwa, K. (2006) 'Careers in forensic psychiatry', *British Medical Journal Careers*, 333: 133–4.

Johnstone, E., Lawrie, S., Cunningham-Owens, D. G. and Sharpe, M. D. (2004) *Companion to Psychiatric Studies*. Oxford: Churchill Livingstone.

Jones, C., Cormac, I., Silveira da Mota Neto, J. I. and Campbell, C. (2004) 'Cognitive behaviour therapy for schizophrenia', *Cochrane Database of Systematic Reviews 2004*, Issue 3. Art. No.: CD000524. DOI: 10.1002/14651858. CD000524.pub2.

Jones, P. B. (1997) 'The early origins of schizophrenia', *British Medical Bulletin*, 53: 135–55.

Jones, R. (2008) *The Mental Health Act Manual*. London: Sweet & Maxwell.

Judge, J., Harty, M. and Fahy, T. (2004) 'Survey of community forensic psychiatry in England and Wales', *Journal of Forensic Psychiatry and Psychology*, 15: 244–53.

Kemshall, H. (2003) 'The community management of high-risk offenders: a consideration of "best practice" – Multi-Agency Public Protection Arrangements (MAPPA)', *Prison Service Journal*, 146: 2–5.

Kennedy, H. G. (2002) 'Therapeutic uses of security: mapping forensic mental health services by stratifying risk', *Advances in Psychiatric Treatment*, 8: 433–43.

Kerr, M. (2004) 'Improving the general health of people with learning disabilities', *Advances in Psychiatric Treatment*, 10: 200–6.

Khalifa, N., Saleem, Y. and Stankard, P. (2008) 'The use of telepsychiatry within forensic practice: a literature review on the use of video link', *Journal of Forensic Psychiatry and Psychology*, 19: 2–13.

Kirmayer, L. J., Groleau, D., Guzder, J., Blake, C. and Jarvis, E. (2003) 'Cultural consultation: a model of mental health service for multicultural societies', *Canadian Journal of Psychiatry*, 48: 145–53.

Koons, C. R., Robins, C. J., Tweed, J. L., Lynch, T. R., Gonzalez, A. M., Morse, J. Q., Bishop, G. K., Butterfield, M. I. and Bastian, L. A. (2001) 'Efficacy of dialectical behaviour therapy in women veterans with borderline personality disorder', *Behaviour Therapy*, 32: 371–90.

Laing, J. L. (1995) 'The mentally disordered subject at the police station', *Criminal Law Review*, May: 371–81.

Lazzaro, T. A., Beggs, D. L. and McNeil, K. A. (2006) 'The development and validation of the self-report test of impulse control', *Journal of Clinical Psychology*, 25: 434–8.

Lart, R., Payne, S., Beaumont, B., MacDonald, G. and Mistry, T. (1999) *Women and Secure Psychiatric Services: A Literature Review*, CRD Report 14. Centre for Reviews and Dissemination: York. Retrieved 4 January 2008 from http://www.york.ac.uk /inst/crd/pdf/crdreport14.pdf.

Lelliot, P., Audini, B. and Duffett, R. (2001) 'Survey of patients from an inner-London health authority in medium secure psychiatric care', *British Journal of Psychiatry*, 178: 62–6.

Leonard, S. (2004) 'The development and evaluation of a telepsychiatry service for prisoners', *Journal of Psychiatric and Mental Health Nursing*, 11: 461–8.

Levenson, J. L. (1985) 'Neuroleptic malignant syndrome', *American Journal of Psychiatry*, 142: 1137–45.

Liechsenring, F., Rabung, S. and Liebing, E. (2004) 'The efficacy of short-term psychodynamic psychotherapy in specific psychiatric disorders: a meta-analysis', *Archives of General Psychiatry*, 61: 1208–16.

Lindqvist, P. and Allebeck, P. (1990) 'Schizophrenia and crime – a longitudinal follow-up of 644 schizophrenics in Stockholm', *British Journal of Psychiatry*, 157: 345–50.

Lindsay, W. R. (2002) 'Integration of recent reviews on offenders with intellectual disabilities', *Journal of Applied Research in Intellectual Disabilities*, 15: 111–19.

Lindsey, M. (2002) 'Comprehensive health care services for people with learning disabilities', *Advances in Psychiatric Treatment*, 8: 138–48.

Linehan, M. M. (1993a) *Cognitive-behavioral Treatment of Borderline Personality Disorder*. New York: Guilford Press.

Linehan, M. M. (1993b) *Skills Training Manual for Treating Borderline Personality Disorder*. New York: Guilford Press.

Linehan, M. M., Schmidt, H., Dimeff, L. A., Craft, J. C., Kanter, J. and Comtois, K. A. (1999) 'Dialectical behaviour therapy for patients with borderline personality disorder and drug-dependence', *American Journal on Addictions*, 8: 279–92.

Linnoila, M. and Virkkunen, M. (1992) 'Aggression, suicidality and serotonin', *Journal of Clinical Psychiatry*, 53: 46–51.

Lipton, D. S., Pearson, F. S., Cleland, C. M. and Yee, D. (2002) 'The effects of therapeutic communities and milieu therapy on recidivism', in J. McGuire (ed.), *Offender Rehabilitation and Treatment: Effective Programmes and Policies to Reduce Re-offending*. Chichester: Wiley.

Lorr, M., McNair, D. M., Klett, C. J. and Lasky, J. J. (1966) *Inpatient Multidimensional Psychiatric Scale (Rev.)*. Palo Alto, CA: Consulting Psychologists Press.

Lösel, F. and Schmucker, M. (2005) 'The effectiveness of treatment for sexual offenders: a comprehensive meta-analysis', *Journal of Experimental Criminology*, 1: 1–29.

Low, G., Jones, D., Duggan, C., Power, M. and MacLeod, A. (2001) 'The treatment of deliberate self-harm in borderline personality disorder using dialectical behaviour therapy: a pilot study in a high security hospital', *Criminal Behaviour and Mental Health*, 29: 85–92.

Lowenkamp, C. T., Latessa, E. J. and Holsinger, A. M. (2006) 'The risk principle in action: what have we learned from 13,676 offenders and 97 correctional programs?', *Crime and Delinquency*, 52: 77–93.

Lyall, M. (2005) 'Should there be separate forensic psychiatry services for ethnic minority patients?', *Journal of Forensic Psychiatry and Psychology*, 16: 370–9.

McGuire, J. (2000) *Think First: Programme Manual*. London: Home Office.

McGuire, J. (2002) 'Integrating findings from research reviews', in J. McGuire (ed.), *Offender Rehabilitation and Treatment: Effective Programmes and Policies to Reduce Reoffending*. Chichester: Wiley.

McMurran, M. (ed.) (2002) *Motivating Offenders to Change: A Guide to Enhancing Engagement in Therapy*. Chichester: Wiley.

McMurran, M. (2006) 'Drug and alcohol programmes: concept, theory, and practice', in C. R. Hollin and E. J. Palmer (eds), *Offending Behaviour Programmes: Development, Application, and Controversies*. Chichester: Wiley.

McMurran, M. (2008) 'Substance abuse', in K. Soothill, P. Rogers and M. Dolan (eds), *Handbook of Forensic Mental Health*. Cullompton: Willan.

McMurran, M. (in press) 'Motivational interviewing with offenders: a systematic review', *Legal and Criminological Psychology*.

McMurran, M. and McGuire, J. (2005) *Social Problem Solving and Offending: Evidence, Evaluation, and Evolution*. Chichester: Wiley.

McMurran M. and Theodosi, E. (2007) 'Is offender treatment non-completion associated with increased reconviction over no treatment?', *Psychology, Crime, and Law*, 13: 333–43.

McMurran, M., Egan, V. and Ahmadi, S. (1998) 'A retrospective evaluation of a therapeutic community for mentally disordered offenders', *Journal of Forensic Psychiatry*, 9: 103–13.

McMurran, M., Fyffe, S., McCarthy, L., Duggan, C. and Latham, A. (2001) '"Stop & Think!" Social problem solving therapy with personality disordered offenders', *Criminal Behaviour and Mental Health*, 11: 273–85.

McMurran, M., Theodosi, E., Sweeney, A. and Sellen, J. (2008) 'What do prisoners want? Current concerns of adult male prisoners', *Psychology, Crime and Law*, 14: 267–74.

McNair, D. M., Lorr, M. and Droppleman, L. F. (1971) *Manual for the Profile of Mood States*. San Diego, CA: Educational and Industrial Testing Service.

Macpherson, G. J. D. (2003) 'Predicting escalation in sexually violent recidivism: use of the SVR-20 and PCL:SV to predict outcome with non-contact recidivists and contact recidivists', *Journal of Forensic Psychiatry and Psychology*, 14: 615–27.

Maden, A. (2007) *Treating Violence: A Guide to Risk Management in Mental Health*. Oxford: Oxford University Press.

Maden, A. (2008) 'The process and systems for adults', in K. Soothill, P. Rogers and M. Dolan (eds), *Handbook of Forensic Mental Health*. Cullompton: Willan.

Maden, A., Rutter, S., McClintock, T., Friendship, C. and Gunn, J. (1999) 'Outcome of admission to a medium secure psychiatric unit: short and long term outcome', *British Journal of Psychiatry*, 175: 313–16.

Maden, A., Taylor, C., Brooke, D. and Gunn, J. (1995) *Mental Disorder in Remand Prisoners*. London: Home Office.

Maden, A., Scott, F., Burnett, R., Lewis, G. H. and Skapinakis, P. (2004) 'Offending in psychiatric patients after discharge from medium secure units: prospective national cohort study', *British Medical Journal*, 328: 15–34.

Marshall, W. L., Fernandez, Y. M., Marshall, L. E. and Serran, G. A. (2006) *Sexual Offender Treatment: Controversial Issues*. Chichester: Wiley.

Martin, C. and Player, E. (2000) *Drug Treatment in Prison: An Evaluation of the RAPt Treatment Programme*. Winchester: Waterside Press.

Martinson, R. (1974) 'What works? Questions and answers about prison reform', *Public Interest*, 35: 22–54.

Maruna, S. and LeBel, T. P. (2003) 'Welcome home? Examining the "re-entry court" concept from a strengths-based perspective', *Western Criminology Review*, 4: 91–107.

Meltzer, R. H., Gill, B. and Petticrew, M. (1995) *The Prevalence of Psychiatric Morbidity Among Adults Aged 16–64, Living in Private Households in Great Britain*. London: Office of Population Censuses and Surveys.

Mental Health Act Commission (2007) *About Us*. Accessed 26 September 2008, from http://www.mhac.org.uk.

Miller, K. and Vernon, M. (2003) 'Deaf offenders in a prison population', *Journal of Deaf Studies and Deaf Education*, 8: 357–62.

Miller, W. R. and Rollnick, S. (2002) *Motivational Interviewing: Preparing People for Change*, 2nd edn. New York: Guilford.

Mind (2006) *Mind Guide to Advocacy*. Retrieved 17 April 2008 from http://www.mind.org.uk/Information/Booklets/Mind+guide+to/advocacy.htm.

Ministry of Justice (2008) *Solicitors Act 1974*. Retrieved 1 May 2008 from http://www.statutelaw.gov.uk.

Monahan, J., Steadman, H. J., Appelbaum, P. S., Robbins, P. C., Mulvey, E. P., Silver, E., Roth, L. H. and Grisso, T. (2000) 'Developing a clinically useful actuarial tool for assessing violence risk', *British Journal of Psychiatry*, 176: 312–19.

Moran, P. (2002) *The Epidemiology of Personality Disorders*. London: Department of Health.

Morris, N. and Rothman, D. J. (eds) (1995) *The Oxford History of the Prison*. Oxford: Oxford University Press.

Mullen, P. E. (2005) 'Facing up to our responsibilities: commentary on … the draft Mental Health Bill in England: without principles', *Psychiatric Bulletin*, 29: 248–9.

Mullen, P. E. (2006) 'Schizophrenia and violence: from correlations to preventative strategies', *Advances in Psychiatric Treatment*, 12: 239–48.

Mullen, P. E. (2007) 'Dangerous and severe personality disorder and in need of treatment', *British Journal of Psychiatry*, 190 (Suppl. 49): ss3–ss7.

Myers, D. H. (1997) 'Mental health review tribunals. A follow-up of reviewed patients', *British Journal of Psychiatry*, 170: 253–6.

National Institute for Health and Clinical Excellence (2002) *Core Interventions in the Treatment and Management of Schizophrenia in Primary and Secondary Care*. Retrieved 23 May 2008 from http://www.nice.org.uk/nicemedia/pdf/CG1NICEguideline.pdf.

National Institute for Health and Clinical Excellence (2006) *The Management of Bipolar Disorder in Adults, Children and Adolescents, in Primary and Secondary Care*. Retrieved 29 May 2008 from http://www.nice.org.uk/nicemedia/pdf/CG38niceguideline.pdf.

National Institute for Health and Clinical Excellence (2007a) *Depression: Management of Depression in Primary and Secondary Care (Amended Version)*. Retrieved 29 May 2008 from http://www.nice.org.uk/nicemedia/pdf/CG23fullguideline.pdf.

National Institute for Health and Clinical Excellence (2007b) *Drug Misuse: Opioid Detoxification*. Retrieved 20 June 2008 from http://www.nice.org.uk/Nicemedia/pdf/CG52NICEGuideline.pdf.

National Institute for Mental Health in England (2003) *Personality Disorder: No Longer a Diagnosis of Exclusion*. London: Department of Health.

National Probation Service (2007) *A Century of Cutting Crime 1907–2007*. Retrieved 26 December 2007 from http://www.probation.homeoffice. gov.uk/files/pdf/A%20Century%20of%20Cutting%20Crime%201907%20-%202007.pdf.

National Treatment Agency for Substance Misuse (2002) *Models of Care for the Treatment of Drug Misusers*. London: NTA. Accessed 20 June 2008 from http://www.nta.nhs.uk/publications/documents/nta_modelsofcare2_2002_moc2.pdf.

Nee, C. and Farman, S. (2005) 'Female prisoners with borderline personality disorder: some promising treatment developments', *Criminal Behaviour and Mental Health*, 15: 2–16.

Newton-Howes, G., Tyrer, P. and Johnston, T. (2006) 'Personality disorder and the outcome of depression: meta-analysis of published studies', *British Journal of Psychiatry*, 188: 13–20.

Norfolk, G. A. (1997) '"Fitness to be interviewed" – a proposed definition and scheme for examination', *Medicine, Science and the Law*, 37: 228–34.

O'Rourke, S. and Reed, R. (2007) 'Deaf people and the criminal justice system', in S. Austen and D. Jeffrey (eds), *Deafness and Challenging Behaviour: the 360° Perspective*. Chichester: Wiley.

Ormerod, D. (2006) *Smith and Hogan Criminal Law: Cases and Materials*, 9th edn. Oxford: Oxford University Press.

Oyebode, F. (2008) *Sims' Symptoms in the Mind: An Introduction to Descriptive Psychopathology*. London: Saunders.

Palmer, B. A., Pankratz, V. S. and Bostwick, J. M. (2005) 'The lifetime risk of suicide in schizophrenia: a re-examination', *Archives of General Psychiatry*, 62: 247–53.

Paris, J. (2003) *Personality Disorders over Time: Precursors, Course, and Outcome*. Arlington, VA: American Psychiatric Publishing.

Parole Board for England and Wales (2007) *Annual Report and Accounts 2006–2007*. London: Stationery Office. Accessed 25 June 2008 from http://www. paroleboard.gov.uk/servefile.aspx?docid=6.

Parole Board for England and Wales (2008) *Parole Board Members*. Accessed 28 January 2008 from http://www.paroleboard.gov.uk/about/parole_board_members.

Peay, J. (1989) *Tribunals on Trial: A Study of Decision Making under the Mental Health Act 1983*. London: Clarendon Press.

Perala, J., Suvisaari, J., Saarni, S. I., Kuoppasalmi, K., Isometsa, E., Pikola, S., Partonen, T., Tuulio-Henriksson, A., Hintikka, J., Kieseppa, T., Harkanen, T., Koskinen, S. and Lonnqvist, J. (2007) 'Lifetime prevalence of psychotic and bipolar disorder in general population', *Archives of General Psychiatry*, 64: 19–28.

Pereira, S., Dawson, P. and Sarsam, M. (2006) 'The national survey of PICU and low secure services: two unit characteristics', *Journal of Intensive Care*, 2: 13–19.

Perry, J. C., Banon, E. and Ianni, F. (1999) 'Effectiveness of psychotherapy for personality disorders', *American Journal of Psychiatry*, 156: 1312–21.

Pharaoh, F., Mari, J., Rathbone, J. and Wong, W. (2006) 'Family intervention for schizophrenia', *Cochrane Database of Systematic Reviews 2006*, Issue 4. Art. No.: CD000088. DOI: 10.1002/14651858.CD000088.pub2.

Picchioni, M. M. and Murray, R. M. (2007) 'Schizophrenia', *British Journal of Psychiatry*, 335: 91–5.

Pratt, D., Piper, M., Appleby, L., Webb, R. and Shaw, J. (2006) 'Suicide in recently released prisoners: a population based cohort study', *Lancet*, 368: 119–23.

Prins, H. (1995) *Offenders, Deviants or Patients?* 2nd edn. London: Routledge.

Prochaska, J. O. and DiClemente, C. C. (1983) 'Stages and processes of self-change of smoking: toward an integrated model of change', *Journal of Consulting and Clinical Psychology*, 51: 390–5.

Puri, B. K. and Hall, A. D. (2004) *Revision Notes in Psychiatry*, 2nd edn. London: Arnold.

Quinsey, V. L., Harris, G. T., Rice, M. E. and Cormier, C. A. (2006) *Violent Offenders: Appraising and Managing Risk*, 2nd edn. Washington, DC: American Psychological Association.

Raynor, P. (2007) 'Risk and need assessment in British probation: the contribution of the LSI-R', *Psychology, Crime and Law*, 13: 125–38.

Reed, J. (2002) 'Delivering psychiatric care to prisoners: problems and solutions', *Advances in Psychiatric Treatment*, 8: 117–27.

Rice, M. E., Harris, G. T. and Cormier, C. A. (1992) 'An evaluation of a maximum security therapeutic community for psychopaths and other mentally disordered offenders', *Law and Human Behavior*, 16: 399–412.

Riordan, S., Wix, S., Kenney-Herbert, J. and Humphreys, M. (2000) 'Diversion at the point of arrest: mentally disordered people and contact with the police', *Journal of Forensic Psychiatry*, 11: 683–90.

Rix, K. (1997) 'Fit to be interviewed by police?', *Advances in Psychiatric Treatment*, 3: 33–40.

Robertson, G., Pearson, R. and Gibb, R. (1995) *The Entry of Mentally Disordered People to the Criminal Justice System*. London: Home Office.

Ross, R. R. and Fabiano, E. A. (1985) *Time to Think: A Cognitive Model of Delinquency Prevention and Offender Rehabilitation*. Ottawa: Air Training and Publications.

Ross, R. R. and Hilborn, J. (2008) *Rehabilitating Rehabilitation: Neurocriminology for Treatment of Antisocial Behaviour*. Ottawa: Cognitive Centre of Canada.

Ross, R. R., Fabiano, E. A. and Ewles, C. D. (1988) 'Reasoning and rehabilitation', *International Journal of Offender Therapy and Comparative Criminology*, 32: 29–35.

Royal College of Psychiatrists (1996) *Health of the Nation Outcome Scales (HoNOS)*. London: Royal College of Psychiatrists.

Royal College of Psychiatrists (1999) *Patient Advocacy*, Council Report CR 74. London: Royal College of Psychiatrists.

Royal College of Psychiatrists (2006) *Psychiatrists and Multi-Agency Public Protection Arrangements: Guidance on Representation, Participation, Confidentiality and Information Exchange*. London: Royal College of Psychiatrists.

Royal College of Psychiatrists (2008) *Psychiatry as a Career – Information for Medical Students*. London: Royal College of Psychiatrists. Accessed 18 June 2008 from http://www.rcpsych.ac.uk/pdf/medical students_2008.pdf.

Sahota, S., Davies, S., Duggan, C. and Clarke, M. (2008) 'The fate of medium secure patients discharged to generic and specialised services', *Journal of Forensic Psychiatry and Psychology* (in press).

Saleem, Y. and Stankard, P. (2006) 'I'm only at the end of a video link', *British Medical Journal Career Focus*, 333: 223.

Scott, J. and Dickey, B. (2003) 'Global burden of depression: the intersection of culture and medicine', *British Journal of Psychiatry*, 183: 92–4.

Scott-Moncrieff, L. and Vassal-Adams, G. (2006) 'Yawning gap: capacity and fitness to plead', *Counsel*, October: 2–3.

Seligman, M. E. P. and Csikszentmihalyi, M. (2000) 'Positive psychology: an introduction', *American Psychologist*, 55: 1–5.

Senior, J. and Shaw, J. (2008) 'Mental healthcare in prisons', in K. Soothill, P. Rogers and M. Dolan (eds), *Handbook of Forensic Mental Health*. Cullompton: Willan.

Shaw, J. and Humber, N. (2007) 'Prison mental health services', *Psychiatry*, 6: 465–9.

Shaw, J., Baker, D., Hunt, I., Moloney, A. and Appleby, L. (2004) 'Suicide by prisoners: national clinical survey', *British Journal of Psychiatry*, 184: 263–7.

Shaw, J., Hunt, I. M., Flynn, S., Meehan, J., Robinson, J., Bickley, H., Parsons, R., McCann, K., Burns, J., Amos, T., Kapur, N. and Appleby, L. (2006) 'Rates of mental disorder in people convicted of homicide', *British Journal of Psychiatry*, 188: 143–7.

Simpson, M. K. and Hogg, J. (2001) 'Patterns of offending among people with intellectual disability: a systematic review. Part 1: Methodology and prevalence data', *Journal of Intellectual Disability Research*, 45: 384–96.

Singleton, N., Farrell, M. and Meltzer, H. (1999) *Substance Misuse among Prisoners in England and Wales*. London: Office of National Statistics.

Singleton, N., Meltzer, H. and Gatward, R. (1998) *Psychiatric Morbidity among Prisoners in England and Wales*. London: Office of National Statistics.

Sjöstedt, G. and Långström, N. (2002) 'Assessment of risk for criminal recidivism among rapists: a comparison of four different measures', *Psychology, Crime, and Law*, 8: 25–40.

Skeem, J. and Cooke, D. J. (in press) 'Is criminal behaviour a central component of psychopathy? Conceptual directions for resolving the debate', *Psychological Assessment*.

Skodol, A. E., Siever, L. J., Livesley, W. J., Gunderson, J. G., Pfohl, B. and Widiger, T. A. (2002) 'The borderline diagnosis II: Biology, genetics and clinical course', *Biological Psychiatry*, 51: 951–63.

Smiley, E. (2005) 'Epidemiology of mental health problems in adults with learning disability: an update', *Advances in Psychiatric Treatment*, 11: 214–22.

Solicitors Regulation Authority (2008) *The Training Regulations 1990*. Accessed 6 March 2008 from http://www.sra.org.uk/documents/students/academic-stage/trainingregs1990.pdf.

Soloff, P. H. (1998) 'Algorithms for pharmacological treatments of personality dimensions. Symptom specific treatments for cognitive-perceptual, affective and impulsive behavioural dyscontrol', *Bulletin of the Menninger Clinic*, 62: 195–214.

Spielberger, C. D. (1999) *STAXI-2: State-Trait Anger Expression Inventory-2*. Odessa, FL: Psychological Assessment Resources.

Steadman, H. J., Mulvey, E. P., Monahan, J., Robbins, P. C., Appelbaum, P. C., Grisso, T., Roth, L. H. and Silver, E. (1998) 'Violence by people discharged from acute psychiatric inpatient facilities and by others in the same neighbourhoods', *Archives of General Psychiatry*, 55: 393–401.

Steele, J., Darjee, R. and Thomson, L. D. G. (2003) 'Substance dependence and schizophrenia in patients with dangerous, violent, and criminal propensities: a comparison of co-morbid and non-co-morbid patients in a high secure setting', *Journal of Forensic Psychiatry and Psychology*, 14: 569–84.

Steels, M., Roney, G., Larkin, E., Jones, P., Croudace, T. and Duggan, C. (1998) 'Discharged from special hospital under restrictions: a comparison of the fates of psychopaths and the mentally ill', *Criminal Behaviour and Mental Health*, 8: 39–55.

Stewart, D., Gossop, M., Marsden, J. and Rolfe, A. (2000) 'Drug misuse and acquisitive crime among clients recruited to National Treatment Outcome Research Study (NTORS)', *Criminal Behaviour and Mental Health*, 10: 10–20.

Stueve, A. and Link, B. G. (1997) 'Violence and psychiatric disorders: results from an epidemiological study of young adults in Israel', *Psychiatric Quarterly*, 68: 327–42.

Swanson, J. W. (1994) 'Mental disorder, substance abuse, and community violence: an epidemiological approach', in J. Monahan and H. J. Steadman (eds), *Violence and Mental Disorder*. Chicago: University of Chicago Press.

Swanson, J., Holzer, C. E., Ganju, V. K. and Jono, R. T. (1990) 'Violence and psychiatric disorder in the community: evidence from the epidemiological catchment area surveys', *Hospital and Community Psychiatry*, 41: 761–70.

Taylor, D., Paton, C. and Kerwin, R. (2007) *The Maudsley Prescribing Guidelines*, 9th edn. London: Informa Healthcare.

Taylor, P. J. and Gunn, J. (1999) 'Homicides by people with mental illness: myth and reality', *British Journal of Psychiatry*, 174: 9–14.

Taylor, P. J., Leese, M., Williams, D., Butwell, M., Daly, R. and Larkin, E. (1998) 'Mental disorder and violence. A special (high security) hospital study', *British Journal of Psychiatry*, 172: 218–26.

Taylor, R. (1999) *Predicting Reconvictions for Sexual and Violent Offences Using the Revised Offender Group Reconviction Scale*, Home Office Research Findings No. 104. London: Home Office.

Tehrani, J. A., Brennan, P. A., Hodgins, S. and Mednick, S. M. (1998) 'Mental illness and criminal violence', *Social Psychiatry and Psychiatric Epidemiology*, 33: s81–s85.

Thomas, F. and Bracken, P. (1999) 'The value of advocacy: putting ethics into practice', *Psychiatric Bulletin*, 23: 327–9.

Thornton, D. (2007) *Scoring Guide for Risk Matrix 2000.9/SVC*. Retrieved 4 December 2007 from http://psg275.bham.ac.uk/forensic_centre/External%20Documents/SCORING%20GUIDE%20FOR%20RISK%20MATRIX(ver-Feb%202007)pdf.

Tiihonen, J., Isohanni, M., Rasanen, P., Koiranen, M. and Moring, J. (1997) 'Specific major mental disorders and criminality: a 26-year prospective study of the 1966 Northern Finland birth cohort', *American Journal of Psychiatry*, 154: 840–5.

Tilt, R., Perry, B., Martin, C., Maguire, M. and Preston, M. (2000) *Report of the Review of Security at the High Security Hospitals*. London: Department of Health.

Tong, L. S. J. and Farrington, D. P. (2008) 'Effectiveness of Reasoning and Rehabilitation in reducing reoffending', *Psicothema*, 20: 20–8.

Tyrer, P. and Bateman, A. (2004) 'Drug treatment for personality disorders', *Advances in Psychiatric Treatment*, 10: 389–98.

Tyrer, P. and Johnson, T. (1996) 'Establishing the severity of personality disorder', *American Journal of Psychiatry*, 153: 1593–7.

Tyrer, P. and Seivewright, H. (2000) 'Studies of outcome', in P. Tyrer (ed.), *Personality Disorders: Diagnosis, Management, and Course*, 2nd edn. Oxford: Butterworth-Heinemann.

Tyrer, P., Joseph, P., Morgan, J., Marriott, S., McEvedy, C. and Cox, S. (1998) 'Work of the Mental Health Act Commission', *Psychiatric Bulletin*, 22: 118–21.

Tyrer, P., Mitchard, S., Methuen, C. and Ranger, M. (2003) 'Treatment-rejecting and treatment-seeking personality disorders: type R and type S', *Journal of Personality Disorders*, 17: 268–70.

Vaughn, C. E. and Leff, J. P. (1976) 'Influence of family and social factors on the course of psychiatric illness', *British Journal of Psychiatry*, 129: 125–37.

Verheul, R., van den Bosch, L. M. C., Koeter, M. W. J., De Ridder, M. A. J., Stijnen, T. and van den Brink, W. (2003) 'Dialectical behaviour therapy for women with borderline personality disorder: 12 month, randomised clinical trial in The Netherlands', *British Journal of Psychiatry*, 182: 135–40.

Waheed, W., Husain, N. and Creed, F. (2003) 'Psychiatric services for ethnic minority groups: a third way?', *British Journal of Psychiatry*, 183: 561–6.

Wallace, C., Mullen, P. E. and Burgess, P. (2004) 'Criminal offending in schizophrenia over a 25-year period marked by deinsitutionalisation and increasing prevalence of comorbid substance use disorders', *American Journal of Psychiatry*, 161: 716–27.

Walsh, E., Buchanan, A. and Fahy, T. (2002) 'Violence and schizophrenia: examining the evidence', *British Journal of Psychiatry*, 180: 490–5.

Ward, T. (2002) 'Good lives and the rehabilitation of offenders: promises and problems', *Aggression and Violent Behaviour*, 7: 513–28.

Ward, T. and Brown, M. (2004) 'The Good Lives Model and conceptual issues in offender rehabilitation', *Psychology, Crime and Law*, 10: 243–57.

Ward, T. and Stewart, C. A. (2003) 'Criminogenic needs and human needs: a theoretical model', *Psychology, Crime, and Law*, 9: 125–43.

Ward, T., Day, A., Howells, K. and Birgden, A. (2004) 'The multifactor offender readiness model', *Aggression and Violent Behavior*, 9: 645–73.

Ward, T., Melser, J. and Yates, P. M. (2007) 'Reconstructing the Risk-Needs-Responsivity model: a theoretical elaboration and evaluation', *Aggression and Violent Behavior*, 12: 208–28.

Ward, T., Polaschek, D. L. L. and Beech, A. R. (2006) *Theories of Sexual Offending*. Chichester: Wiley.

Webster, C. D. and Bailes, G. (2004) 'Assessing violence risk in mentally and personality disordered individuals', in C. R. Hollin (ed.), *The Essential Handbook of Offender Assessment and Treatment*. Chichester: Wiley.

Webster, C. D., Douglas, K. S., Eaves, D. and Hart, S. D. (1997) *HCR-20: Assessing Risk for Violence*. Burnaby, BC: Simon Fraser University.

West, D. J. and Walk, A. (1977) *Daniel McNaughton: His Trial and the Aftermath*. London: Royal College of Psychiatry.

West, R. (2005) 'Time for a change: putting the transtheoretical (stages of change) model to rest', *Addiction*, 100: 1036–9.

Wolff, K., Farrell, M., Marsden, J., Monteiro, G., Ali, R., Welch, S. and Strang, J. (1999) 'A review of biological indicators of illicit drug use, practical considerations and clinical usefulness', *Addiction*, 94: 1279–98.

World Health Organisation (1992) *10th Revision of the International Classification of Diseases (ICD-10)*. Geneva: WHO.

World Health Organisation (1997) *Multiaxial Presentation of the ICD-10 for Use in Adult Psychiatry*. Cambridge: Cambridge University Press.

Yacoub, E., Hall, I. and Bernal, J. (2008) 'Secure in-patient services for people with learning disability: is the market serving the user well?', *Psychiatric Bulletin*, 32: 205–7.

Young, A., Monteiro, B. and Ridgeway, S. (2000) 'Deaf people with mental health needs in the criminal justice system: a review of the UK literature', *Journal of Forensic Psychiatry*, 11: 556–70.

Zigmond, T. (2004) 'A new mental health act for England and Wales', *Advances in Psychiatric Treatment*, 10: 161–3.

Zigmond, T. (2007) *Mental Health Bill, Newsletter No. 14*. London: Royal College of Psychiatrists.

Index

Added to a page number 'f' denotes a figure and 't' denotes a table.

abnormality of mind 66, 67
absolute discharge 17, 63
abstinence-oriented TCs 135
abuse 51
academic stage
  barrister training 180
  solicitor training 179
accelerated discharge programme 80
accident 65
accreditation, treatment programmes 123–4, 125t
accuracy, risk prediction 107
acquisitive crime 52, 127t
action stage (change model) 130
actuarial risk assessment 113–14
actus reus 64
advocacy *see* Mental Health Advocacy
advocate-solicitors 178
aetiology 29
affect 29
affective disorders 29, 158t
African-Caribbean patients 83, 84
aftercare, duty to provide 23
aggression 132, 159

alcohol abuse
  among prisoners 71t
  detoxification 161
  and personality disorders 48
  and violent crime 52
  violent recidivism 110t
  withdrawal state 161
amitriptyline 148t
anankastic personality disorder 45
antidepressants 146–50, 157
antipsychotics 141–4, 157
antisocial lifestyle, and general recidivism 113
antisocial personality disorder 43–4, 46, 47, 48, 110t, 112, 153–4
anxious avoidant disorder 45
'any disorder or disability of mind' 13–14
appeals
  against convictions 8, 9
  against detention 15, 16, 19
Approved Mental Health Professional (AMHP) 15, 16, 99
Approved Social Workers 98–9
aripiprazole 158t
arrest-referral scheme workers 55
arson 75
art therapists 101

art therapy 100–1
Ashworth 74, 81
Asian patients 83
assessment
    of arrested persons 55
    compulsory admission for 15, 20
    of dangerousness 58
    for reports to court 59
    see also gatekeeping assessment; risk assessment
Assessment, Care in Custody and Teamwork (ACCT) 73
attitudes, and violent recidivism 110t
atypical antipsychotics 143
augmentation therapy 150
automatic life sentence 171
automatism 67–8
avoidant disorder 45, 47

Bar Council 180
Bar Standards Board 180
barring orders 16
barristers 178, 180
basic intent 64
Baxtrom, Johnny 106
behaviours, challenging 159–60
bench (Magistrates' Court) 6
Bennett, David 84
benzodiazepines 161
biological tests 162, 163t
bipolar affective disorder 33
    treatment 146–52
    see also depression; mania
black and minority ethnic (BME) groups 83–4, 136
borderline personality disorder 42, 44, 47, 112, 154
British Medical Association (BMA) 12
British Psychology Society 93, 94–5
Broadmoor 74, 79, 81
buprenorphine 162
Butler Report (1975) 75

carbamazepine 150, 151t
Care Programme Approach (CPA) 75, 81, 139–40, 180
categorised prisons 10
challenging behaviour 159–60
change, motivation of offenders 124–30
change model 130
change statements 129
charities, mental health 186
child abusers, reoffending 52
child aggression 132
chlordiazepoxide 161
chlorpromazine 141
Circular 66/90 (Home Office) 54
citalopram 148t
citizen advocacy 184
Civil Division (Court of Appeal) 8
clinical psychologists 56, 93–4
clozapine 143
Codes of Practice (PACE) 4
cognitive behavioural programmes 124–34, 135, 145, 154
cognitive-perceptual symptoms, medication 158t
Commission Board 181, 183
commissioners 181–2
'common mental health problems' 30
communication, in nursing 95
community mental health services 84–7
community psychiatric nurses 55, 58, 72
community treatment orders 19–23
complaints, MHAC investigations 183
compulsory hospital admission see hospital admission
compulsory treatment 12
concept therapeutic communities 135, 136
conditional discharge 17, 166–7
confidentiality 178
consent to treatment 24

contemplation stage (change model) 130
correctional treatments see treatments
'Count Me In' census 81–2
Court of Appeal 7f, 8
courts
 automatism 67–8
 diminished responsibility 66–7
 fitness to plead 61–4
 infanticide 67
 insanity 65–6
 mental health professionals' reports to 58–61
 pre-trial diversion from custody 58
 psychiatric defences 64–5
 see also Crown Court; Her Majesty's Court Service; Magistrates' Court; Youth Court
creative thinking 133
crime, and intent 64
Crime and Disorder Act (1998) 86
Criminal Division (Court of Appeal) 8
criminal history, violent recidivism 110t
criminal justice
 cooperation between health and social services and 54
 liaison workers 55
 process 3f
Criminal Justice and Court Services Act (2000) 175
criminal justice system
 agencies 1–8
 diversion 3, 54–69
 government departments responsible for 2
 inappropriate interventions for Deaf people 82
 video links for child testimony 86
Criminal Procedure (Insanity) Act (1964) 62

Criminal Procedure (Insanity and Unfitness to Plead) Act (1991) 62
criminal psychology 94
criminogenic needs 122
critical reasoning 133
Crown Court 6–8, 16, 17
Crown Prosecution Service (CPS) 2, 5–6, 54
cultural consultation model 84
cultural issues, in healthcare 84
custodial sentences 171

dangerous and severe personality disorder (DSPD) 47
 criticisms of concept 79
 illustrative case 80
 services 78–9
dangerousness, assessment of 58
Deaf mentally disordered offenders, services for 82–3
defect of reason 66, 67
deferred discharge 166
Delivering Race Equality in Mental Health Care 84
delusion 29
Department of Health 78, 88
dependence 51
dependent disorder 45, 47
depot antipsychotics 143
depression 33–5
 ICD-10 features 34
 levels of severity 35
 and offending 36
 prevalence 34
 treatment
  antidepressants 146–50, 157
  electroconvulsive therapy 150–2
  psychological therapies 152
detection, learning disability and offending 51
detention see hospital detention
determinate sentences 170, 171
detoxification 160–1

diagnostic systems *see* DSM-IV; ICD-10

dialectical behaviour therapy (DBT) 154

diazepam 161

difference, making a 90t

diminished responsibility 66–7, 68

Diploma in Forensic Psychology 94

Director of Public Prosecutions (DPP) 5

discharge *see* hospital discharge

disclosure 178

discretionary life sentence 171

'disease of mind' 66

dissocial disorder 43–4

district judges 6

divalproex 158t

diversion 3f, 54–69

diversity, respecting 90t

doctors' holding power 20

Domestic Violence, Crime and Victims Act (2004) 62, 66

dopamine 143

Dovegate 73

Down's syndrome 159

drama therapists 101–2

drama therapy 100

drug abuse *see* substance abuse

DSM-IV (Diagnostic and Statistical Manual of Mental Disorders) 28–30
    learning disability 48
    personality disorder 41, 42, 43–5
    substance abuse disorders 51

duloxetine 149t

dynamic risk factors 109

'either-way' offences 8

electroconvulsive therapy (ECT) 152

emergency, admission for assessment 20

emotional support, for prisoners 72–3

emotionally unstable personality disorder 42, 44

'end-to-end' offender management 9, 136

ethical dilemmas, involvement of mental health professionals 59–61

ethical issues, risk assessment/ management 139

ethical practice 90t

exclusion criteria, hospital admission 14

expert witnesses 5–6, 58

extended sentences 171

external readiness conditions, to change 129

Fallon Inquiry 74

false negatives 107, 108t

false positives 107, 108t

family therapy 146

female offenders, dialectical behaviour therapy 154

female sentenced prisoners, substance abuse 51

fitness for interview 56–7

fitness to plead 61–4

fluoxetine 158t

forensic mental health services
    in the community 84–6
    in prisons 70–3
    referrals 58
    secure hospitals 73–8
    specialised 78–84
    telepsychiatry 86–7
    see also multidisciplinary teams

forensic mental health system
    entering 54–69
        police custody 55–7
        courts *see* courts
        prison transfers 69
    leaving 165–86
        Mental Health Review Tribunals 165–9
        Parole Board 170–5

Multi-Agency Public
Protection Arrangements
175–8
legal representation 178–80
Mental Health Act
Commission 181–3
Mental Health Advocacy 183–5
voluntary groups 185, 186
forensic physicians 55, 56
forensic psychiatrists 56, 58, 72,
89–93, 138
forensic psychiatry 72, 75, 91–2
forensic psychologists 58, 94–5
Forum for Preventing Death in
Custody 183
Frankland 79

Gartree 73
gatekeeping assessment 74
Glancy Report (1974) 75
Good Lives Model (GLM) 134
Grendon Underwood 73, 135
group advocacy 184

hair analysis 163t
hallucination 29
haloperidol 158t
Hare's Psychopathy Checklist
– Revised (PCL-R) 42–6, 112–13,
114–15
harm reduction strategies, substance
misuse 162
hazardous drinking see alcohol
abuse
hazards 105
HCR-20 115–17
Health Professions Council 99
healthcare assistants 96–7
Her Majesty's Court Service
(HMCS) 6, 7f
High Court 7f
high risk offenders, benefit from
treatment 122
high-secure (special) hospitals 74–5
admission of women to 79–80

co-occurring substance misuse
and personality disorder 52
'unfitness to plead' admissions 63
histrionic disorder 44, 47
Home Office 2, 54, 71–2, 78
Homicide Act (1957) 66
hospital admission (compulsory)
for assessment 15, 20
criteria for 14
exclusion criteria 14
legal sections authorising 20–2
for treatment 16, 20
hospital detention
appeals against 15, 16
at high-secure units 74
learning disabled 82
legal sections authorising 15,
16–17
in medium-secure units 77
hospital discharge
absolute 17, 63
accelerated programme for
women patients 80
barring orders to prevent 16
conditional 17
MHRT powers 166–7
reconvictions after 75, 77
hospital orders 16–17, 21, 63
hospital transfers see transfers
hospitals see secure hospitals
House of Lords 7f, 8
hypnotic withdrawal state 161
hypomania 29, 152

ICD-10 (International Classification
of Diseases) 28, 30
bipolar affective disorder 33
depression 34, 35
learning disability 48, 49
mania 35
personality disorders 41, 42, 43–5
psychiatric morbidity among
prisoners 71t
schizophrenia 32
sexual preference disorders 53

substance abuse disorders 51
imprisonment, aims of 9
imprisonment for public protection
  (IPP) 171
impulsive behavioural dyscontrol
  158t
indeterminate sentences 171, 173
inequality, challenging 90t
infanticide 67, 68
Infanticide Act (1938) 67
information-sharing 178
injectable antipsychotics 143
Inns of Court 180
inpatient services 73
insane automatism 67–8
insanity 63, 65–6
intelligence, juvenile delinquency
  and low 50
intelligence quotient (IQ), and
  learning disability 48, 49
intensive care beds, in prisons 73
intent 64
internal readiness conditions, to
  change 129
interpersonal cognitive problem-
  solving 133
intoxication 51

juries 8
juvenile delinquency
  and low intelligence 50
  see also Youth Court

Knowledge and Skills Framework
  (DoH) 88, 89

lamotrigine 151t, 158t
Law Lords 8
Law Society 179
learning, personal development and
  91t
learning disability 48–51
  associated disorders 50
  challenging behaviour 159–60
  ICD-10 features 49

mental health issues 159
mental health services 81–2
offending 50–1
prevalence 50
terminology 48
treatment 159–60
treatments 136
unfitness to plead 63
leave, grant of 19
legal representation 178–80
Level of Service Inventory – Revised
  (LSI-R) 119
Level of Service/Case Management
  Inventory (LS/CMI) 119
Ley Prison Programme 135
life sentences 171
lithium carbonate 150, 151t, 152
local area commands (LACs) 4
local prisons 10
lofepramine 148t
lorazepam 161
Lords of Appeal in Ordinary 8
low risk offenders, treatment and
  recidivism 122
low secure units (LSUs) 77, 78
low-secure mental health services
  77–8
Lunacy Act (1891) 11

magistrates 6
Magistrates' Courts 4, 6, 16, 17
maintenance stage (change model)
  130
male sentenced prisoners, substance
  abuse 51
mandatory life sentence 171
mania 35–6
  defined 29
  ICD-10 features 35
  and offending 36
  treatment 152
manic depression 33
medical treatment see treatment(s)
medication
  administration of 182

personality disorders 156–7, 158t
see also antidepressants;
   antipsychotics
medium-secure units 75–7
   admission of women patients 79
   for Deaf people 83
   quality principles for 76
   telepsychiatry service in 86–7
mens rea 64, 67
Mental Capacity Act (2005) 64
mental disorder(s)
   co-morbidity 28
   legal definitions 13–14
   prevalence among prisoners 70–1
   Second Opinion Appointed
      Doctor service 182–3
   terminology and classification 27,
      28–30
   see also learning disability; mental
      illness; personality disorders;
      substance abuse disorders
Mental Health Act (1959) 12, 165
Mental Health Act (1983) 11
   concerns about operation of
      12–13
   exclusion criteria 14
   hospital orders 16–17
   medical treatment 14
   mental disorder definition and
      categories 13
   MHRTs 165
   safeguards for patients 12, 181
Mental Health Act (2007) 11, 13
   civil sections authorising hospital
      detention 15
   community treatment orders
      19–23
   consent to treatment 24
   duty to provide aftercare 23
   example of appropriate use of
      25–6
   hospital admission 14, 16, 20–2
   leave 19
   medical treatment 14
   mental disorder definition 13–14

mental health advocacy 185
professional roles 14–15
removal from a public place to a
   place of safety 23
restriction orders 17, 18–19
right to enter premises 23–4
transfer of sentenced prisoners to
   hospital 18
transfer of unsentenced prisoners
   to hospital 18
treatment orders 16, 19–23
Mental Health Act Commission
   181–3
functions 181
investigation of complaints 183
organisation 181–2
responsibility 181
roles 183
Second Opinion Appointed
   Doctor service 182–3
visits to mental health facilities
   182
Mental Health Advocacy 183–5
independence 184
mental health legislation 185
models 184–5
mental health advocates 185
Mental Health Alliance 12
mental health charities 186
mental health facilities,
   commissioner visits to 182
Mental Health Foundation 185
mental health in-reach teams 72
mental health legislation
brief history 11–13
see also individual acts
mental health professionals
advocacy 184
assessment of arrested persons 55
ethical dilemmas of involving
   59–61
as expert witnesses 5–6, 58
help in management of mental
   disorder and risk 9
reports to the court 58–61

standard diagnostic criteria 28–30
see also community psychiatric
nurses; forensic psychiatrists;
forensic psychologists
Mental Health Review Tribunals
165–9
application to and powers of
166–7
function 165, 166
legal representation 179–80
potential criticisms 169
structure and proceedings 167–9
mental health services
exclusion of individuals with
personality disorders 153
see also forensic mental health
services
mental illness
definition 13
offending 36–40, 109–12
personality disorders in
association with 41
see also bipolar affective disorder;
schizophrenia; severe mental
illness
mental impairment 13
mental retardation 48
Mental Treatment Act (1930) 11–12
mentally disordered offenders
diversion from custody 54–69
falling within the remit of
MAPPA 176–7
leaving mental health system
165–86
mental health services 70–87
motivation to change 124–30
treatments see treatments
meta-cognition 133
methadone 161, 162
mild learning disability 49, 50, 51
Ministry of Justice 2, 17, 18, 63
Minnesota Model 135
mirtazapine 149t
M'Naughten, Daniel 65
M'Naughten test of insanity 66

moclobemide 148t
moderate learning disability 49, 50
Modernising Medical Careers 92
mood stabilisers 150, 151t, 152
motivation (of offenders) to change
124–30
motivational interviewing 162
Multi-Agency Public Protection
Arrangements (MAPPA) 11,
175–8
multi-agency working 96
multi-axial presentation, diagnostic
systems 28–30
multidisciplinary teams 88–104
art, drama and music therapists
100–2
clinical psychologists 93–4
essential shared capabilities 90–1t
forensic psychiatrists 89–93
forensic psychologists 94–5
healthcare assistants 96–7
nurses 95–6
occupational therapists 99–100
pharmacists 102–3
social workers 97–9
teamwork example 103–4
Multifactorial Offender Readiness
Model (MORM) 129
music therapists 102
music therapy 100

narcissistic personality disorder 41,
44, 47
National Health Service Act (1977)
74
National High-secure Healthcare
Service for Women (NHSHSW)
81
National Offender Management
Information System (NOMIS) 9
National Offender Management
Service (NOMS) 8–11, 136
National Probation Service see
Probation Service
needs principle (RNR model) 122

negligence 65
neurosis 29, 71t
non-disclosure 178
non-sexual violence, predictor of 113
noradrenaline 146–50
North West Area Therapeutic
    Community 135
nortriptyline 158t
nurses 95–6
    holding power 21
    see also community psychiatric
        nurses
nursing, core competencies for 95–6

obsessive-compulsive personality
    disorder 45, 47
occupational standards of practice
    97–8
occupational therapists 99–100
occupational therapy 145
Offender Assessment System
    (OASys) 119, 136
Offender Group Reconviction Scale
    (OGRS) 118
Offender Group Reconviction Scale
    – Revised (OGRS2) 118–19
Offender Management Model 9
offenders
    with common mental health
        problems 30
    see also mentally disordered
        offenders
offending
    learning disability and 50–1
    mental illness and 36–40
    personality disorder and 47–8
    substance abuse and 52
    treatment programmes 126t
    see also reoffending; sexual
        offending; violent offending
Office of the Attorney General 2
olanzapine 143, 152
opioid detoxification 161
opioid withdrawal state 161
oral antipsychotics 143

oral hearings (Parole Board) 173–4
oxazepam 161

paper panels 172–3
paranoid personality disorder 43, 47
paranoid schizophrenia 31–2
paraphilias (sexual preference
    disorders) 52, 53
Parole Board
    decision-making
        oral hearings 173–4
        paper panels 172–3
        public protection priority 172
        recall cases 174
    future of 175
    role and function 170–2
    transfer of prisoners to
        psychiatric hospital 174–5
partnership working 90t
patients
    black and ethnic minority 83, 84
    grant of leave 19
    in high-secure hospitals 74–5
    in medium-secure units 77
    in multidisciplinary teamwork
        (example) 103
peer advocacy 184
peers, and violent recidivism 110t
personal development 91t, 96
personality, reliability of interviews
    56
Personality Disorder: No Longer a
    Diagnosis of Exclusion 153
personality disorders 40–8
    among prisoners 71t
    in association with mental illness
        41
    definition 41
    and offending 47–8
    psychopathy 42–7
    rate and prevalence 42
    risk of recidivism 112–13
    and substance abuse 52
    treatment 153–7, 158t
    types 41–2, 43–5

white patients likelihood of
diagnosis 83
see also severe personality
disorders
pharmacists 102–3
pharmacology *see* medication
phenelzine 148t, 158t
physical health, promoting 96
physical security 73, 138
police 4
right to enter premises 22, 23–4
right to remove persons to a
place of safety 23
Police and Criminal Evidence Act
(1984) 4, 57
police custody 55–7
police interviews 4, 57
Poor Law (1601) 11–12
positive psychology 134
Prader-Willi syndrome 160
pre-sentence reports (PSRs) 10
pre-trial diversion from custody
58
precontemplation stage (change
model) 130
premises, power to enter 22, 23–4
primary healthcare, in prisons 72
Prison Service 9–10
risk assessment procedures
118–19
treatments *see* treatments
prison transfers *see* transfers
prisoners
emotional support for 72–3
numbers, England and Wales
(2007) 9
prevalence of mental disorders
70–1
substance abuse 51
transfers *see* transfers
prisons
categories 10
current numbers 10
mental health services 70–3
treatments in *see* treatments

Prisons Partnership 12-Step
Programme 135
Pritchard 61
probation caseload 10
probation hostels 11
probation officers 10–11
Probation Service 10–11
risk assessment procedures
118–19
treatments *see* treatments
procedural security 73, 138
prodromal period 31
professional advocacy 184
professional development 96
professional roles 14–15
profound learning disability 49, 50
prognosis, defined 29
psychiatric defences 64–8
psychiatric intensive care units
(PICUs) 77, 78
psychiatrists *see* forensic
psychiatrists
psycho-education 145, 154–6
psycho-social interventions 145
psychoanalytically oriented partial
hospitalisation 154
psychological interventions 152,
153–6, 162
psychologists *see* clinical
psychologists; forensic
psychologists
psychopathic disorder 13, 46–7
psychopaths, and recidivism 112–13
psychopathy 42–7
checklist *see* Hare's Psychopathy
Checklist – Revised (PCL-R)
psychosis 29, 71t, 74, 145
psychotherapy 100
public protection 171, 172, 176
Public Protection Advocates 173
pupillage, barrister training 180

quality
medium secure units 76
treatment programmes 124

quetiapine 152

race equality, in mental health
    services 84, 85
Rampton 74, 79, 81
Rapid Risk Assessment for Sexual
    Offence Recidivism (RRASOR)
    113
rapists, reoffending 52
readiness to change 129
Reasoning and Rehabilitation 133
reboxetine 149t
recall panels (Parole Board) 174
recall to hospital 166–7
receptor blockade, antipsychotic
    medication 144
recidivism
    and mental illness 109–12
    and personality disorder 112–13
recklessness 64–5
reconvictions, after discharge 75, 77,
    86
recovery, promoting 90t
Reed Report (1992) 84
referrals
    to mental health services 58
    to secure hospitals 73
rehabilitation see treatments
Rehabilitation of Addicted Prisoners
    Trust Programme (RaPT) 135
relapse prevention 133–4, 145, 146,
    163
relational security 73, 138
reliability, of interview material
    57
remand to hospital 21
remand for treatment 21
reoffending
    by rapists and child abusers 52
    personality disorders and 48
    prediction of sexual 117
Responsible Clinician (RC) 14–15,
    16, 17, 19
Responsible Medical Officer (RMO)
    14

responsivity principle (RNR model)
    122
restriction orders 17, 18–19
'rights of audience' 178
risk
    elimination of 105
    level of security in hospitals 73–4
risk assessment 105–20
    empirically-based 106–9
    ethical issues 139
    forensic mental health
        base rates 113
        mental illness and violent
            recidivism 109–12
        personality disorder and
            recidivism 112–13
    instruments 113–19, 176–7
    of offenders subject to MAPPA
        176–7
risk management 96, 105, 106, 139
Risk Matrix 2000 176
risk prediction 107, 108t
risk principle (RNR model) 122
Risk of Sexual Violence Protocol
    (RSVP) 118
risk-needs-responsivity (RNR) model
    121–2, 123t, 134
risk-taking, promoting positive 91t
risperidone 143, 152, 158t
Royal College of Psychiatrists 92
Royal Medico-Psychological
    Association 12

safety
    promoting 91t
    removal of persons to a place of
        22, 23
saliva testing 163t
sane automatism 68
schizoid personality disorder 43, 47,
    112
schizophrenia 31–3
    co-occurring alcohol problem
        52
    family therapy 146

ICD features 32
paranoid 31–2
positive and negative symptoms 31
prevalence 141
prodromal period 31
prognosis 32–3
treatment
    antipsychotic medications 141–4
    cognitive-behavioural therapy 145
    NICE guidelines 142
    psycho-social interventions 145
unfitness to plead 63
and violence 36–40
schizotypal disorder 41, 43, 47
Second Opinion Appointed Doctor service (SOAD) 182–3
secondary healthcare, in prisons 72
secure hospitals 73–4
transfers see transfers
see also high-secure (special) hospitals; low-secure mental health services; medium-secure units
security, prison categorisation 10
sedative withdrawal state 161
selective serotonin re-uptake inhibitors (SSRIs) 148t, 149, 157
self-advocacy 184
self-control 130–2, 133
self-harm 50, 71, 159, 160
sentences, custodial 171
sentencing 6, 8
Serious Fraud Office 2
serotonin 146–50, 156–7
sertraline 148t
severe learning disability 49, 50
severe mental illness 30
severe mental impairment 13
severe personality disorders
    exclusion of individuals from services 12

see also dangerous and severe personality disorder
sexual criminal history, and violent recidivism 110t
sexual deviance 52, 110t
sexual offending
    admission to high-secure hospitals 75
    among Deaf people 82
    risk assessment 113, 176–7
    self-control 130–1
    sexual deviance and 52
    treatment programmes 128t
sexual preference disorders (paraphilias) 52, 53
sexual reoffending 117
sexual violence, assessment 117–18
Sexual Violence Risk-20 117–18
sign, psychiatric definition 29
A Sign of the Times 83
Smith and Hogan Criminal Law – Cases and Materials 65
social interventions 145
social skills 133
social workers 58, 97–9
sodium valproate 150, 151t, 152
solicitors 178, 179–80
Solicitors Act (1974) 179
Solicitors Regulation Authority 179
special hospitals see high-secure (special) hospitals
'special verdict' 66
specific intent 64
specific responsivity 122
stage model of change 130
static risk factors 108, 113
STATIC-99 113
stimulant withdrawal state 161
structured risk assessments 114
substance abuse
    admission to high-secure hospitals 74–5
    among prisoners 71t
    personality disorders and 48, 52
    violent recidivism 110t

substance abuse disorders 51–2
  screening 161–2, 163t
  treatments 160–3
    CBT programmes 127t
    concept TCs 135, 136
    detoxification 160–1
    harm reduction strategies 162
    major domains 160
    motivational interviewing 162
    psychological components 162
    tiers 160
    withdrawal state 161
suicide
  and mental illness 33, 34
  prevention 72–4
  in prisons 71
supervision orders 63
symptom, defined 29
symptom-based approach, too
  medication 158t

telepsychiatry 86–7
therapeutic communities (TCs) 73,
  122, 134–5, 136, 156
thiamine (vitamin B1) 161–2
thinking skills, enhancing 132–3
thought disorder 29
topiramate 151t, 158t
training
  art therapy 100
  barristers 180
  clinical psychology 93–4
  forensic psychiatry 91–2
  forensic psychology 94–5
  solicitors 179
training prisons 10
transfers
  between hospitals 167
  restriction orders 18–19
  of sentenced prisoners to hospital
    18, 22, 69, 174–5
  of unsentenced prisoners to
    hospital 18, 22
treatability test 12
treatment orders 16, 19–23

treatment(s)
  mental health settings 138–64
    against patient's will 15
    availability of appropriate 14
    Care Programme Approach
      139–40
    compulsory admission 12, 15,
      20
    consent 24
    definition of medical 14
    learning disability 157–60
    mental health problems 141–57
    substance abuse 160–3
  prison and probation services
    121–37
    risk-needs-responsivity 121–2,
      123t, 134
    programme accreditation
      123–4, 125t
    cognitive behavioural
      programmes 124–34, 135
    accredited therapeutic
      communities 134–5
    effectiveness 135–6
    sentence management and
      throughcare 136
    development 136
    risk reduction 106
tricyclic antidepressants 146, 148t,
  150
true negatives 107, 108t
true positives 107, 108t
typical antipsychotics 143

unemployment, and recidivism 110t
unfitness to plead 62, 63
urine analysis 163t
user-centred care 90t

values, in nursing 95
values enhancement 133
venlafaxine 148t
verdicts 8, 66
Victim Personal Statements 173
video conferencing 86

Violence Risk Appraisal Guide
(VRAG) 113
violent offending
admission to high-secure
hospitals 75
and alcohol 52
among Deaf people 82
and mental disorders
mental illness 36–40,
109–12
mild/borderline learning
disability 51
personality disorders 47–8
risk assessment 113, 115–17
self-control 131–2
treatment programmes 126t
see also sexual violence
vocational stage

barrister training 180
solicitor training 179
voluntary groups 185, 186

Whitemoor 79
wing listeners 72–3
witness care units (WCUs) 5
women
forensic mental health services
79–81
see also female offenders; female
sentenced prisoners
Women Enhanced Medium Secure
Services (WEMSS) 81
Women's Mental Health: Into the
Mainstream (DoH) 80

Youth Court 4, 6